HOLLYWOOD VAMPIRE
THE APOCALYPSE

By the same author:

Slayer: The Revised and Updated Unofficial Guide to Buffy the Vampire Slayer

Slayer the Next Generation: An Unofficial and Unauthorised Guide to Season Six of Buffy the Vampire Slayer

Slayer the Last Days of Sunnydale: An Unofficial and Unauthorised Guide to the Final Season of Buffy the Vampire Slayer

Slayer: A Totally Awesome Collection of Buffy *Trivia*

The Complete Slayer: An Unofficial and Unauthorised Guide to Every Episode of Buffy the Vampire Slayer

Hollywood Vampire: An Expanded and Updated Unauthorised and Unofficial Guide to Angel

High Times: An Uofficial and Unauthorised Guide to Roswell

Inside Bartlet's White House: An Unofficial and Unauthorised Guide to The West Wing (2 editions)

By the same author with Paul Cornell and Martin Day:

The New Trek Programme Guide
X-Treme Possibilities
The Avengers Dossier

By the same author with Martin Day:

Shut It! A Fan's Guide to 70s Cops on the Box

HOLLYWOOD
VAMPIRE
THE APOCALYPSE

An Unofficial and Unauthorised Guide
to the Final Season of *Angel*

Keith Topping

First published in Great Britain in 2005 by
Virgin Books Ltd
Thames Wharf Studios
Rainville Road
London
W6 9HA

A catalogue record for this book is available from the British
Library.

ISBN 0 7535 1000 6

Typeset by TW Typesetting, Plymouth, Devon
Printed and bound in Great Britain by
Mackays of Chatham PLC

Contents

Hollywood Vampire: The Apocalypse
is thoroughly dedicated to
all of my pals on *Outpost Gallifrey*
and *Buffy Watchers*.

Keep the faith.

Acknowledgements

The author wishes to thank the following for their encouragement and contributions to all four editions of *Hollywood Vampire*: Ian and Janet Abrahams, Sean Brady, Jo Brooks, Anthony Brown, Suze Campagna, Paul Cornell and Caroline Symcox, Allison Costa, David Darlington, Dan Erenberg, Irene Finn, the Godlike Genius of Jeff Hart, Claire Hennessy, David Howe, Michael Lee, Dave and Lesley McIntee, Ian McIntire, David Miller at *Shivers*, Ian Mond, Tara O'Shea, Leslie Remencus, Jill Sherwin, Mick Snowden, Tom Spilsbury, Jim Swallow and Mandy Mills, Susannah Tiller, Jason Tucker, Yochanan and Veda Urias, (the real) Maggie Walsh, Bill and Jacque Watson, Garth Wilcox, Michael Zecca, and the Fat Dragon Ladies.

My gratitude is due to numerous website custodians who spared the time to answer my, no doubt annoying, emails. Everyone at Gallifrey One and CONvergence (including fellow campaigners for a Tasteful-Lesbian-Shower-Scene, Anna Bliss, Stephanie Lindorff, Jody Wurl and Windy Merrill). Not forgetting Jason Boulter, Matt Boughton, Paul Condon, Dave Cook, Jonn Elledge, Jonathan Gatenby, Kathy Hill, Scott Matthewman, Jim Sangster, Chris Weimer and Alicia White.

A special thank you to my Scooby Gang: my long-suffering editor Kirstie Addis, Martin Day (*my* Watcher and my crashing computer's saviour, *yet again*), Diana Dougherty, Clay Eichelberger, Rob Francis, Robert Franks, Tony and Jane Kenealy, Shaun Lyon, Paul Simpson (who provided unedited transcripts of his interviews with many of the cast and crew), Kathy Sullivan (without whom there would have been no *Hollywood Vampire*), Graeme Topping, Deborah Williams and Mark Wyman – all of whom loaned this ongoing project their boundless enthusiasm and talent.

And, as always, to my family for their support and sage advice when I needed it.

This book was written – on location – in Newcastle upon Tyne, Van Nuys, North Hollywood, Minneapolis, London, Paris, Madeira, Sorrento and Lübeck. And various airports and hotels in-between.

Cue the cellos . . .

Preface

It started out as a generic ten-words-or-less idea for a spin-off series. *Vampire with soul seeks redemption and fights demons in LA.* Who would have predicted just how far *Angel* would eventually come? Set up during *Buffy the Vampire Slayer*'s critically acclaimed third season (1999), and debuting a year later, *Angel* had rather schizophrenic beginnings, seemingly unable to decide what sort of show it wanted to be. Whereas, with *Buffy*, it had been quickly established that the main reasons viewers were watching was related to the ensemble cast and the soaplike story arcs, on *Angel* it was initially felt that the series would work best as an anthology, in which guest characters were often the central focus. That theory lasted about half-a-dozen episodes before the production got the dichotomy right and started telling more personal tales from the underground. In doing so, *Angel* became, over the subsequent years, arguably an even more consistent show than *Buffy*. It may never, quite, have hit the inventive dramatic heights of *Buffy* episodes like 'The Body', 'Doppelgängland', 'Hush' or 'Once More, With Feeling', but *Angel* seldom produced a duff note. In its own quiet way, *Angel* built up a stunning back-catalogue of 110 episodes for syndication and the DVD age.

Angel was tough, dark and gritty (all of the things that a series dealing with the soft underbelly of the superficially glamorous City of Angels was expected to be). Yet it also had wisdom, profundity, poetry and *soul* in its creative locker. It was often funny, occasionally sad, but always impressive, cutting-edge, dangerous. It was good. *Really* good. And then, on Friday 13 February 2004, in the middle of a critically lauded fifth season, while achieving some of its best-ever ratings figures on The WB network, *Angel* was inexplicably, some would argue cynically, cancelled.

The cancellation was a stake through the heart for *Angel*'s many fans who had loyally stuck with the show –

and the network – through two previous threatened cancellation crises (in 2001 and 2003). On the *Angel* Internet posting board, Joss Whedon wrote to thank fans for all their support, community and devotion and asked them to remember the words of the poet: ' "Two roads diverged in a wood, and I took the road less travelled . . . and they *CANCELLED MY FRIKKIN' SHOW*. I totally shoulda took the road that had all those people on it." ' We *all* knew how he felt. As the final half-a-dozen episodes played out over the following weeks, most *Angel* fans and many critics in the media expressed, essentially, the same incredulity: They're cancelling *this* show while others which aren't fit to lick its – metaphorical – boots in dramatic terms are to continue? *Angel* still clearly had stories to tell and things to say. Perhaps, one day, it will (see **Grr! Arrrgh!**). There's no doubt that Joss Whedon is a remarkable man, with a remarkable ability to sell apparently dead concepts to a living market. Who else could take a four-year-old flop movie and make it into a cult TV classic that ran for seven years? Who else could take a gone-before-its-time TV show that ran 15 episodes and turn it into a $50 million SF blockbuster? Maybe *Angel*'s time has not, yet, passed.

But, even if it never returns in any form, *we* know *Angel*'s true worth, right?

One of the best television series of the last decade.

Headings

Dreaming (As *Buffy* Often Proves) is Free: Lots of series do cool dream sequences. *Angel* (and *Buffy*) did *magnificent*, surreal, scary, funny ones. You'll find them listed here.

Dudes and Babes: A meditation on all the pretty girls and boys that flitted across our screens. Even more than Sunnydale, Los Angeles is full of beautiful people. Most have a story to tell.

It's a Designer Label!: In the first episode of *Buffy*, Cordelia Chase was envious of the new girl in school who had recently arrived from Los Angeles. 'I'd kill to be that close to *that many shoes*,' she noted. In *Angel*, she was, and her clothing budget ran to a few expensive items. We check out the quality *and* feel the width.

References: Joss Whedon's shows always took great delight in slipping pop-culture and Generation X references into both the dialogue and the visuals. This category tries to catch all of them.

'West Hollywood?': The debate in fandom about whether Angel was gay or not was always a fierce one. The *Angel* writers were, it appears, not oblivious to this and, after many fans misheard Doyle's question 'Are you game?' in **1, 'City Of'** as 'Are you gay?' the writers seemed to use several scripts to indulge us with a few 'slash-fiction' fantasies via some of the filthiest innuendo this side of *Round the Horne*!

LA-Speak: S'up, homie? 'From the netherworld known as the 818 area code', this category lists as much *valley-slang* as requires an explanation. *Totally.*

Sex and Drugs and Rock 'n' Roll: In LA *all* are rife, even in TV shows. The city may have, as Raymond Chandler noted, 'the personality of a paper cup', but it's a place where literally *anything* goes.

Logic, Let Me Introduce You to This Window: An acknowledgement that even in the best shows there are sometimes logic flaws, bits of bad continuity or plain foul-ups. Part of the *job* of being a fan is looking for these, laughing at them when they occur and then aggressively defending them to your non-fan friends.

Quote/Unquote: Dialogue that's worth stopping the video for.

Other categories appear occasionally, including a few old friends and some new to this edition. Most should be self-explanatory. **Critique** details what the reviewers had to say while **Comments** from the cast and crew have been added where appropriate. **Soundtrack** highlights *Angel*'s excellent use of music. Each episode concludes with a review and copious notes on continuity and other general trivia that don't fit in anywhere else.

Keith Topping
Escaping by Canoe
Merrie Albion
October 2004

Previously on *Angel*

'A vampire in love with a Slayer. It's rather poetic. In a maudlin sort of way.'

Buffy: 'Out of Mind, Out of Sight'

Born in Galway in the eighteenth century, a young man named Liam was, according to Margaret (one of his subsequent victims), 'A drunken, whoring layabout and a terrible disappointment to your parents'. Though, as he would tell his vampire sire Darla: 'With the exception of an honest day's work, there's no challenge I'm not prepared to face.' Asking Darla to show him her world, Liam became a vampire in 1753. He has remained 27 years old ever since. Angel is the nickname of his possessing demon, *Angelus* ('the one with the angelic face').[1] He created havoc and terror across Europe for decades and was, according to the elite vampire The Master, 'The most vicious creature I ever met'. Angelus's modus operandi involved sending his victims insane, first by killing their family and friends before finally murdering them without mercy or pity. However, all bad things come to an end and, in 1898 after he murdered a Romanian gypsy from the Kalderash Clan, Angelus was cursed by her people to regain his soul and have knowledge of the dreadful crimes he had committed against humanity.

Damned to walk the Earth, Angel (the vampire with a soul) spent most of the following century in misery over his past deeds, shunning other vampires, coming to America and living in the gutter. Rescued by a friendly demon, Whistler, in New York in 1996, and shown a path of hope in the shape of the Vampire Slayer Buffy Summers, Angel

---

[1] Angel is, essentially, three separate personalities that all inhabit one body. For the purposes of simplicity, in this book all references to Liam refer to Angel's human persona during the years 1726–53. The difference between Angelus and Angel is a simple one – Angelus doesn't have a soul, Angel *does*.

accepted that he had a destiny and travelled to Sunnydale and the Hellmouth.

Over the next two years Angel helped the Slayer and her friends – Willow, Xander, Cordelia, Giles and Oz – to fight vampires, demons and the forces of darkness. He killed his sire and nemesis Darla and assisted Buffy in her defeat of The Master and prevention of the opening of the Hellmouth. Briefly, Angel lost his soul again after enjoying a single moment of happiness with Buffy and returned to his evil ways, killing Giles's friend Jenny Calendar and stalking Buffy with the aid of his offspring, the English vampire couple Spike and Drusilla. Angel was eventually cured by a reversal spell performed by Willow and sent to Hell by Buffy to save the world from the coming of the demon Acathla.

On his return, Angel slowly regained his humanity and resumed his relationship with Buffy. But he spent much time questioning the reason why he was allowed to escape from Hell by The Powers That Be. Realising that there could be no future in a lasting relationship with Buffy, and after helping her to defeat the apocalyptic schemes of Mayor Wilkins and the rogue Slayer Faith, Angel left Sunnydale for the glamour and lights of Los Angeles.

Settling in the City of Angels and trying to forget all about the girl he left behind, Angel spends his days brooding and his nights fighting evil and an ever-present craving for blood. Fortunately, he is contacted by half-human demon Francis Doyle, who points out the dangers of his current lifestyle – for Angel and others – and informs him that The Powers That Be have chosen him for a special mission. Guided by Doyle's visions Angel tries to save the life of Tina, a coffee bar waitress, who is being stalked by evil businessman and vampire Russell Winters. Sadly, Angel fails, but does succeed in killing Winters and saving Cordelia Chase, one of Buffy's Scooby Gang who has recently relocated to LA in the hope of becoming an actress. Doyle, Cordy and Angel decide that they should start an agency to 'help the hopeless' and Angel Investigations is born ('City Of'). However, Angel has made a dangerous enemy in the form of evil law firm Wolfram & Hart and, specifically, lawyer Lindsey McDonald.

In a city singles bar, a demonic body-stealing entity is decimating the customers ('Lonely Heart'). Angel saves the day but seems in danger of losing his own heart to attractive police detective Kate Lockley. Meanwhile, in Sunnydale, Spike has been searching for the famed Gem of Amara (a vampire Holy Grail that grants the undead invulnerability to staking and sunlight). Buffy obtains the gem and sends it to Angel via Oz. However, Spike follows and, in an attempt to retrieve the gem, kidnaps Angel and, with a psychopathic accomplice, subjects him to unbelievable torture ('In the Dark').

The gang investigate a stalker who has the ability to detach parts of his own body and send them out to prey on the object of his obsession ('I Fall to Pieces'). This case is remarkable in proving that, occasionally, the team *can* save the damsel *and* make money. Distressed by her sub-standard apartment, Cordy is delighted when Doyle finds her new, plusher lodgings. The only snag is a resident ghost. But, even the toughest spook is no match for the nastiest girl in Sunnydale ('Rm w/a Vu'). The LAPD tries a sensitive approach to policing, with predictably chaotic results ('Sense and Sensitivity') and Doyle's former wife turns up wanting his blessing for her forthcoming wedding to a demon whose family want to eat Doyle's brains ('The Bachelor Party').

Doyle's attempts to pluck up the courage to ask Cordy on a date seem doomed to failure. Angel's love life is also in crisis as a pissed-off Buffy arrives in LA seeking a confrontation. An encounter with a Mohra demon breaks up the argument and restores Angel's humanity. After one perfect day of savouring the pleasures of the flesh Angel, unable to protect Buffy in his human form, asks the Oracles – The Powers' representatives – to fold back time. Angel is once again a vampire and only he retains his memory of the day he spent with Buffy ('I Will Remember You'). Doyle's visions lead the gang to a group of terrified demons who are hiding from The Scourge, an army of pure-bred demons intent on racial purification. Doyle, having confessed both his own demonic nature and his love for Cordy, makes the ultimate sacrifice. He destroys The Scourge's death-ray at the price of his own life ('Hero'). A grieving Cordelia discovers that Doyle's parting kiss to her was more than a sweet goodbye to the object of his desire and she now has to contend with painful visions and an empath demon named Barney who wants to sell her gift of vision on the open market ('Parting Gifts'). Angel is assisted in saving her by rogue demon hunter and former Watcher Wesley Wyndam-Pryce. Another ex-Sunnydale resident, Wesley subsequently joins Angel Investigations.

Angel is tortured by dreams of his murderous past and is horrified when these dreams appear to be manifesting themselves in reality. The culprit, it turns out, is Penn, a serial-killing vampire sired by Angelus in his heyday. Angel tracks down Penn but in the process is forced to reveal his own vampiric nature to Kate Lockley ('Somnambulist'). Cordelia indulges in a one-night stand and wakes up to find herself instantly and hugely pregnant. Thanks to Angel and Wesley, she is rescued and spawn-free within the day ('Expecting'). Angel encounters Jheiera, a militant feminist member of the Vigories – pan-dimensional female warriors who battle male oppression. Angel is sympathetic but cannot allow tourists to go around torching locals, however worthy their cause ('She'). Cordelia's visions enable the gang to save the life of a demonically possessed boy. An exorcism is arranged, but all is not as it seems. When Wesley confronts the released demon and taunts it with not getting the little boy's soul, it replies 'What soul?' ('I've Got You Under My Skin').

Angel takes a flashback visit to his human past, his awkward relationship with his father and his first, heady days as Angelus while in the present, trying and failing to save Kate's father, Trevor, from death at the hands of drug-dealing demons and their vampiric henchmen. It is a failure that further distances Angel from Kate ('The Prodigal'). Hired to investigate a kidnapping, Angel finds himself trapped in a demon fight-club and forced to battle for his life and freedom while trying, with limited success, to incite his fellow prisoners to revolt ('The Ring'). Angel also meets another Wolfram & Hart nemesis, the alluring Lilah Morgan. Hollywood is a tough place for actors and soap star Rebecca Lowell, upon discovering that Angel is a vampire, and desperate to retain her own youth and beauty, feeds an unwitting Angel drugged wine, thus briefly releasing his demonic persona Angelus ('Eternity').

The rogue Slayer Faith arrives in town direct from battling Buffy in Sunnydale and is recruited by Wolfram & Hart with a view to eliminating Angel ('Five by Five'). Capturing her former Watcher, Wesley, Faith subjects him to horrific torture as her real objective becomes clear. She wants to get Angel angry enough to kill her. Angel, however – despite the fierce opposition of Cordelia, Wesley and, especially, Buffy – decides to try rehabilitating her instead ('Sanctuary'). As Faith turns herself in and begins a prison sentence for her crimes, Angel encounters Charles Gunn, the leader of a street gang of itinerant vampire hunters. Gunn, while deciding that Angel poses no threat, is contemptuous of the idea of a good vampire, particularly one who is white and middle class. Meanwhile, Cordy considers prostituting herself to millionaire computer geek David Nabbit, whose path briefly crosses with Angel Investigations ('War Zone').

Angel encounters Wolfram & Hart's blind assassin, Vanessa Brewer, and, seeking the identity of Brewer's next target, infiltrates the firm. In the process, and much to his surprise, Angel gains a new temporary ally – an emotionally conflicted Lindsey McDonald. However, Lindsey is subsequently lured back to the dark side by his boss, Holland Manners. Angel also acquires the mythical Scrolls of Aberjan ('Blind Date'). Wolfram & Hart, intent on destroying Angel's link to The Powers That Be, summon the demon Vocah in an attempt to regain the scrolls. Angel, with Wesley's help, learns the meaning of the Aberjan prophecy's key phrase, 'Shanshu': that the vampire with a soul will play an important part in the coming apocalypse and will then die . . . to live again. In other words, he will become human.

Meanwhile, Wolfram & Hart recapture the scrolls to raise from Hell the very thing that will tear Angel away from The Powers That Be – his sire Darla ('To Shanshu in LA').

Inspired by the prophecy Angel starts to calculate his good deeds. However, his record suffers a setback when, due to mistaken identity, he kills the demon protector of a pregnant woman whose unborn child will have a significant future. Angel is compelled to become the woman's champion in a cross-dimensional trial of combat. Angel, Cordelia and Wesley also meet the Host – a green-skinned empath demon who runs a downtown karaoke bar, Caritas. Meanwhile, Darla is recovering in the offices of Wolfram & Hart ('Judgment'). Wesley and Cordelia research the violent past of the abandoned Hyperion hotel and are startled to learn that Angel was a resident there during the 1950s. Angel, attempting to help a young woman on the run from the police, was lynched by a paranoid mob of residents influenced by a Thesulac demon. Having abandoned both the hotel and the occupants to their fate, Angel is horrified to discover that the demon and his final victim are still in residence ('Are You Now or Have You Ever Been?'). Cordelia, Wesley and Angel also find the time to help Gunn battle with the demon Deevak after which Gunn becomes a member of the Angel Investigations team ('First Impressions'). Angel goes to the rescue of a lone girl menaced by thugs in an alley. But Bethany, aided by her telekinetic powers, is more than capable of looking after herself. The abused Bethany is actually being manipulated by Lilah Morgan for nefarious purposes ('Untouched'). Angel dreams of his first encounter with Drusilla and, unexpectedly, discovers that Darla is alive and has lured him into a trap. Lindsey McDonald reveals that Wolfram & Hart's plan is not to kill Angel but to awaken his uglier urges in preparation for a forthcoming apocalypse ('Dear Boy'). Seeking spiritual guidance, Angel visits an upstate swami who isn't all that he seems. In Angel's absence, Wesley assumes the vampire's identity and, despite some bumbling along the way, manages to save the day *and* get the girl – a beautiful heiress, Virginia Bryce ('Guise Will Be Guise').

Angel continues to brood about Darla; the now-human Darla starts to feel the guilt and horror of her violent past. Lindsey, meanwhile, finds himself increasingly attracted to Darla and at odds with his superiors' plans for her. When Wolfram & Hart decide to terminate their experiment, Lindsey gives this information to Angel, enabling the vampire to save his sire. A distraught Darla, tormented by her reacquired soul, begs her former lover to make her a vampire again. Angel, focused as ever on the possibility of redemption, refuses ('Darla'). Gunn's cousin becomes embroiled in an elaborate demon plot to steal the mythical Shroud of Rahmon – a cloth reputed to cause madness. Angel and Gunn infiltrate the gang but Wesley fears for Angel's sanity, especially after he, apparently, bites Kate Lockley during a confrontation ('The Shroud of Rahmon'). Darla's past, in the unwelcome shape of a syphilitic heart condition, finally catches up with her and Angel must choose between siring her again or watching her die. The Host, however, offers him another option: Angel can win a new life for Darla by submitting himself to three deadly trials. Sadly, there's a flaw in the plan and Angel, having endured excruciating torments, is told that Darla has already had her second chance. The pair decide to live out Darla's remaining days together but Wolfram & Hart have other ideas and bring Drusilla to LA where she makes Darla a vampire again ('The Trial').

A desperate Angel searches for Darla's corpse, hoping to kill her before she can rise, but he's too late and Drusilla and Darla hit the streets on a murderous killing spree. An enraged Angel takes a terrible revenge on Wolfram & Hart, doing nothing to prevent Drusilla and Darla's massacre of the top echelon of the law firm, including Holland Manners. Returning to the Hyperion, he continues this flirtation with the dark side by firing Wesley, Cordelia and Gunn ('Reunion'). As his friends adjust to unemployment, Drusilla and Darla begin to recruit muscle for their own gang. But Angel gives the ladies a warmer welcome than they'd anticipated ('Redefinition'). Discovering that Wolfram & Hart are siphoning monies raised for a teen shelter, Angel visits the organiser, former Sunnydale resident Anne Steele. He subsequently calls in a favour from fellow demon, Boone, to disrupt a charity function and expose the firm's criminal activities. Meanwhile, Cordelia, Wesley and Gunn decide to continue helping the helpless without their mentor ('Blood Money').

Gene, a brilliant scientist heartbroken at hearing that his girlfriend plans to ditch him, decides to use his latest invention to trap himself and his lover forever in a single perfect moment of time. Unfortunately a demon sect alter his calculations hoping to freeze the entire world. The Host and Angel prevent an apocalypse and comfort the hapless Gene while the Angel Investigations gang celebrate the successful conclusion of their first – solo – case ('Happy Anniversary'). The streets of LA seem to be getting safer, but it's not down to Angel or his friends. Rather, a squad of zombie policemen who are keen on justice, if not mercy, are terrorising Anne's street kids. Wesley helps Gunn to solve the problem but ends up in hospital with a near-fatal gunshot wound. Kate's career is placed on the line after she tries to help Angel ('The Thin Dead Line'). Things aren't going well for Wesley, Cordelia and Gunn's new business after a client refuses to pay their bill. Meanwhile, Wolfram & Hart are gearing up for the 75-year review and, facing the arrival of a senior partner, nervous lawyers seek help via evil rituals. It seems that a Wolfram & Hart contract extends well beyond death as Holland Manners takes Angel on a trip to the Home Office revealing, in the process, that Los Angeles is (as many had believed all along) Hell. As both Cordelia and Kate face mortal danger, Angel succumbs to the pleasures of Darla's bed and staggers into the rain in agony, just as he once did after having sex with Buffy ('Reprise').

However, this is an epiphany of perfect despair rather than happiness and Angel, much to Darla's disgust, emerges from his night of passion with his soul intact. Kate attempts suicide, but Angel, with some supernatural help, saves her. Then, guided by the Host's warning that his friends are in danger, he attempts to rebuild some burned bridges. Lindsey, meanwhile, has a few scores of his own to settle with Angel. Having saved Cordelia's life Angel tells Wesley that he doesn't want his friends to return to work for him. Rather, having seemingly recovered his taste for their mission, he would like to work for them ('Epiphany').

Harmony Kendall drops in to visit her old friend Cordelia, but Harmony has changed since her Sunnydale days – she's now a vampire and part of a vampiric pyramid scheme. Meanwhile, Angel discovers that there's an even bigger bitch than Harmony – atonement ('Disharmony'). Lindsey's life was difficult with the prosthetic hand that he was forced to wear after Angel chopped off his own, but his newly acquired replacement proves to be a mixed blessing. Cordelia's latest horrifying vision leads the team to Wolfram & Hart's body-parts farm. Lindsey leaves Wolfram & Hart and Angel intervenes to save his nemesis's life – but he cannot resist one final bit of payback ('Dead End'). Cordelia's dreams of acting stardom are compromised by a lecherous director and Angel's protective attitude, while a disturbance at Caritas has the Host seeking Angel's help. The trail leads to a library, a missing student and a mysterious book in an unreadable language. The Host reveals that he is Lorne (Krevlonswath of the Deathwok Clan), a native of another dimension, Pylea. He finds himself face to face with a past that he would rather forget when Cordelia is sucked through a portal to his former home ('Belonging').

In Pylea, Cordy is treated as a slave and meets another LA resident, missing physicist Fred Burkle, who has been stuck there for five years. Back in LA, the gang frantically search for a way to rescue their colleague. Arriving in Pylea, Lorne mourns the presence of his far-from-loving family (although it's hard not to love his brother, the dancing Numfar) while Angel celebrates the fact that the suns in this world are both of the non-fatal variety. Cordelia's visions surprisingly elevate her status from slave to princess. Her would-be rescuers, on the other hand, are captured ('Over the Rainbow'). Cordelia quickly finds that she is nothing more than a figurehead monarch but is happy to meet her handsome half-human champion, the Groosalugg. Pylea brings out the worst in Angel – quite literally ('Through the Looking Glass'). Angel, with Fred's help, battles his manifest demon while Wesley and Gunn become freedom-fighters in a revolutionary cause. Lorne loses his head which, luckily, proves not to be fatal. Having set Pylea on the road to freedom and independence, the gang help Fred to reopen the portal and return to LA. There, Willow waits for them with the terrible news of Buffy's death ('There's No Place Like Plrtz Glrb').

Fred has difficulties adjusting to life back in her own dimension as Angel returns from a summer in Sri Lanka where his attempts to come to terms with Buffy's demise have been hampered by the attentions of some demon monks. His first mission back in LA involves liquidating a group of vampires whose number includes Elizabeth, the eternal love of James – one of Angelus's protégés during the 1760s. Heartbroken at Elizabeth's death and swearing revenge James visits a demon doctor who renders him temporarily invincible. Angel ultimately defeats James, but is left to question his own response to the death of his true love. Meanwhile, in Nicaragua, a heavily pregnant Darla seeks some answers of her own ('Heartthrob'). Cordelia's visions begin manifesting themselves in a physical way. However, as the gang seek a mystical cure, Lorne reveals that the visions are being sent not by The Powers but, rather, by Wolfram & Hart, who need Angel to open a door between dimensions and spring one of their clients from Hell. Angel overcomes Skip, a demonic prison guard, rescues his charge and ensures that Lilah Morgan will never again attempt to use Cordelia as a pawn ('That Vision Thing'). An outbreak of seemingly random killings of the LA demon community leads Gunn to his old gang and a hard decision as to where his loyalties lie. Cordelia seeks the help of the Transuding Furies (who seem *very* well acquainted with Angel) to temporarily lift the protective Sanctorium spell on Caritas and enable him to rescue his friends from a lengthy stand-off. Gunn decides that his old gang have lost the mission and that his allegiance is with Angel ('That Old Gang of Mine').

Investigating a series of bizarre deaths, Angel visits a health club and, subsequently, a retirement home. There he encounters Marcus, an elderly man who has, literally, recaptured his youth by taking over the bodies of healthy young men. In Angel, Marcus finally finds a body that may be strong enough to withstand this process for longer than a single night. Angel finds himself trapped in the body of a weak-hearted old man until his friends realise what has happened and reverse the spell ('Carpe Noctem'). Fred is visited by her parents and must finally face up to what happened to her in Pylea. While largely supportive of her new lifestyle and friends, the Burkles offer Fred the sanctuary of a return home. She chooses to stay at the Hyperion where her intellect and inventiveness are proving increasingly helpful in the fight against evil ('Fredless'). Billy Blim, the demonic captive whom Angel rescued from hellfire, wastes no time in unleashing the primal rage inherent in any male he touches; his victims fall prey to murderous misogynistic urges. Wesley, Gunn and Angel are no exception and Fred and Cordelia must fight for their lives until Lilah, having been savagely beaten by her colleague Gavin Park, sends Billy back to Hell. Wesley, devastated by his actions towards Fred, struggles to regain his sense of self despite Fred's assurances that he is a good man ('Billy'). As a hugely pregnant Darla arrives at the hotel, Angel is forced to contemplate the seemingly impossible consequences of his night of passion with her some months ago. His friends also discover that the child of two vampires is the subject of yet another ancient prophecy. Meanwhile Sahjhan, a non-corporeal demon, concerned that Angel's yet-to-be-born child is a threat to his life, releases Angel's old enemy, the vampire hunter Daniel Holtz, from a stone sarcophagus in which he had been encased for two centuries ('Offspring'). Wolfram & Hart are intent on capturing Darla for their own nefarious purposes and Angel must protect her both from the law firm and a sinister vampire cult who believe that their baby is The Miracle Child. Holtz catches up on the events of the past 227 years and plans revenge for Angelus and Darla's heartless murder of his family ('Quickening'). Darla, influenced by the soul of her unborn child, experiences love for the first time, but Holtz is on the trail and attacks Caritas, forcing the gang to flee to an alley where Darla, unable to give birth, makes the ultimate sacrifice, staking herself to save her child's life. Thus, she leaves Angel to face fatherhood and the possible consequences of the prophecy alone ('Lullaby'). As Angel seeks to protect his newborn son, Connor, from the assaults of the demon underworld and the machinations of Wolfram & Hart, Holtz recruits a troop of individuals who have lost their family to vampires, including the beautiful and dangerous Justine Cooper. Under siege from his enemies, Angel flees the Hyperion with Connor in his arms and lures the warring factions into an explosive trap in the desert ('Dad'). On her birthday, Cordelia experiences a vision so intense that she leaves her body. As her friends struggle to bring her back from the astral plane, Cordy takes a trip with the demon Skip, who tells her that she was never meant to have the visions and offers her a chance to change her life. In the ensuing alternate reality, Cordelia becomes a successful sitcom actress haunted by the vague feeling that her destiny remains elsewhere. When she meets this universe's shattered version of the Angel Investigations team, she asks Skip for her old life back. Since, as a human, the visions will ultimately prove fatal, Skip demonises Cordelia, giving her pain-free visions and, as a bonus, the gift of levitation ('Birthday').

Angel becomes obsessed with the need to provide for his family and advertises for clients, thus unwittingly leading his team into danger from a group of demons who want Fred's head for their dying leader ('Provider'). An evening at the ballet takes a sinister turn as Angel spots something odd about this particular production – it seems to have remained remarkably unchanged for over a century. Angel and Cordelia go backstage to investigate and are possessed by the spirits of unrequited lovers. Meanwhile Wesley plucks up the courage to profess his love to Fred, unaware that Gunn has similar ideas ('Waiting in the Wings'). Fred and Gunn embark on a romantic relationship just as Angel finds his relationship with Cordelia altered by the arrival from Pylea of the handsome Groosalugg. Not only is Angel forced to confront his own shortcomings as a champion but he also agrees to help Cordelia find a magical prophylactic that will enable her to consummate her passion for Groo without losing her visions ('Couplet').

Wesley investigates a prophecy which suggests that Angel will eventually kill Connor. To his distress the signs of the prophecy's fulfilment all seem to be coming true ('Loyalty'). Angel, unaware that his food has been spiked with his son's blood by Wolfram & Hart, is behaving in an erratic fashion, terrifying Wesley, who kidnaps Connor in an attempt to keep the baby safe. Sadly, he plays into the hands of Holtz and Justine and is left for dead with his throat cut as Holtz takes Connor through a dimensional portal to Quor-Toth, darkest of the dark dimensions ('Sleep Tight'). A grief-stricken Angel seeks revenge on Wesley, attempting to suffocate him in his hospital bed. Wesley finds himself ostracised by his friends as Fred, Gunn and Angel pay a visit to the chaos-loving guardian of Wolfram & Hart's White Room. Angel conjures dark magic in an attempt to rescue his son from the Hell dimension. But the portal to Quor-Toth can only be opened once; a second attempt would endanger the universe ('Forgiving'). A depressed Wesley learns from Fred that the prophecy for which he almost gave his life was a fake and his efforts were for nothing. A supernatural debt collector has come to collect from Gunn – his soul, signed away in return for a truck. Angel is forced to put his own soul on the line to save that of his friend ('Double or Nothing'). As a result of Angel's use of dark magic, the Hyperion is infested with supernatural parasites which inhabit and dehydrate their victims. Fred is infected and her friends must turn to Wesley for help. Meanwhile, Cordelia discovers that she possesses new and shocking powers and the team learn of the coming of The Destroyer as an unexpected guest arrives at the hotel ('The Price').

Connor returns from Quor-Toth as a feral teenage warrior who has been taught to hate his biological father and to seek vengeance for the deeds of Angelus. When his attempt to kill Angel fails, Connor must learn to adapt to life alone in a bewildering and terrifying city ('A New World'). Angel and Connor reunite and fight side by side, but Holtz has a final devious plan, staging his own death at the hands of Justine and framing Angel for the deed ('Benediction'). As Lilah and Wesley enter into a sexual alliance, Connor, enraged by Holtz's death, plans revenge on his father. Unaware of this, Angel and Cordelia arrange to meet and discuss their relationship but en route Cordelia is sent a message from The Powers That Be and, escorted by Skip, ascends to her destiny as a Higher Being. Connor ambushes Angel and, assisted by Justine, locks his father in a steel coffin that they sink to the bottom of the ocean ('Tomorrow').

With Angel starving and hallucinating on the ocean floor and Cordelia bored on a different plane of existence, Fred and Gunn search for clues as to where their friends have disappeared. However, salvation for Angel comes from an unlikely source as Wesley holds Justine hostage to aid in a search-and-rescue operation. Meanwhile, Connor finds his double-dealing exposed and is brought face to face with his father who, after telling him that he loves him, kicks him out of the Hyperion to fend for himself ('Deep Down'). The search for Cordelia continues and, guided by Wesley, Angel visits Dinza, a Dark Goddess of the lost, who tells Angel about the Axis of Pythia, a mystical antiquity that can locate souls. Angel, Gunn and Fred break into an auction house to recover the artefact, only to discover that Gwen Raiden, a glamorous cat burglar with electrical superpowers, has beaten them to it ('Ground State'). In need of a break, Angel and his friends head for Las Vegas to visit Lorne, who has become a huge cabaret celebrity. But all is not well with the empath demon as he is being forced to read the minds of his audiences and help crooked casino owner Lee Demarco steal their destinies ('The House Always Wins'). An amnesiac Cordelia returns to this plane of existence. Angel decides to protect her from the full reality of her past. But Lorne's attempt to read Cordelia and thus help her to regain her memories backfires when Wolfram & Hart brain-suck him, stealing what he saw in Cordelia's mind ('Slouching Towards Bethlehem'). Fred has a physics article published and is invited to speak at a high-profile symposium. During her speech a dimensional portal opens and she narrowly escapes being drawn into it. Research shows that Fred's old professor has been banishing his brightest students to other dimensions, including Fred herself to Pylea. Enraged, Fred plots a suitable revenge but, at a terrible cost to their relationship, Gunn prevents her from committing murder. Meanwhile, Cordelia bonds with Connor and slowly pieces together some aspects of her past life ('Supersymmetry'). Lorne casts a spell to restore Cordelia's memory with disastrous effects as all of the Angel Investigations team regress to their teenage personas. Once the spell is broken, however, Cordelia's memory returns ('Spin the Bottle').

As Angel and his friends struggle to deal with a sudden spate of biblical plagues, Cordelia has a vision which is beyond her worst nightmares. With Lilah's reluctant help, Angel, Wesley, Gunn and Lorne investigate and meet a formidable new enemy, The Beast. As fire rains down on Los Angeles, Connor and Cordelia take their relationship to a disturbing new level, unaware that Angel is watching them ('Apocalypse Nowish'). The Beast kills its way through LA, trapping Connor inside Wolfram & Hart as Angel and his friends find their rescue mission complicated by hordes of zombie employees. At the Hyperion, Angel confronts Cordelia and instructs her to take her new boyfriend and get the hell out ('Habeas Corpses'). The Beast is systematically exterminating all five members of the Ra-Tet, an ancient mystical order. Once he accomplishes his goal, he will be able to blot out the sun, plunging LA into eternal darkness. Gwen helps the team by providing a refuge for Manjet, the last of the five, but even she is unable to prevent Manjet's murder. Learning from Cordelia that Angelus has a past history with The Beast, the team decide that it's time to call back Angel's own personal demon ('Long Day's Journey'). As LA stews in its own darkness, Wesley summons a mystic shaman to release Angelus. Angel experiences a fantasy of a perfect day. But, as he achieves perfect happiness in the arms of Cordelia, his soul is extracted and stored in a mystical vessel, and Angelus returns ('Awakening'). As Connor valiantly struggles to contain the crime wave that engulfs the city, Angelus uses mockery to sow the seeds of discord among the Angel Investigations team. Cordelia offers to sacrifice herself to Angelus in return for information. Intrigued, Angelus agrees ('Soulless'). The team discover that Angel's soul is missing and Cordelia has a vision telling her how to restore it; despite the apparent success of the ritual, though, Angelus is still very much in charge of Angel's body. He's also free from his prison, as Lilah discovers when she arrives at the Hyperion armed with a crowbar and intent on revenge. However, it is *not* Angelus who kills Lilah soon afterwards, but rather Cordelia who has, seemingly, planned Angelus's escape ('Calvary'). Believing that Angelus was responsible for Lilah's death, Wesley decapitates her corpse to prevent her from rising. Angelus enjoys his freedom and discovers that something other than The Beast is behind the apocalyptic events in LA. He also discovers, to his annoyance, that killing The Beast restores the sun to the city. Meanwhile, Wesley helps rogue Slayer Faith to stage a jail break in order to recapture Angelus. And Cordy tells Connor that she is expecting his child ('Salvage').

As Cordelia's pregnancy advances at unnatural speed, she begins to exhibit strange new powers. Faith tracks and fights Angelus who is being guided by a strange inner voice, who he believes to be The Beast's master. But in biting and drinking from Faith, Angelus unwittingly finds himself drugged by her tainted blood ('Release'). Angelus takes a nightmare trip into his own past, accompanied by the Slayer. Fred seeks help from Sunnydale, contacting Willow to find and restore Angel's soul ('Orpheus'). While the team come to terms with the ramifications of Cordelia's pregnancy and seek the identity of The Beast's master, Gwen asks for Gunn's help in freeing a kidnapped child. However, Gwen is not telling the whole truth and Gunn finds himself helping her to steal a device that will enable Gwen to control her powers. Back at the Hyperion, Cordelia's perfidy is exposed ('Players'). Seeking answers about who, or what, is controlling Cordy, Angel pays a visit to Skip. The answers that he receives are profoundly disturbing and leave the team contemplating their lack of free will. Cordy, meanwhile, enlists Connor's help in obtaining the ingredients required for a protective ritual and, despite an attempted intervention by his ghostly mother Darla, he assists in the murder of a young girl as Cordelia goes into supernatural labour. Angel tracks her down but is unable to kill her before her child is born. At which point, he and Connor fall to their knees in awe as Jasmine enters the world ('Inside Out').

The messianic Jasmine, a Power That Was, announces her intent to save the world from itself and she is welcomed with open arms by Angel and his friends, who become her devoted disciples. But, although Jasmine radiates peace and happiness, Fred sees her true face after coming into contact with her blood. As Jasmine gathers new converts, Fred is forced to flee ('Shiny Happy People'). Los Angeles is rapidly becoming a Utopian paradise in which Jasmine eating a few of her own acolytes goes quietly unnoticed amid the atmosphere of peace, love and harmony. Fred researches mind-control techniques and realises that blood is the key to stopping Jasmine. She devises a plan to enable the team to see the true face of their Goddess. However, although she is mostly successful, the revelation fails to work on Connor ('The Magic Bullet'). Angel and his friends flee underground to escape the wrath of Jasmine's followers. Wesley learns that Jasmine is from another dimension and that the answer to how to destroy her is learning her true name. Angel and Wesley obtain a blue orb that enables Angel to open a portal to Jasmine's home dimension ('Sacrifice'). There, Angel climbs a mountain and battles with the keeper of the sacred word. He is victorious and, returning to our reality, the keeper speaks Jasmine's name, revealing her true face and causing panic and mayhem. Seeking vengeance, Jasmine intends to destroy humanity but she is killed by Connor before she can carry this out ('Peace Out'). Jasmine's death puts an end to world peace and Angel and his friends face the consequences of their actions. The shattering of Connor's illusions leads him to become unstable, Cordelia remains in a coma and Lilah returns from the dead to make the team an unbelievable offer: to take over Wolfram & Hart. Each member is tempted, Wesley by unlimited access to books and texts, Fred by the scientific research department of her dreams, Lorne by the prospect of working with everyone he's ever wanted to meet, while Gunn has a life-changing encounter with a black panther in The White Room. Angel, ultimately, makes the decision on their behalf. Offered the chance to bend time and give the tormented Connor a normal life, he signs on the dotted line and a new era begins for the Angel Investigations team ('Home').

Angel – Season Five (2003–2004)

Mutant Enemy Inc/Kuzui Enterprises/Sandollar Television/
20th Century Fox

Created by Joss Whedon and David Greenwalt
Consulting Producer: David Greenwalt
Producers: Steve S DeKnight, Kelly Manners
Supervising Producer: Ben Edlund
Co-Producers: Skip Schoolnik, James A Contner (90, 109)
Co-Executive Producers: David Fury, Jeffrey Bell
Executive Producers: Sandy Gallin, Gail Berman, Fran Rubel Kuzui, Kaz Kuzui, Joss Whedon

Regular Cast:
David Boreanaz (Angel/Angelus)
Charisma Carpenter (Cordelia Chase, 100, 109[2])
Glenn Quinn (Allen Francis Doyle, 100[3])
Sarah Michelle Gellar (Buffy Summers, 90[4], 98[5])
Christian Kane (Lindsey McDonald[6], 96, 98, 100, 105, 109–110)
James Marsters (Spike)
Alexis Denisof (Wesley Wyndam-Pryce, 89–95, 97–110)
Julie Benz (Darla, 108)
J August Richards (Charles Gunn)
Amy Acker (Fred Burkle/Illyria)
Andy Hallett (Lorne)
Juliet Landau (Drusilla, 108)
Julia Lee (Anne Steele, 110)
Mercedes McNab (Harmony Kendall, 89–90, 93, 96–100, 102–104, 106–110)
Jennifer Griffin (Trish Burkle, 103–104, 108)
Gary Grubbs (Roger Burkle, 103, 108)
Jack Conley (Sahjhan, 106)
Vincent Kartheiser (Connor Riley, 106, 110)
Jonathan Woodward (Knox, 89, 93, 95, 102–104)

---

[2] Uncredited. Archive footage from **100**, 'You're Welcome' used in **109**, 'Power Play'.
[3] Uncredited. Archive footage from **9**, 'Hero' used in **100**, 'You're Welcome'.
[4] Uncredited. Archive footage from *Buffy*: 'Chosen' used in **90**, 'Just Rewards'.
[5] Uncredited. Voice-only; archive soundtrack from *Buffy*: 'Bad Eggs' and 'The Prom' used in **98**, 'Soul Purpose'.
[6] Uncredited in **96**, 'Destiny' and **98**, 'Soul Purpose'.

Sarah Thompson (Eve, 89, 92–93, 95–96, 98, 100, 103–105, 110)
Marc Vann (Doctor Sparrow, 89, 102, 104)
TJ Thyne (Lawyer, 89, 93[7], 100)
Jenny Mollen (Nina Ash, 91, 102, 109)
Leland Crooke (Sebassis, 93, 109–110)
Ryan Alvarez (Demon Slave, 93, 100, 110)
Michael Halsey (Rutherford Sirk, 96)
Tom Lenk (Andrew Wells, 99, 108)
Mark Colson (Izzy, 100, 109–110)
Alec Newman (Drogyn, 103, 109)
Adam Baldwin (Marcus Hamilton, 105–107, 109–110)
Dennis Christopher (Cyvus Vail, 106, 109–110)
Stacey Travis (Senator Bruckner, 109–110)

89
Conviction

US Transmission Date: 1 October 2003[8]
UK Transmission Date: 13 January 2004

Writer: Joss Whedon
Director: Joss Whedon
Cast: Rod Rowland (Corbin Fries), Dane Northcutt (Hauser),
Jacqueline Hahn (Judge), Michael Shamus Wiles (Spanky),
Pete Breitmayer (Desmond Keel), Kelv'i (Sam),
Jordan Garrett (Matthew), Marissa Tait (Woman),
Danielle Kuhn (Notary), Chris Eckles (Special Ops Guy),
Susan Slome (Cindy Rabinowitz), Christopher Leps (Vampire)[9]

Angel and his friends find themselves in charge of the LA
offices of a multidimensional legal corporation with many
evil clients – and more than a few evil employees. Can the
champions remain incorruptible in the face of such obvious
temptations? Will they find a way to prevent a threatened
demon holocaust if one of the scum they are reluctantly
defending is jailed for his numerous ghastly crimes? And
who sent the package containing a strange mystical amulet
that arrives on Angel's desk?

---

[7] Credited as Employee #1 in **93**, 'Life of the Party'.
[8] All US transmission details refer to The WB network. UK transmission details
refer to those on Sky One.
[9] Uncredited.

A Little Learning is a Dangerous Thing: Corbin Fries is one of Wolfram & Hart's primary clients – and has been since the days of Holland Manners. (Thus, he's been around at least since Manners was murdered by Darla and Drusilla in **32**, 'Reunion' and probably a good deal longer.) Considered by Wesley to be the lowest piece of pond-scum that he has met in several hours, Fries is involved in smuggling Asian immigrants into the US for cheap labour, prostitution, kidnapping, gun-running, pimping and drug trafficking. Currently on trial for some of these offences, Fries, if convicted, will serve at least twenty years in jail. (Wesley thinks that the least he deserves is to be eaten alive by weasels.) Fries is, needless to say, less than keen on this potential outcome and feels that his Wolfram & Hart lawyer, Desmond Keel, isn't doing enough to avert it. To ensure the best efforts of the firm's new leadership, Fries has placed – in his son Matt – a lethal retrovirus that will be released when Fries says a specific word. Fries's trial is eventually declared a mistrial when Gunn alleges that the judge has financial ties to one of Fries's businesses. Fries remains free awaiting a retrial while Fred and Wesley's departments work to neutralise the viral bomb.

The Conspiracy Starts at Home Time: When the gang are reading through Wolfram & Hart's files, Lorne notes that Joseph Kennedy (1888–1969)[10] once tried to get out of his deal with the firm. Lorne continues that George Bush Snr,[11] seemingly, was more clever and actually *read* the fine print.

---

[10] Born in Boston, the son of Irish immigrants, Kennedy attended Harvard. Later, he worked in investment banking, movie theatres and film production and made a fortune during the 1920s and 1930s, when he was an active supporter of Franklin Roosevelt. He was rewarded with the ambassadorship to Great Britain (1938–40). There were always dark rumours, however, that at least a portion of Kennedy's millions was made through illegal activities (including bootlegging alcohol during prohibition and various deals made with the Mafia). Four of his sons were subsequently groomed for political greatness but either died in tragic circumstances (Joseph Jnr – killed in a flying accident during World War II; John and Robert – both assassinated, one while president, the other while running for office) or were tainted by scandal (Edward).

[11] George Bush Snr (b. 1924), the 41st President of the US (1988–92). Father of George W Bush, the 43rd President.

Work is a Four-Letter Word: Agent Hauser is the leader of Wolfram & Hart's Special Operations Team, which traditionally handles all of the firm's wet-works. Hauser's team follows Angel through a tracking device secreted in his jacket lapel.

It's a Designer Label!: Fred's birthday-cake-like blue dress and later her silver boots. Also, Lorne's various (perfectly hideous) threads, Harmony's red dress and Eve's gold frilly skirt.

References: Lorne has a telephone conversation, pitching a film project to a client. It is, he notes, *Joanie Loves Chachi* meets *The Sorrow and the Pity*: 'It's *Joanie Loves Pity!*' The former was a short-lived spin-off from *Happy Days* starring Erin Moran and Scott Baio. The latter was Marcel Ophüls's devastating 1969 documentary about the Nazi occupation of France. Rabinowitz was the name of the owner of one of the storefronts which feature prominently in the opening scenes of Sergio Leone's *Once Upon a Time in America*. Also, Marvel superhero comics' *The Punisher* and *X-Men*, Patient Zero,[12] Sarin gas,[13] *Die Hard* ('you're not part of the solution'), *Apollo 13* ('work the damn problem'), *The Godfather* (allusions to a severed horse's head), *All the President's Men* ('the cleaners'), *JFK*, *Hansel & Gretel* (Fred notes that someone has eaten her trail of breadcrumbs), *Towering Inferno* and OJ Simpson's performance in it, Radio Shack, twins Mary-Kate and Ashley Olsen (stars of the TV series *Full House*), the children's game 'Mother, May I?', William S Gilbert (1836–1911) and Arthur Sullivan (1842–1900) and their operetta *The Pirates of Penzance*, the *Our Gang* film series of the 1930s (aka:

---

[12] This refers to the initial patient in any epidemiological investigation. The most famous such description, and the probable influence for this reference, was Gaëtan Dugas (1953–1984), a Canadian airline steward who was Patient Zero for an early study on HIV by the Centers for Disease Control.

[13] Sarin or GB (O-Isopropyl methylphosphonofluoridate) is a nerve agent first discovered by German scientists in 1938. Its most infamous usage was in the shocking Tokyo subway attack of March 1995 by Aum Shinrikyo, the leader of a Japanese doomsday cult, which killed 12 and injured more than 5,000.

The Little Rascals) and one of the series' stars, Spanky McFarland.[14] When Gunn finally sees Dr Sparrow he makes a sarcastic comment about the age of the copy of *Scene* magazine in the waiting area, referring to the 1987 break-up of Emilio Estevez and Demi Moore. Fred hangs a Dixie Chicks poster in her office. She also possibly makes an oblique allusion to The Machine That Goes Ping from *Monty Python's Meaning of Life*. Eve's first scene is replete with numerous allusions to Genesis 3 (Angel taking a bite from the apple that Eve gives him).

The Lack of Charisma Show: Cordelia is still in a coma (see **83**, 'Inside Out'; **88**, 'Home'). Harmony is told about her former best friend's condition and seems, briefly, upset (Cordy was, after all, her role model). But she gets over it quite quickly.

'West Hollywood?' (Fetish Supplement): Lorne tells Angel that Spanky, a mystic occasionally employed by Wolfram & Hart, is mentioned in Fries's file. When Angel pays Spanky a visit, Spanky apologises for being all sweaty as he has been working out and offers Angel a daiquiri. Angel, instead, admires Spanky's wall of paddles and tawses. Spanky tells Angel that he doesn't spank men and mentions that he has his own fetishist website. When Angel asks about the job that Spanky did for Fries, Spanky explains that he built a mystical container that would hold anything until it's dissolved by a magic word. As the conversation continues, Spanky gets Angel in a headlock and notes that he's putting pressure on Angel's windpipe and Angel will soon pass out. Angel explains that he's not actually using his windpipe. He breaks the stranglehold, grabs one of the paddles off the wall and whacks Spanky across the room noting that he has *no* problem spanking men.

Awesome!: 'Conviction's opening scene mirrors the beginning of **3**, 'In the Dark' (which was, of course, the last time

---

[14] Confusingly, there was also a mid-1960s Californian soft-rock group named Spanky and Our Gang (a sort of poor man's The Mamas and the Papas). Spanky *may* have been a fan of them rather than the films that inspired their name.

Spike appeared in Angel's world). The hilarious following sequences concern the changing scenario that Angel is now a, very unwilling, part of. Change is in the air on *Angel*, yet the opening moments seem deliberately designed to reassure the viewer that it's the same old show: a vulnerable woman in a back alley is attacked by a vampire assailant; Angel charges to the rescue, saves her from dark horror, and then swans away like a magnificent nancy boy while she asks how she can ever thank him. If the scene had ended there, this could have been an episode from any era of the past. But things are different now and, as a consequence, it doesn't. Instead a whole retinue of Wolfram & Hart flunkies appear, turning a heroic selfless act into a comedic exercise in bureaucracy. This, the scene suggests, is the way that it's going to be for the hero from now on.

Wesley believes that Fred's new habit of adding a 'y' to the end of people's names (Knoxy, for example) could be considered unseemly. Gunn wonders, therefore, if he'll have to start called Wesley 'Wesle'.

'You May Remember Me From Such Films and TV Series As . . .': Born in Canada in 1980, the daughter of former Huddersfield Town, Arsenal and England football legend Bob McNab, Mercedes McNab appeared in *Escape From Atlantis* and *Beer Money*, played the young Sue Storm in *The Fantastic Four* and was Amanda Buckman in *The Addams Family* and *Addams Family Values*. Like numerous teenage actresses in Hollywood in 1996, she auditioned for the role of Buffy Summers. Although unsuccessful, along with fellow shortlistees Elizabeth Anne Allen and Julie Benz, she was rewarded with a recurring role in *Buffy*. Marc Vann's CV includes *The Forsaken*, *When Billie Beat Bobby*, *CSI* and *The Shield*. Jonathan Woodward appeared in *Pipe Dream* and *Still Life*. Sarah Thompson played Danielle in *Cruel Intentions 2* and Dana Poole in *Boston Public*. Rod Rowland's CV includes *Shade*, *Space: Above and Beyond* and *The X-Files*. Dane Northcutt appeared in *Tigerland*, *Murdercycle* and *24*. Jacqueline Hahn was in

The Division and *JAG*. The excellent Michael Shamus Wiles appeared in *Rock Star*, *Pearl Harbor*, *Magnolia*, *Fight Club*, *The X-Files* and *Roswell*. Pete Breitmayer's movies include *Jingle All the Way*. TJ Thyne was in *How High*, *The Sky is Falling*, *What Women Want* and *Ghost World*. Jordan Garrett's movies include *Hidden Agenda*. Marissa Tait played Ashley in *The Biggest Fan*. Chris Eckles was in *CSI: Miami*. Danielle Kuhn featured in *Hulk* and *Bring It On*. Susan Slome appeared in *Scrubs*, *Friends* and *The Woman Every Man Wants*.

Behind the Camera: Stuntman Christopher Leps's work can also be seen on *The Handler*, *Firefly*, *Alias*, *CSI* and *Pirates of the Caribbean*. Casting director Barbara Stordah's CV includes *Dawson's Creek*, *The Practice* and *Tru Calling*. Her colleague, Angela Terry, worked on *Band of Brothers* and *The X-Files*. Costume designer Shawna Trpcic's CV includes *Leather Jackets* and *The Red Shoes Diaries*. Production co-ordinator David Eck previously worked on *Roswell*, *Office Space*, *Hollyweird* and *Dante's Peak*.

Not Exactly a Haven For the Bruthas: The office that Gunn has chosen for himself has a view of the Santa Monica mountains that run through LA. Gunn jokingly notes that he's lived in the city all his life and never realised that it had mountains before – adding that a brutha ought to be told about such things.

Logic, Let Me Introduce You to This Window: In addition to the severe provocation caused by the defence's endless procrastination, the judge in Fries's trial seems overtly hostile towards them. Indeed, as Gunn notes upon entering the court, she makes two prejudicial comments in the space of about twenty seconds. *That* should be grounds for a mistrial on its own without the *McCracken vs. The State of Maine, 1954* precedent that he comes up with. Why is a professional wrestler delivering mail at Wolfram & Hart? (See **94**, 'The Cautionary Tale of Numero Cinco' for a not-particularly-interesting explanation.) If everybody has forgotten about Connor and everything related to him (see

88, 'Home'), then how does Wesley believe Cordelia got into her coma? For that matter, does Lorne remember why Caritas was destroyed for a second time (see **52**, 'Quickening')? Do all the gang remember Darla or Jasmine or any of the other events that directly included Connor during the last two years of their lives? (There is an attempt to answer this in **106**, 'Origin', but it's only partly successful.) LA is a city of some strange sights but doesn't *anyone* notice the wholly conspicuous green man (wearing shades and a hat just to make him stand out a bit more) sitting in the courtroom of a major criminal trial? From this moment on it seems as though the production team just gave up on the concept of Lorne's appearance being, in any way, unusual. The obvious logic question in this episode involves who, exactly, went into the crater that used to be Sunnydale and retrieved the amulet that Angel gave to Buffy and which Spike used to close the Hellmouth (see **88**, 'Home'; *Buffy*: 'End of Days'; 'Chosen'). However this is, eventually, explained (see **98**, 'Soul Purpose'; **100**, 'You're Welcome' – although, again, only in a somewhat roundabout way). As an ex-Watcher, Wesley obviously has much knowledge of events that he, himself, had no direct involvement in. However, it's worth noting that when Spike appears, Wes, who – to the best of the viewer's knowledge – has never met the (second) vampire-with-a-soul, instantly knows who he is before Angel (or Harmony) says *anything*.

I Just *Love* Your Accent: When Gunn throws a basketball at Wesley, the latter notes that he prefers cricket. Well, of *course* he does, he's English – it's part of the culture. Actually, it's not hard to imagine Wesley as a decent middle-order batsman, sharp fielder in the covers and with a bit of useful leg spin in his armoury, plying his trade for some village team in the Cotswolds.

Motors: Not only does Angel discover that he owns numerous classic cars – much to his delight – but he also has access to his own helicopter.

Quote/Unquote: Wesley: 'Feng Shui'. Gunn: 'What's that mean again?' Wesley: 'That people will believe anything.'

Angel's speed-dialer: 'You have reached Ritual Sacrifice. For Goats, press one or say "Goats".'

Angel: 'I'm not allowed to hit people?' Wesley: 'Not people capable of genocide.' Angel: 'Those are *exactly* the types of people I *should* be allowed to hit!'

Hauser: 'You pathetic little fairy.' Angel: 'I'm *not* little.'

Notes: 'You really think you can solve the problem? Come into Wolfram & Hart and make everything right? Turn night into glorious day?' 'Conviction' sees the Angel Investigations team a few days into their running of Wolfram & Hart. Angel himself views it all as a challenge and *loves* his fleet of cars, though he feels that the Special Ops team which dog his footsteps somewhat cramp his style. Fred is having a lot of fun with her new toy – the Practical Science department. Gunn acquires some important knowledge that the team can put to good use and Lorne is already comfortable in his new surroundings, hanging out with the many celebs that the company has as clients. Only Wesley, it seems, sees any downside to their new position. The 'pedaconferencing' aesthetic, patented by *LA Law* and especially *The West Wing*, is used very effectively in initial scenes which suggest that things are always more complicated than they may, at first, seem. An intended theme of the season, it appeared, was to be the exploration of how corrupting their new environment would prove to be to the previously incorruptible gang.

Just in case the audience was wondering if this was an entirely new show, there are continuity references to Cordelia, Connor and Holland Manners, a reappearance of Harmony (a somewhat bizarre, but comedically inspired, choice as Angel's new PA) and the beginnings of an explanation of Gunn's madcap adventures in The White Room from **88**, 'Home'. The episode's highlights are, mostly, comedic but, just to remind us that this *is Angel* we're watching, there's at least one epic action sequence and a *faux-naïf* allusion to a romantic avenue that is effectively closed before the viewer can get bored with it. Oh yes, and Spike appears at the end.

This episode takes place approximately one week after Angel assumed control of Wolfram & Hart (see **91**, 'Unleashed'). Angel, Wesley and Gunn are visited by the self-assured Eve who introduces herself as the team's connection to The Senior Partners. Wesley notes that Eve is in a very powerful position for such a young woman. Eve asks him how he knows that she's either of those things (and, indeed, subsequent episodes reveal that she's neither; see **105**, 'Underneath'). Eve and Angel have a brief conversation about Connor living with a normal family (see **88**, 'Home'; **106**, 'Origin') and she reminds Angel that Wolfram & Hart are a multi-dimensional corporation (see **43**, 'Through the Looking Glass'; **105**, 'Underneath'). Angel tries to reassure the girl he rescues from a vampire attack that he's only interested in helping the helpless (see **4**, 'I Fall to Pieces'; **56**, 'Provider'). Wesley and Gunn have adjacent offices across the lobby from Angel's while Fred apparently works upstairs in the Practical Science department. After reading some of the horrible details in the Wolfram & Hart files, Fred says that she's lost her appetite. She suggests that this is a first. Among the personal items she has in her office is a wooden duck. Having spoken to The Conduit (the black panther previously seen in The White Room in **88**, 'Home' – and, presumably, the replacement for the Ra-Tet entity killed by The Beast in **74**, 'Habeas Corpses'; see, also **75**, 'Long Day's Journey') and subsequently to Eve, Gunn visits Dr Sparrow and undergoes a painful scientific procedure. This is, basically, a huge information dump of legal knowledge (and, as a minor extra, the works of Gilbert and Sullivan) into his brain. This turns him almost immediately into the best lawyer at Wolfram & Hart's disposal. Gunn believes that most of the Wolfram & Hart staff are not evil, per se, simply opportunistic, and will happily go with the flow of whatever changes Angel intends to initiate. Nevertheless, Lorne is given the task of reading the auras of the employees to ascertain who *is* evil and who isn't. Lorne's rating system is OKAY; ON THE BUBBLE; EVIL; TO BE FIRED; YIKES! Knox assures Fred that *he* isn't evil, he just makes the potions (however, see **103**, 'A Hole in the World'; **104**, 'Shells'). He believes that Wolfram & Hart have contained more plagues than those they've actually been responsible for.

The address of the Wolfram & Hart offices is 1127 Spring Street, Los Angeles, CA 90008. Harmony is hired, seemingly by Wesley, as Angel's assistant (or secretary, her exact job title is never made abundantly clear). She lists her potential assets to Angel: she is strong, quick, sycophantic (assuming that the word means what Wesley told her it meant) and she types like a superhero. Plus she and Angel, as vampires, keep the same hours. Harmony's drink of choice is pig's blood, with a dash of otter. Angel seems to quite like it. She mentions the time that she tried to kill Angel and his friends (see **39**, 'Disharmony'). Wolfram & Hart offers all of its employees medical and dental benefits. Fries's previous dealings with the firm involved the use of illegal pesticides. The technician who helped Fries to create the lethal virus was named Lopez. He was subsequently fired, notes Knox, before he rereads the computer document and informs Fred that, actually, Lopez was set *on fire*. Lopez belonged to a cult called the Black Tomorrow which specialised in viruses. The Los Angeles District Attorney, seemingly, employs shamans. They appear to have cast a mystical shield around the jury in Fries's case. Spanky's address is on Temple Street in Echo Park. At the climax Angel opens the mysterious package sent to him and the amulet that Lilah gave him to help Buffy (see **88**, 'Home') falls to the floor. Then it starts glowing and, in a whirlwind of special effects, a screaming Spike materialises. A delighted Harmony calls her ex-boyfriend 'blondie-bear' (see *Buffy*: 'The Harsh Light of Day', 'The Initiative', 'Out of My Mind', 'Crush').

Soundtrack: When reading the staff's minds for evil intent, Lorne has Cindy Rabinowitz sing the opening verse from the Broadway standard 'There Once Was a Man (Who

Loved a Woman)'. Much use was made in trailers for this, and several future episodes, of Jet's thrash-rocker 'Are You Gonna Be My Girl?'

Critique: In a controversial article on the website *salon.com*, critic Laura Miller described the new season of *Angel* as 'methadone for *Buffy* addicts in withdrawal. A Wednesday night palliative for the pangs left by that big void on Tuesdays, almost the real thing but not quite.' Needless to say, the website was bombarded with angry comments. Other reviewers were more impressed, including Kathie Huddleston of *Science Fiction Weekly*, who noted that '*Angel* has been producing not just great episodes but great *seasons* for years now. The two-part season premiere, written and directed by Whedon, offers the clever dialogue, humor and drama that make his shows so rich and rewarding.'

In Britain, Sky One's website trailed the new season noting that 'LA's brooding vampire-with-a-soul returns to help the hopeless. Having launched in the States to some of its highest-ever ratings, British audiences can sink their teeth into an irresistible new season.' Meanwhile, the *Cleveland Plain Dealer* described the series as concerning 'the vampire with a heart of gold trying to do good deeds in a bad place'.

Did You Know?: Most TV actors use their summer hiatus to make movies. Amy Acker, by contrast, got married. On 25 April 2003, Amy and her boyfriend, *The Punisher* actor James Carpinello, tied the knot at a winery in the Napa Valley. 'Then we went to Europe on honeymoon.' After a two-week stay on the Amalfi Coast in Italy, the couple visited London where Amy was one of several high-profile guests at a British convention. 'They were so nice,' Amy noted. 'They know more about the characters than we do.'

Cast and Crew Comments: Sarah Thompson did not have any reservations about entering such an established cast; however, she noted that she was nervous immediately prior to her first day of shooting. 'I felt like it was my first day at school and everybody knew each other,' she told the website *cityofangels.com*. New to the fantasy genre, Sarah noted most of the acting work that she had done – in series like *Boston Public* and *Line of Fire* – 'all have very realistic storylines . . . So it's fun to do something like this because it's like learning a new language.'

In another interview, with Steve Eramo, Sarah noted that 'I loved filming the scene where Eve explains why she is there. There was so much dialogue, my biggest concern was making sure I'd get everything right.'

Joss Whedon's Comments: 'It was clear, when I first devised the *Buffy* pilot, that Angel was the one character bigger than life in the same way that Buffy was, a superhero,' Joss told *TNT*. The setting was vitally important too: 'LA is not only a very funny place, it's also incredibly scary. It is a minefield for horror.'

Previously on *Buffy the Vampire Slayer*: With the information that Lilah provided, Angel travels to Sunnydale and gives Buffy the amulet to help the Slayer and her friends in their battle against The First. Aided by this powerful device, which Spike uses at the cost of his own destruction, and Willow's spell to turn the potential Slayers into warriors, the Hellmouth is closed for good.

90
Just Rewards

US Transmission Date: 8 October 2003
UK Transmission Date: 20 January 2004

Writers: David Fury, Ben Edlund
Story: David Fury
Director: James A Contner
Cast: Victor Raider-Wexley (Magnus Hainsley),
William Utay (Manservant), Bill Escudier (Hainsley Demon),
Joshua Hutchinson (Novac)

A necromancer – enraged that various Angel-initiated policies at Wolfram & Hart have denied him a supply of recently deceased corpses – intends to extract a price from Angel. His soul. Meanwhile, the gang have a new, and most unhappy, partner in their ranks – all the way from Sunnydale.

Dudes and Babes: Spike's arrival in Angel's office is made all the more dramatic by the fact that, as he soon discovers, he's non-corporeal. Harmony offers the opinion that he's a ghost. When Spike disagrees, Harmony notes that it's a reasonable assumption considering that he's currently sticking out of a desk. In the lab, Fred scans Spike and tells Angel that she's getting electromagnetic readings consistent with spiritual entities, but there's no ectoplasmic matrix, which makes ghosts visible. She adds that usually ghosts make the area around them cold, but Spike – while she doesn't consider him hot, exactly – is at least lukewarm. Wesley doesn't know what Spike is, but says that his presence is clearly tied to the amulet that his essence was held within. Wes wonders if Spike remembers any strange sensations when the amulet released its energy. Spike asks if he means skin and muscle burning away from the bone, organs exploding in his chest, eyeballs melting in the sockets and the like (see *Buffy*: 'Chosen'). Subsequently, Spike disappears and reappears on several occasions. He finally tells Fred that he feels as if he is slipping. It is, he explains, like the ground beneath him is opening and he finds himself straddling a great chasm, with Hell below (see **92**, 'Hellbound').

A Little Learning is a Dangerous Thing: Demons with four horns, Groxlars are notorious for eating the heads of babies. This part of their culture seems to be negotiable, however, as the head of the clan has a three o'clock appointment with Angel and Gunn to discuss the matter. Angel mistakenly attacks and kills the Groxlar leader. However, this may ultimately work to his advantage as Groxlars are known to respect someone who takes a strong opening position.

Denial, Thy Names Are Liam and William: Spike jealously notes that Angel has had it good with his cars, comfort and power. Spike, by contrast, saved the world and threw himself onto the proverbial hand grenade for all the *right* reasons. Yet what was his reward? (see *Buffy*: 'Chosen'). Angel is incredulous since Spike *wanted* a soul. Angel, on the other hand, had no choice in the matter – and it almost killed him. He says that he spent a hundred years trying to come to terms with infinite remorse (see *Buffy*: 'Becoming' Part 1; **24**, 'Are You Now or Have You Ever Been?'; **29**, 'Darla'; **81**, 'Orpheus'). Spike, alternatively, spent three weeks moaning in a basement and, thereafter, he was fine (see *Buffy*: 'Lessons', 'Beneath You', 'Same Time, Same Place', 'Sleeper', 'Lies My Parents Told Me').

The Conspiracy Starts at Home Time: Magnus Hainsley is a necromancer with power over the dead. He appears to specialise in transferring demons into the bodies of recently deceased humans. One of Wolfram & Hart's oldest clients (in this and other dimensions) and with connections in entertainment and politics, Hainsley relies on the newly defunct Internment Acquisitions Department for a sizeable proportion of his showroom full of corpses. Despite Angel having Hainsley's assets frozen, the necromancer does not want to risk insulting The Senior Partners by killing Angel outright (they have plans for Angel). Instead, he conspires with Spike to hijack Angel's body and displace his soul, leaving Spike running the show.

It's a Designer Label!: Gunn's sharp business suit. Fred's microdot miniskirt (see **89**, 'Conviction') puts in another appearance. There are several tasty shirts on display, including Angel's crimson effort and Wesley's tasteful royal-blue affair.

References: The character of Mr Green Jeans from the children's TV show *Captain Kangaroo* is alluded to. While Angel and Spike argue about which of them loved Buffy more, Lorne tells Wesley that it's a great story – the Slayer both men loved and both men lost. He thinks he could easily sell the movie rights to every studio in town. He's thinking Johnny Depp[15] and Orlando Bloom[16] for the lead roles. Then again, he admits, he thinks about them rather a lot. So do most of the girls who've seen the pair in *Pirates of the Caribbean*, it must be said. Also, *Casper the Friendly Ghost*, *The Littlest Hobo*, *The Tick* ('A spoon!'), *The Wizard of Oz*, Shirley Temple Black, *Road Trip*, Patrick Swayze and his role in the film *Ghost*, the *Tarzan* movies and *Peter Pan*. Wesley alludes to Exodus 21:23 ('an eye for an eye') and Hainsley to Revelation 20 ('the dead shall rise'). Spike paraphrases Olivia Newton-John's 'Physical'.

Bitch!: About 42 minutes of it – every scene involving Boreanaz and Marsters, basically.

Gruesome!: Hainsley's bloodthirsty butler sends Mr Novac, formerly of Wolfram & Hart's Internment Acquisitions Department, back to Angel in enough pieces to fill three buckets. When the butler tries a repeat performance on Angel, however, he ends up with a teaspoon imbedded in his skull. Equally outrageous as a method of dispatch is Angel decapitating Hainsley with a tray.

'You May Remember Me From Such Films and TV Series As . . .': Victor Raider-Wexley appeared in *Minority Report*, *John*, *The Lot* and *The West Wing*. William Utay's CV includes *Ali*, *Days of Our Lives*, *Species* and *ER*. Bill Escudier did voice work on *Family Guy*. Joshua Hutchinson appeared in *Charmed*.

Behind the Camera: Ben Edlund is best known as the writer and illustrator of the influential comic *The Tick*. Director/producer James A Contner's CV includes *Midnight Caller*, *21 Jump Street*, *Wiseguy*, *The Equalizer*, *Miami Vice*, *The Flash*, *SeaQuest DSV*, *Lois & Clark: The New Adventures*

---

[15] Previously referred to in **3**, 'In the Dark', Depp is one of this author's favourite actors; a celebrity *Fast Show* fan and occasional Oasis slide-guitarist, he's also the star of *21 Jump Street*, *Cry-Baby*, *Edward Scissorhands*, *Ed Wood*, *Donnie Brasco*, *Fear and Loathing in Las Vegas*, *Sleepy Hollow*, *Chocolat*, *Blow*, and *From Hell*.

[16] The latest British heartthrob in Hollywood, Bloom's movies include *The Lord of the Rings* trilogy, *Black Hawk Down*, *The Calcium Kid*, *Troy*, and *Wilde*.

of Superman, Roswell, Hercules: The Legendary Journeys, Dark Skies, American Gothic, The X-Files, Smallville, Enterprise, Firefly, The Dead Zone and *Charmed*. He was a cinematographer on movies such as *Heat, Monkey Shines, Jaws 3-D, The Wiz, Superman* and *Times Square*. It's his camera work on the concert footage in *Rock Show: Wings Over the World* (1976). There's a fine *Angel*-related Six-Degrees-of-Kevin-Bacon question: Paul McCartney to David Boreanaz, in one.

Set designer Andrew Reeder previously worked on *Austin Powers: The Spy Who Shagged Me*. Set decorator Sandy Struth's work can be seen on *Boogie Nights, S.F.W.* and *Payback*. Leadman Chris Carrivcau worked on *Hyperion Bay, Strip Poker* and *From Dusk Till Dawn*. Production sound mixer Beau Baker's movies include *Lolita*.

Sex and Drugs and Rock'n'Roll: When Spike and Angel argue about Buffy, Harmony realises for the first time that Spike's fatal obsession with the Slayer, which she observed before leaving Sunnydale (see *Buffy*: 'Out of My Mind', 'Family', 'Crush'), developed somewhat in her absence. She's, quite simply, *appalled* by the thought of what went on between them.

Logic, Let Me Introduce You to This Window: Given that, presumably, he's never heard of necro-tempered windows, Spike shows a remarkable lack of surprise at being able to walk in sunlight in Angel's office. Like Wesley (see **89**, 'Conviction'), Gunn has heard of Spike even if he hasn't actually met him. However, this is probably understandable. Firstly, Gunn has previously shown a good deal of knowledge concerning Angel's history (note, for instance, him telling Fred details about both Darla and Buffy in **51**, 'Offspring'). Additionally, as a teenage vampire hunter before he met Angel (see **20**, 'War Zone') it makes sense that Charles would have acquired considerable knowledge about the species and, particularly, those who were likely to show up in Los Angeles – Spike, after all, had been in the city as recently as 1999 (**3**, 'In the Dark'). Given that, as Wesley notes, Spike's reign of terror is, in vampire

history, second only in terms of violence to that of
Angelus, it makes sense for Gunn to have known all about
the notorious William the Bloody long before he actually
meets him in this episode.

Spike refers to Angel as his 'grandsire' directly contra-
dicting information previously given in *Buffy*: 'School
Hard' and 3, 'In the Dark', but confirming events wit-
nessed in *Buffy*: 'Fool for Love', 'Lies My Parents Told
Me'; 27, 'Dear Boy' and 29, 'Darla' (see also 96, 'Destiny').

Timescale query: In 88, 'Home', Angel is offered the
opportunity to run Wolfram & Hart by Lilah; she also
gives him the amulet which, after a short stop to make sure
Connor's new life is going OK, Angel subsequently gives
to Buffy (one would presume this happened on the same
day – it's only an eighty mile drive from LA to Sunnydale).
The next day, Buffy and her friends fought The First Evil's
forces and Spike closed the Hellmouth. Back in LA, it's
reasonable to assume that Angel and co. spent a couple of
days tying up their affairs at the Hyperion and moving into
Wolfram & Hart (indeed, in 89, 'Conviction', Fred is seen
carrying a box of her things into the firm as though it's her
first day). It is, however, established during that episode
that Angel and co. have been at Wolfram & Hart for 'a
few days' (perhaps as much as a week). The events of
'Conviction' take place over the course of one day and, at
the end of it, Spike arrives. At the beginning of this episode
the viewer is informed that the events of *Buffy*: 'Chosen'
happened nineteen days ago when, in the timeline established, it should have been no more than eight or nine (see
91, 'Unleashed' for further complications).

I Just *Love* Your Accent: Spike calls Wesley 'Percy', a
crude-but-amusing English euphemism for a penis. Of
course, having Spike around suddenly increases the use of
English slang expressions a dozen-fold. It's so nice to hear
a word like 'geezer' casually cropping up in *Angel* as easily
as it once did in *Buffy*.

Motors: One of Angel's new cars is a stunning 1991 Dodge
Viper.

Quote/Unquote: Spike: 'I must be in Hell.' Lorne: 'No, LA. But a lot of people make that mistake.'

Fred: 'If he's a ghost, technically we shouldn't be able to see him. And I'm detecting brainwave activity.' Angel: 'On Spike? That *is* weird.'

Angel: 'I'm in a meeting, Spike.' Spike: 'Oh, I'm sorry. I didn't care.'

Spike: 'That's how you're going to fight the forces of evil now? Call the IRS?'

Notes: 'I know what's down there . . . and it's not the place heroes go. It's the other one, full of fire and torment. And I'm terrified.' If the rumours are true and the sole reason that *Angel* got a fifth season *at all* was due to Mutant Enemy giving in to The WB's demands that James Marsters should come on board, then it was either an incredibly brave or a very foolish decision to have his introduction delayed in such a fashion. Whichever, the ploy works brilliantly and Spike utterly dominates the episode – one that would, in other circumstances, be a rather forgettable one. If **89**, 'Conviction' was a pilot for *Angel Law*, then 'Just Rewards' travels another route: *Angel and Spike (Deceased)* – Spike even alludes to himself as a 'wisecracking ghost sidekick' at one point. The bickering between Boreanaz and Marsters is, inevitably, priceless and the pair are given some reasonable dramatic conceits amid a bunch of one-liners that threaten to turn them into the best TV double act since Morecambe and Wise. The sitcom, buddy-cop shenanigans of this oddest of odd couples, bound together by destiny, works just as well as the previous episode's evocation of monsters as a metaphor for corporate America. Nevertheless, there *are* more serious elements if you look hard enough. Gunn is really cool in his new, augmented role while the addition of Harmony is a comedy masterstroke. Mercedes McNab's effortless abilities around a pithy quip are put to great use. Harmony is effectively given the former Cordelia role and she fills it with great aplomb. Amid some flowery and poetic dialogue, there are also hints of a developing relationship between Spike and Fred. With questions of atonement and fate, allusions to The Senior Partners' future plans for Angel and Spike's wish to be saved from Hell, *Angel* effectively reformatted itself within two episodes and with some class. These, then, are two pilots for the parallel paths that *Angel* would hope to walk in the coming year.

Angel has a rather palatial bedroom somewhere in the Wolfram & Hart building (it's subsequently discovered to be upstairs from his office). Angel tells Spike that Buffy is currently in Europe (see **97**, 'Harm's Way'; **99**, 'Damage'; **108**, 'The Girl in Question'). Angel has told Wesley some of the details concerning Spike having allied himself with Buffy. However, he left out both of the important points: that Spike now has a soul (see *Buffy*: 'Grave') and that he, seemingly, died saving the world. Spike's essence was contained in the mystical amulet and he has no memories of what has happened to him since his apparent death. The amulet also, in some unspecified way, prevents Spike from leaving LA. Any attempt to do so seems to return him to the Wolfram & Hart building. The amulet can only be destroyed on hallowed ground. Spike has heard of Wolfram & Hart, noting that they represent the worst evil in the universe. Gunn has fired forty employees during recent days (it's unclear whether these terminations simply mean the sack for those employees concerned or whether some of them have been as permanent, and as bloody, as the one subsequently seen in **97**, 'Harm's Way'). He mentions that the legal knowledge he was given in **89**, 'Conviction' included interdimensional and other demon laws. Wolfram & Hart have a Voodoo Division. Someone in there has been attempting to hex Gunn.

Soundtrack: Robert Kral was assisted in providing the music for *Angel* for much of Season Five by Douglas Romayne Stevens whose previous work includes *Paper Cuts*, *In Between Days*, *Wolf Girl* and *Big Fat Liar*.

Critique: 'They're classics,' wrote TNT's David Martindale concerning *Buffy* and *Angel*. 'A couple of small-screen masterpieces, scarier than most horror movies, funnier than most sitcoms and more action-packed than a John Woo flick. But the quality that makes [them] truly special is a depth of feeling and intelligence that's exceptionally rare on TV.' In four years, Martindale continued, the character of Angel has saved the world from the horror of permanent darkness and explored the highs and heartaches of fatherhood. 'Yet, at its core, *Angel* remains a meditation on redemption and the qualities that make a hero.'

'How *Angel* does after *Smallville* may well be the make-or-break point as to whether this series has a future on The WB,' noted Kathie Huddleston. 'I hope so. I'm not ready to tune in to a television season that doesn't have a Joss Whedon series. This is one show we don't want to lose.'

Did You Know?: On *The Bronze* Posting Board during 2002, Joss Whedon noted that when he was doing the rewrite on Spike's scenes in *Buffy*: 'Lover's Walk' – the episode which first reintroduced Spike to the show – he locked himself in a hotel room and listened to Hüsker Dü's *Candy Apple Grey* and the Replacements' *Let it Be* non-stop. He did this, he noted, to get into an appropriate depressive and angry my-girlfriend's-dumped-me mind-set.

Ratings: By its second episode, the total audience for *Angel* was up a staggering 21 per cent to 5.1 million viewers – the show's best-ever figure – compared to the same period during 2002 when it drew approximately 4 million. That included a jump of 62 per cent among the precious 18-to-34-year-old demographic.

Cast and Crew Comments: 'One thing I wanted to make sure of before accepting Joss's offer [to move from *Buffy* to *Angel*] was that David was OK with playing a storyline between his character and Spike and the conflict that would result,' James Marsters told *TV Zone*. 'Happily he was. The best thing about my time on *Angel* has been getting to know David. He's a real stand-up guy with an honest passion for the work.'

Joss Whedon's Comments: 'We definitely want Charisma [back] again . . . to bring some closure,' Joss told Associated Press in October 2003 (see **100**, 'You're Welcome').

Responding to comments attributed to Charisma in the *Boston Herald* ('I started that show. Not to be finishing it is a pretty big deal for me'), Joss told *TV Zone* that 'we didn't want to start doing hollow riffs on what we'd [already] done. It *was* discussed with her when the decision had been made.'

As for the one definite new recruit to *Angel*, Joss was happy to note: 'What Spike will bring to the show is a little anarchy and a little blond. Two things that we need.'

91
Unleashed

US Transmission Date: 15 October 2003
UK Transmission Date: 27 January 2004

Writers: Sarah Fain and Elizabeth Craft
Director: Marita Grabiak
Cast: John Billingsley (Evan Royce), Heidi Dippold (Jill),
Sascha Shapiro (Amanda), Braeden Marcott (Jacob Crane)

Angel heroically destroys a werewolf, but the creature's intended victim, a young woman named Nina Ash, having been bitten by the creature, flees the scene of the attack. A desperate search to find Nina ensues, before she succumbs to the beast incubating within her. But, inevitably, it's not just Angel and his friends who are searching for the girl.

Dudes and Werewolves: Lycanthropis Exteris is a rare breed of werewolf, previously uncatalogued in North America, distinguished from the standard genus (Willow's ex-boyfriend Oz, for instance) by a bipedal nature, longer teeth and greater armspan. The first known case was a man named McManus who Wolfram & Hart spent some time tracking; he left his family and spent years moving around in isolated locations in an attempt to prevent himself from harming anyone. However, he eventually stopped trying to control his inner demons. Upon attacking Nina, McManus was killed by Angel using Wesley's silver pen. Nina, an art student who lives with her sister Jill and nine-year-old niece Amanda, is infected. However, with the help and resources of Angel, she will be able to at least live with her condition (see **102**, 'Smile Time').

Dreaming (As *Buffy* Often Proves) is Free: The day after being bitten, Nina has a horrific waking-vision of slashing Amanda's throat.

The Conspiracy Starts at Dinner Time: Jacob Crane is an evil restaurateur catering to the very wealthy. Crane captures various beasts and serves them to his exclusive clientele at his Bistro of the Bizarre.

Dr Evan Royce is a cryptozoologist on Wesley's staff at Wolfram & Hart. He uses calendula to prevent Lorne from discerning that he's passing information to Crane. Bitten by Nina in her lycanthropic form, he is scheduled to be served as dinner to Crane's patrons at the time of the next full moon.

Work is a Four-Letter Word: There are, apparently, Paranormal Sporting Groups – as *Buffy*: 'Phases' had previously hinted. Lorne mentions organised vampire hunts in Eastern Europe.

It's a Designer Label!: Fred's red jacket and flared jeans. Nina's several extremely revealing T-shirts and pink jogging suit. Lorne's mustard-coloured jacket.

References: Lorne is a fan of 60s chanteuse Nancy Sinatra ('These Boots Are Made For Walking', 'You Only Live Twice'). Also, allusions to *Frankenstein*, the Church of Scientology (founded in 1952 by SF author L Ron Hubbard and registered as a bona-fide religion in the USA), the nursery rhyme 'Pop Goes the Weasel', Raku pottery, Jenny Craig – the creator of a popular weight-loss programme, *Chicken Soup for the Soul*, Sasquatch – the Native American Indian name for the mythical Bigfoot,

EM Forster's *A Room with a View*, Ayn Rand's *Atlas Shrugged* and Jolly Rancher candy. The plot concerning people dining on an exotic forbidden food may have been influenced by the Marlon Brando/Matthew Broderick comedy *The Freshman* and/or the 80s horror movie *Society*. The scenes of Nina becoming lupine were undoubtedly inspired by Rick Baker's Oscar-winning special effects in *An American Werewolf in London*.

'You May Remember Me From Such Films and TV Series As . . .': Jenny Mollen played Grace Robin in *Searching for Haizmann*. Most famous for his role as Doctor Phlox in *Enterprise*, John Billingsley has also appeared in *High Crimes*, *The Glass House*, *Crocodile Dundee in Los Angeles*, *Stargate SG-1*, *The Others*, *Kate's Addiction*, *Eden*, *I Love You to Death*, *Roswell*, *The West Wing*, *Gilmore Girls*, *Felicity* and *NYPD Blue*. Heidi Dippold was in *Stardom*, *Alias* and *The Sopranos*.

Behind the Camera: Writing duo Elizabeth Craft and Sarah Fain's work can be seen on *All About Us*, *Glory Days* and *The Shield*. Marita Grabiak directed episodes of *ER* and *Firefly*. Previously, she was script supervisor on movies such as *Bat*21*, *Young Guns* and *Mother's Boys*. *Angel*'s stunt co-ordinator Mike Massa was Ben Affleck's double on *Pearl Harbor*. His CV also includes *Miss Congeniality*, *Magnolia*, *Seven Days*, *America's Most Wanted*, *Roswell* and *Superboy*. When Mike himself isn't doubling for David Boreanaz, that job belongs to Chad Stahelski who has also worked on *Kung Pow: Enter the Fist*, *Wild Wild West*, *The Matrix*, *8MM*, *Alien: Resurrection*, *Escape from LA*, *The Crow* and *Vampires*. Key grip Andre Sobczak previously worked on *The Forsaken*, *Beyond Belief: Fact or Fiction* and *Schindler's List*. Hair stylist Diana Acrey's movies include *Illegal in Blue* and *Divided by Hate*.

LA-Speak: Gunn: '*Damn*, it feels good to get my violence on!'

Cigarettes & Alcohol: Lorne is busy making cocktails for himself (and, presumably, the rest of the gang) at the end of the episode while they wait for their food to arrive.

Lorne notes that he is, currently, up to his horns schmoozing with starlets and boozing with hipsters. It's a dirty job, but somebody's got to do it.

Sex and Drugs and Rock'n'Roll: During the gang's conversation about how trustworthy the Wolfram & Hart employees are, Wesley blurts out that he doesn't trust Knox (see **88**, 'Home') and he doesn't think Fred should either.

Fred says that Royce blocked Lorne from reading him by using calendula. This is the same, she notes, as people taking Valium in preparation for a Polygraph Test.

Logic, Let Me Introduce You to This Window: It's very obvious that Crane's restaurant uses the same (redressed) set as Magnus Hainsley's showroom from **90**, 'Just Rewards'. When did Angel or Wesley acquire replacement clothes for Nina? It's unlikely they used some of Fred's as she and Nina seem to be completely different sizes (particularly in the chest department). Since when did Fred become such an accomplished shot and so useful in a fight with three, presumably well-trained, kidnappers? Lorne says that Spike showed up on Angel's 'first day in the Wolfram & Hart saddle'. However, **89**, 'Conviction' clearly took place several days after the events of **88**, 'Home' (see also **90**, 'Just Rewards').

I Just *Love* Your Accent: Spike uses the word bloody so casually in his conversation that, after a while, Fred starts to drop it into hers too.

Wesley wonders if he can acquire a craving for Sasquatch soup. Gunn speculates that it's something the English eat with their beans on toast.

Motors: Wolfram & Hart have access to traffic cameras all around LA (Nina was spotted by one at 10.19 the night of her attack). Nina drives a 1992 Honda Civic (2ABM-543).

Wesley's big chopper (see **10**, 'Parting Gifts'; **25**, 'First Impressions') is glimpsed again.

Cruelty to Lycanthropes: Someone really ought to inform People for the Ethical Treatment of Werewolves (see *Buffy*:

'Phases') about Crane and his activities. Crane notes that he once tasted werewolf flesh in Sofia. The chef there used an understated mole sauce to bring out the meat's flavour. His own chef, Renaud, swears that serving Nina *en neige*, with a light drizzle of truffle oil, will be surprisingly delicious.

Quote/Unquote: Angel, to Spike: 'You know that *whoosh* thing you do, when you're suddenly not there anymore? I *love* that.'

Gunn, on Wolfram & Hart: 'Everybody here got something out of this.' Angel: 'Fear. Mistrust. Great motor pool.'

Nina, on Angel: 'He saves a lot of girls?' Fred: 'Girls, guys, puppies. He's pretty much an equal opportunity saver.'

Spike, on why he can't ask Wesley for help: 'It was a long time ago. He was a young Watcher, fresh out of the academy, when we crossed paths ... Blood was spilled.' Fred: 'My God. You're so *full of crap!*'

Notes: 'Tonight may not be salvageable, but my guests have paid a high price ... and I promised them a werewolf.' There is much discussion about dysfunctional family values in 'Unleashed'. The story is bookended by two *terrific* conceptual sequences in which the gang, despite a growing paranoia about internal factions within Wolfram & Hart, are clearly becoming more confident about their ability to help the helpless. Spike's lying hasn't improved much since Sunnydale, though Fred's gullibility towards such smooth-talking claptrap, clearly *has*. In one of the episode's finest scenes, Lorne yet again has to tell Angel some necessary home truths about a frequently unfair world and his place within it. A homage to every werewolf movie ever made, the first half of 'Unleashed' is truly magnificent – a sympathetic and beautifully characterised half-story about inner demons, life choices, world views and the idea of control in all its various forms. The second half of the episode, unfortunately, is less successful, involving a bizarre plot about high-class monster cannibalism that appears from absolutely nowhere and is wrapped-up far too easily. Thankfully, there are two exquisite codas, which reinforce the episode's twin themes and end a patchily good piece on a very positive note.

Angel and friends regularly order Chinese food from a local restaurant (although this appears to be the first time that they've done so since they moved into Wolfram & Hart). Angel's impressive artistic ability (*Buffy*: 'Passion'; **10**, 'Parting Gifts'; **27**, 'Dear Boy') is seen again. When Fred mentions that the kidnappers were almost military in their precision, Wesley notes that an underground, mon-ster-hunting, military organisation has existed before (The Initiative, seen in various *Buffy* Season Four episodes; indeed, as subsequent *Buffy* episodes like 'Out of My Mind', 'Listening to Fear' and 'As You Were' make clear, in one form or another, the government *still* maintains a group for such purposes). Fred mentions having spent five years in a demon dimension, until Angel rescued her (see **42**, 'Over the Rainbow'; **43**, 'Through the Looking Glass'; **44**, 'There's No Place Like Plrtz Glrb'). From Angel's apartment Fred believes that she can see their former base of operations, The Hyperion. Spike says that he once fought a werewolf for over an hour and that he almost lost his hand in the battle. He notes that each time he disappears (**90**, 'Just Rewards') it feels as if something is trying to pull him towards whatever is on the other side (see **92**, 'Hellbound'). Some of the psychics employed by Wolfram & Hart are able to create photographic images by touching a person's blood. Nina's address is given as 2315 Harvard.

Soundtrack: 'La Cienga Just Smiled' by Ryan Adams is used during the scene of Nina and Angel sitting in the car. Royce sings a verse and chorus of Rick Springfield's 'Jessie's Girl' to Lorne.

Critique: One of *Buffy* and *Angel*'s most vocal supporters over several years in the US press was Robert Bianco, the TV critic of *USA Today*. In an article entitled 'TV Shows Worth Making Time For', Bianco noted that, 'I know most of you *aren't* going to watch *Angel*. Which is a shame, because new blood and an altered format have [turned the show into] TV's best fantasy.'

Did You Know?: Following a very impressive performance during the opening two weeks of the season, 'Unleashed' saw *Angel*'s first significant ratings dip of the year. This probably wasn't a comment on the quality of the episode, however. Rather, it was because of Fox's decision to air a Florida Marlins versus Chicago Cubs baseball game in this slot. Given the daunting opposition that it was already facing in its 9 p.m. Wednesday slot – ABC's popular reality show *The Bachelor*, NBC's acclaimed drama *The West Wing*, the sitcoms *The King of Queens* and *Becker* on CBS and the sci-fi series *Jake 2.0* on UPN – *Angel*'s ratings were remarkably consistent. It was even suggested on several websites during this period, including the normally reliably informed *E!Online*, that a sixth season of *Angel* was already assured for 2004–05.

Cast and Crew Comments: 'It's brought a new energy to [the show], having the characters relocate to the enemy's quarters and become the generals of the opposing team,' Alexis Denisof told CNN. 'I think there's a lot of territory to explore in how the characters respond to their new environment, how they'll pull together [or] pull apart.'

'It was just a matter of trying to change the dynamics of it in order to pump it up,' David Boreanaz said when asked by Associated Press about the cast changes prior to Season Five. 'We've been a show that's pretty much been under the radar.'

Joss Whedon's Comments: The development of first *Buffy* and then *Angel* had been close to what Joss envisioned when he began, he told David Martindale. 'Except it grew up a lot more. I didn't know [the] full potential. I didn't know how good my actors would be. The basic idea was always there. But it grew beyond my best imagination.'

92
Hellbound

US Transmission Date: 22 October 2003
UK Transmission Date: 3 February 2004

Writer: Steven S DeKnight
Director: Steven S DeKnight
Cast: Simon Templeman (Matthias), Dorie Barton (Claire),
Willow Greer (Glass Woman), Peter Kanetis (Lawyer #1),
Judson Pearce Morgan (Bloody Lawyer), Elliot Gray (Hanging Man),
Allison Barcott (Armless Woman)

If Fred can defy most of the laws of physics, she believes that she can make Spike corporeal again. Spike, meanwhile, is suffering from a series of terrifying hallucinations. Could it be that what the other ghosts are telling him is true – The Reaper is coming for him?

Really Disturbing Visions (As *Buffy* Often Proves) Are Free: Around Wolfram & Hart, Spike suffers a series of horrific visions: a woman with no arms, another with a jagged piece of glass sticking from her eye, a man mutilating himself by sawing off his own fingers. They all appear to be previous employees of the firm who died within the building at various times (most, seemingly, by suicide). Believing them, at first, to be ghosts like himself, Spike eventually realises that they are, in fact, illusions created by his new nemesis, The Reaper.

Dudes and Babes: Matthias Pavayne, The Reaper, was an eighteenth-century surgeon forced to flee Europe after being caught performing unnecessary – lethal – surgical procedures. Pavayne settled in California while it was still under Spanish rule. There, he conducted a series of ritualistic murders over the course of twenty years. His reign of terror was ended by the embryonic Wolfram & Hart, who used his blood to deconsecrate the site of a Spanish mission. This would, ultimately, become their Los Angeles Branch. Pavayne's knowledge of the dark arts, however, allowed him to avoid dropping into Hell and his sadistic doings have continued in the realm between the living world and the afterlife. Using a supply of recently deceased souls from Wolfram & Hart's employees, he sends *them* to Hell in his place. Responsible for Spike's intermittent disappearances (see **90**, 'Just Rewards'; **91**, 'Unleashed'), Pavayne has the knowledge and power to avoid detection by Wolfram & Hart's mystics. He can also bend reality to his own will and affect the physical world too (for example, he's able to attempt to strangle Fred and to choke the psychic). Once Spike discovers Pavayne's weaknesses, a device constructed by Fred to return Spike to corporeal form instead works on Pavayne. Angel's punishment for The Reaper is to lock him deep within the bowels of Wolfram & Hart. Trapped forever, he is unable to move, although, because Angel included a window in his cell, he *does* have a permanent view of the corridor outside.

Denial, Thy Name is Angel: Gunn tells Angel that there are 3,200 different references to The Dark Soul in the various research indices they have access to. Four of them are about Angel himself. Angel is horrified, reading the references and muttering how grossly unfair they are.

Denial, Thy Name is Spike: Strip away the surface of Spike, Pavayne notes, get rid of the rebellious clothes and the cocky attitude, and underneath he's just a whimpering nancy boy crying for his mother. (Which, to be fair, might not be an entirely inaccurate assessment – see *Buffy*: 'Lies My Parents Told Me'.) The soul that blesses you, Pavayne continues, also damns you to suffer forever. Subsequently, Spike discovers more about Pavayne's abilities and realises that Pavayne's comments about bending reality are the key to his powers. Just as Spike managed to write a message for Fred on the glass of the shower, if he wants to do something badly enough, he can make it happen. With this knowledge, Spike gives Pavayne a fearful shoeing. Pavayne, however, then presents Spike with a classic dilemma by threatening to kill Fred. Spike will be able to save her but only at the cost of losing a race against time to restore his corporeal form. Spike chooses the former option and kicks Pavayne into Fred's circle-device which corporealises Pavayne instead of Spike. Fred is disappointed that her only apparent shot at making Spike solid again has gone, but Spike himself isn't overly upset, noting that he's learned a thing or two from Pavayne. To prove this, if he concentrates hard enough, he's able to pick up small objects like a coffee cup.

The Legal Issues Start at Home Time: After Spike tells the gang that he is being haunted, Gunn notes that seeing people who aren't there is grounds for involuntary committal under the Lanterman-Petris-Short Act.

It's a Designer Label!: Highlights include Fred's summery dress, Eve's tight black miniskirt, Lorne's silk cravat, Angel's rich-blue shirt and the psychic's red dress.

References: Allusions to Gwyneth Paltrow (*Se7en*, *Shakespeare in Love*, *The Talented Mr Ripley*) and Indian spiritual leader and politician Mahatma Gandhi (1869–1948). Spike notes that he and Angel seem to be stuck together in some kind of permanent double act, like Bob Hope and Bing Crosby. From the mention of Crosby, his train of thought wanders to a litany that includes Stephen Stills and Graham Nash (formerly of Buffalo Springfield and The Hollies respectively and, together with David Crosby and Neil Young, members of CSNY) and then, bizarrely, on to the 70s buddy-sitcom *Chico and the Man* (starring the late Freddie Prinze). There are also references to Sid and Marty Kroft's *Land of the Lost*, David Cronenberg's memorably sick horror film *Scanners*, *The Lord of the Rings*, the exercise regime the Pilates Method (see **48**, 'Carpe Noctem'), *Pinocchio* (Spike wondering if Fred can make him a real boy again – see **98**, 'Soul Purpose') and, obliquely, Hitchcock's *Psycho*. There are conceptual and visual allusions to *Ghost*, *They Came From Within*, *The Vault of Horror*, *Hellraiser* and (especially) *Resident Evil* and *Ghost Story*. Spike makes a possible allusion to the Smiths' 'Handsome Devil' (see also *Buffy*: 'Fool for Love').

Bitch!: Angel, on Spike's hair: 'What colour do they call that? Radioactive?'

The Odd Couple: Angel finds Spike waiting for him in his apartment. Flustered, he suggests that Spike return to haunt him tomorrow. Spike thought they could just hang out like they used to in the old days. Angel asks if Spike is starting to feel how close he is to Hell. Spike notes that it can't be that big a deal, if Angel managed to break out (see *Buffy*: 'Faith, Hope and Trick'). Angel explains that he didn't escape from Hell, he merely received a short reprieve, which makes Spike accuse Angel of having a martyr complex. He continues, saying that Fred told him all about the Shanshu Prophecy (see **22**, 'To Shanshu in LA'). Angel says that all prophecies are rubbish, with nothing ever written in stone (see **58**, 'Couplet'; **59**, 'Loyalty'; **96**, 'Destiny'; **110**, 'Not Fade Away' etc.). All that will ever count, Angel continues, is the lives that they both destroyed. Spike laments that he's going to burn for eternity but he's glad that at least he'll have Angel for company. The pair then exchange a few childish insults, Spike noting that he never much cared for Angel, even when they were both evil. At this point, Angel makes a surprise confession: he quite liked William's bloody awful poetry (see *Buffy*: 'Fool for Love', 'Lies My Parents Told Me'; **110**, 'Not Fade Away'). Angel was *also* a Barry Manilow fan, notes Spike with pungent sarcasm (see **23**, 'Judgment'; **81**, 'Orpheus'). What does *that* say about his taste? At this point Spike looks up and sees another vision – a man hanging from the ceiling. When it becomes obvious that Angel does not see the man, Spike tries to pass this event off as merely his reaction to all the talk of fire and brimstone. However, the sightings continue.

'West Hollywood?': Gunn alludes to one of Spike's more disturbing habits: suddenly appearing when Charles is in the men's room and, apparently, commenting about the size of Gunn's penis.

Gruesome!: The woman-ghost with the shard of glass sticking out of her eye is one of the most repulsive images

ever seen on television. And she's on screen for a disquiet-
ingly long period of time.

**'You May Remember Me From Such Films, TV Series and
Video Games As':** Simon Templeman is best known as the
voice of Kain on the video game series *The Legacy of Kain*.
His CV also includes *Live Nude Girls*, *24* and *Star Trek:
The Next Generation*. Dorie Barton played Tess Farraday
in *Stark Raving Mad* and also appeared in *I'm With Her*
and *Nowhere Man*. Judson Pearce Morgan's movies include *Strangers with Candy*. Elliot Gray appeared in *CSI*
and *The Practice*. Allison Barcott was in *Audrey's Rain*.

Behind the Camera: Steadicam operator Michael Stumpf
also worked on *Celebrity Temps*, *The Cricket Player*,
Myopia, *Popular* and *Blade*. Key set production assistant
Bryan Kalfus's CV includes *Bully*, *This Girl's Life* and *Kiss
the Bride*. Amy Acker's stunt-double Cassandra Crider
previously performed the same duty for Emma Caulfield
on *Buffy*. She has also worked on *Boomtown*, *Alias* and
Charmed.

LA-Speak: Psychic: 'Zip it and let me do my sweet funky.'

Cigarettes & Alcohol: In his apartment, Angel relaxes with
a glass of whisky.

Logic, Let Me Introduce You to This Window: As far as we
know, the last time that Angel met Spike, prior to
Sunnydale 1998 (see *Buffy*: 'School Hard') was in 1943 (see
101, 'Why We Fight'). So, how does Spike know that
Angel was a Barry Manilow fan during the 1970s? The
slash mark on Spike's face appears in a shot seconds before
the actual attack on him. How long has elapsed since the
gang took charge of Wolfram & Hart? Wesley says that it's
been approximately one month; however, Spike tells one of
the spirits that are haunting him that he's been knocking
around the land of the lost for months (plural).

Cruelty to Animals: When Gunn introduces Angel to The
Conduit, Angel notes that he's more of a dog person.

Quote/Unquote: Spike: 'Then why even bother? Try to do the right thing, make a difference.' Angel: 'What else are we gonna do?'

Spike, finding Fred's lab empty: 'Never a fetching mad scientist about when you need one.'

Fred, at the séance: 'Should we hold hands?' Psychic: 'Only if you're lonely.'

Notes: 'You get to live forever, unable to move, to touch, or to feel . . . Welcome to Hell.' An episode containing lots of random horror-movie clichés (including – get this – an entire shower scene), 'Hellbound's central theme is voiced by Fred early in the episode. The help that she is trying to give Spike, she tells Angel, is about 'doing what's *right*'. Spike and Fred's ongoing relationship is very intriguing, ultimately rather charming, and very well played by both actors. Indeed, most of the regulars are given plenty to do here (the exception is Lorne, who disappears completely after one scene). There are more White Room shenanigans for Gunn to endure, and a great sequence between Spike and Angel talking about the old days and bickering, brilliantly, like a divorced couple. The episode's main plot, surrounding the spirit of a malevolent eighteenth-century serial killer, includes a nice mixture of gross-out horror and pithy irony. And, the climax is a satisfyingly upbeat one in which the series' core value of redemption through work ethic is reaffirmed.

Wesley is in charge of Research & Intelligence. Fred's Practical Science department has exceeded its quarterly budget by $800,000 in an effort to help Spike. Fred's technique of writing on walls, and her claim that she's not crazy again, refer to the difficulties that she experienced in adapting to life back in Los Angeles after Pylea (**45**, 'Heartthrob'). When Fred explains to the others how she may be able to recorporealise Spike, she notes that she'll need a massive surge of dark-energy, the equivalent of nuclear-evil. Wesley starts to tell of a legend concerning a volcano deep in the jungles of South Africa. Gunn interrupts and says that he knows a place somewhat closer to home. He then takes Angel to The White Room (see **61**, 'Forgiving'; **74**, 'Habeas Corpses'; **75**, 'Long Day's Journey') where they meet The Conduit – the black panther that Gunn previously encountered in **88**, 'Home'. From The Conduit, they acquire a piece of itself (some whiskers). However, Gunn tells Fred to use the material wisely as they won't be getting any more. Angel says that he didn't hear The Conduit speak. Gunn merely notes that perhaps Angel wasn't listening closely enough. Spike's radiant heat signature has dropped; Fred believes this is due to Spike's lack of particle cohesion possibly explained by the fact that the amulet that held him was a transreality amplifier.

The mystics employed by Wolfram & Hart can, usually, sense the presence of non-corporeal entities within the building. Pavayne is listed as Dark Soul #182 in one of Angel's numerous reference books. There are several allusions to Buffy and to both Angel and Spike's past relationships with her. Among the items that Fred asks Wesley to procure for her are *The Magdalene Grimoire*, *Necronomicon des Mortes* and Hochstadter's *Treatise on Fractal Geometry in 12-Dimensional Space*. Wes notes that if he exploits all the connections that he's made over the last month, he should be able to acquire these in . . . twenty minutes. Eve tells Angel that if there's one thing that Wolfram & Hart are good at it's keeping their unmentionables unmentioned.

The episode's first US broadcast began with a caption: 'Tonight's presentation contains graphic and disturbing violent images, and partial nudity. Viewer discretion [is] advised.'

Soundtrack: No non-source music was used, but viewers will hopefully be as disturbed by Robert Kral's eerie *musique concrète*-influenced score as by some of the episode's visual imagery.

Critique: 'Theological concerns aside, I liked what they did with the episode,' wrote SF author and critic Peter David. 'The concept of Spike (or any vampire) being haunted by the dead is nothing new, and it almost seemed as if they tried to make up for the lack of novelty by ratcheting up the gore level so you wouldn't notice.'

Did You Know?: Fans may have noticed a new look for David Boreanaz in the early episodes of Season Five. After many years with short, spiky, gelled hair, Angel was, during this period at least, sporting a smooth, combed-back style. 'A little slicker look for him,' Boreanaz told *Zap2it.com*'s Kate O'Hare. Those who attended The WB's summer press party in July 2003 had seen Boreanaz with the swept-back long hair that he wore on the recent shoot of his movie *The Crow: Wicked Prayer*. In this, Boreanaz plays Luc Crash, the leader of a satanic biker gang who murders Edward Furlong and Emmanuelle Chriqui as part of a ritual to make Crash immortal. In true *Crow* tradition, of course, his victims rise from the dead to take revenge. Tara Reid, Dennis Hopper and Macy Gray also feature in the movie. 'I was a bad guy,' Boreanaz noted, 'the leader of this gang called The Four Horsemen of the Apocalypse. I had a lot of fun. It was a hard-paced film. We shot [it] in just 23 days.'

Cast and Crew Comments: Jeffrey Bell told *Sci-Fi Wire* that the series would be significantly lighter in tone this year. 'Then again,' Bell noted, 'we're not hosting an apocalypse. It's very hard to do some funny story when the sun has been blotted out and a beast has ripped out your innards and killed 5,000 people.' Bell said that choices made early the previous season forced the writing staff to turn out darker episodes. Now, with Cordelia in a coma, Connor given a new home, and Angel and his friends ensconced in Wolfram & Hart, *Angel* would be much more in keeping with the episode-to-episode tonal changes of its first three years.

'Hellbound' was extremely difficult to shoot, Steven DeKnight told *Xposé*. 'Every single scene was shot nine different ways. It was a technical nightmare and had a huge amount of special effects which are so time-consuming. It was an unpleasant directing experience.'

Joss Whedon's Comments: 'The WB hoped for a show that would be a little more stand alone-y,' Joss told CNN. 'When a show is in its fifth year, they don't expect it to get any sudden heat. They were hoping to pump the audience . . . with episodes people could jump into without being confused.'

93
Life of the Party

US Transmission Date: 29 October 2003
UK Transmission Date: 10 February 2004

Writer: Ben Edlund
Director: Bill Norton
Cast: Michael Maize (Artode), Jim Blanchette (Devlin),
David Mattey (Behemoth Lorne)[17]

The organisation of Wolfram & Hart's annual Halloween party (it's a *Hell* of a good time) inevitably falls to Lorne. However, the Pylean has taken some desperate measures to find the time in his bulging schedule for this onerous task. With potentially hilarious consequences. For everyone except him.

Dreaming (As *Buffy* Often Proves) is Free: Lorne, having had his sleep removed a month previously by Wolfram & Hart to enhance his performance as Head of Public Relations, unwittingly unleashes his subconscious on his friends. Lorne's sleep removal process took just twenty minutes and, he notes, left no scars. As an empath, Lorne normally reads the destiny of others. However, separated from his subconscious, he instead creates new destinies for those to whom he speaks, without being aware of it. Thus, at the party, he causes Wesley and Fred to be drunk despite their lack of alcohol, Gunn to stake out his territory by urinating around the office, Angel and Eve to

---

[17] Uncredited.

have sex with each other and Spike to become disarmingly cheerful. In addition, having removed the ability to sleep but not the need, Lorne is unable to resolve personal conflicts which exist in his subconscious, forcing it to peel away from his mind and – literally – force its way into reality. Manifesting as a green behemoth, Lorne's alter ego destroys Artode and Devlin. When Fred restores Lorne's sleep the entity disappears.

Dudes and Babes: Demonic royalty and the commander of more than forty legions of demons, Archduke Sebassis is the crown jewel of the underworld jet-set and, thus, the most courted guest for Angel's first Halloween party at Wolfram & Hart. This demon literally has blue blood – which he also drinks, as supplied from the wrist of a naked slave he keeps on a chain. Sebassis is disdainful of attending the party but, after Angel and Lorne personally invite him, and in the mood for intrigue, he attends the function with a retinue of bodyguards and functionaries. Armed to the teeth and prepared to kill everyone present if the party turns out to be the trap his right-hand demon Artode believes it to be, Sebassis ultimately rather enjoys the evening.

Denial, Thy Name is Lorne: Lorne says that Angel has no idea what Lorne has to deal with day to day. His position basically involves hand-holding and ego-stroking a lot of very insecure people. He is, he notes, the centre of gravity in a town full of borderline-disorder celebrities and power-brokers. What with all the meetings and clients and the 4 a.m. suicide threats, he simply can't keep up with it all.

It's a Designer Label!: Lorne admires Artode's jacket and is told that it is Pylean. Lorne happily acknowledges that Pylea is his home dimension (see **41**, 'Belonging'; **42**, 'Over the Rainbow'; **43**, 'Through the Looking Glass'; **44**, 'There's No Place Like Plrtz Glrb'). Artode corrects him. It was not made in Pylea, it was made *from* a Pylean. Artode skinned the creature himself. He wonders, idly, if it was anyone Lorne knew. That's just not com-shucking right. Other highlights include Lorne's threads generally, Gunn's red shirt and Harmony's pink party dress. There is another look at Eve's gold skirt (see **89**, 'Conviction': Angel considers that she's banging it out to the cheap seats while wearing it). Worst shirt seen this season by a mile: Angel's hideous orange abomination.

References: Allusions to TV and movie producer Jerry Bruckheimer and director James Cameron, *The Wicker Man*, the Beatles' 'We Can Work It Out', Fatboy Slim's 'Acid 8000' ('party's already dead') and the movie *Spider-Man* (Lorne's mirror reflection talking to him). Also, John Steinbeck's *The Grapes of Wrath* and its chief protagonist Tom Joad (as played by Henry Fonda in John Ford's 1940 film version), Looney Tunes cartoons and the character of Tweetie Pie, *Angel Heart*, *Legal Eagles*, Nextel, Richard Attenborough's epic war movie *A Bridge Too Far*, the Hanna-Barbera cartoon *Top Cat*, Mister Magoo, Bobby Pickett and the Crypt Kickers' kitsch hit 'The Monster Mash', Raggedy Ann dolls, the song 'Ya Got Trouble' from *The Music Man* ('Starts with P, that rhymes with me'), *Julius Caesar* ('Et tu, Brutuses?'), Sergio Leone's *The Good, the Bad and the Ugly*, disgraced former home and garden guru Martha Stewart, *South Park* ('Oh my God, they shot Lorne . . .'), board game Stratego, the Doors' 'Ship of Fools' and Italian actor Roberto Benigni (*Life is Beautiful*). Matsuda is a Japanese fashion line. There's an allusion to the popular car sticker 'My other car's a Lamborghini.' Lorne's inner demon resembles the Incredible Hulk. Some of the dialogue in the final scenes seems inspired by the *Black Adder II* episode 'Beer'. Also, visual allusions to *The Godfather – Part II* and *Almost Famous*.

Awesome!: A drunk Wesley and Fred dancing and Fred challenging a demon to a fight after he bumps into her. 'Positive' Spike. Angel and Eve's tryst. The extraordinary opening sequence – Lorne's mirror arguing with him.

'You May Remember Me From Such Films and TV Series As . . .': Leland Crooke's CV includes *Key West*, *F/X*

2, *Dead Man Walking* and *Melrose Place*. Michael Maize appeared in *The '60s*. Jim Blanchette was in *Starforce* and *Scrubs*. David Mattey played Big Dave in *The Incredible Torture Trio*.

Behind the Camera: Assistant production co-ordinator Kimberley Bellanger also worked on *The X-Files*. Unit production manager Robert Nellans's CV includes *Beverly Hills 90210*, *The Abyss*, *Home Fires Burning* and *The Dukes of Hazzard*. Visual effects supervisor Loni Peristere, in addition to legendary work on *Buffy* and *Angel*, also provided the effects for *Volcano*.

LA-Speak: Lorne: 'Here's the snafu in a nutshell, Top Cat.'
Harmony: 'Somebody really dipped his chip.'

Cigarettes & Alcohol: Lorne drinks whisky in the back of Angel's limo, something blue that came out of the slave's vein when visiting Sebassis, and a Seabreeze at the party (see **27**, 'Dear Boy'). Among the other booze being downed at the party, Wesley's drinking (a very small amount of) beer, and Gunn is on something considerably harder.

Knox fondly recalls the previous year's party at which a bunch of cows were put in a giant wicker effigy of Krishna and doused with Sambuca.

Sex and Drugs and Rock'n'Roll: Eve arrives at Angel's apartment noting that he certainly takes a long shower for a guy. Was he, she wonders, having some gentleman's time. Eve says that she understands – Angel is, after all, running the whole circus, now, which is a lot of pressure for him, especially with his hands-on policy (no pun intended, she assures him). While the pair are arguing at the party, Lorne wanders by and notes that one could cut the sexual tension between them with a knife. He suggests that they get a room and get on with it. Angel and Eve, acting on this subconscious command, move into Angel's office and begin kissing passionately, even though both wonder aloud if this isn't all a little sudden. They subsequently indulge in what appears to be some rather fantastic sex behind Angel's conveniently placed leather sofa. Even their discovery that their attraction is Lorne-influenced doesn't put a stop to it, much to a watching Spike's delight. Eve subsequently assures Angel that this isn't the first time she's had sex under a mystical influence noting that she did, after all, attend the University of Santa Cruz.

Logic, Let Me Introduce You to This Window: How did Lorne's subconscious kill the demon and place him on the buffet table without any of the guests noticing him?

Quote/Unquote: Angel: 'It's a perfect recipe for an out-of-control bloodbath.' Lorne: 'You're describing every good party I've ever been to.'

Lorne, on Angel: 'He's doing great. He's already *not* killed, like, a hundred guests.'

Angel: 'Eve, you stay here with me and we'll have more sex.'

Spike: 'You pissed in the big man's chair? That's fantastic.' Gunn: 'Can you please turn off that warm-fuzzy?' Spike: 'The Lorne thing? Wore off. I just think that's *bloody fabulous.*'

Notes: 'Man, this is lame. I mean, where's the ritual sacrifice?' The long-awaited Lorne-centric *Angel* episode finally arrives. With its garish 70s disco colours and glitterball lighting, the episode appears, at first glance, to be a moderately funny, if somewhat inconsequential, conceit with lots of pithy dialogue but little actual substance. Closer inspection, however, reveals a dark and troubling story about confusion, awareness and self-loathing. Another, very subtle variant on the standard *Buffy*-universe allegory concerning the truism 'be careful what you wish for, it might come true', 'Life of the Party' contains brilliant moments of dramatic subversion to separate the witty one-liners and bold action sequences. This is particularly notable when the production contrived to play clever intertextual games with somewhat clichéd and deep-set elements such as Spike's snarling cynicism, Wesley's painfully unrequited love for Fred and Angel and Eve's unresolved sexual tension. ('Angel's getting some,' notes Spike happily, when finding the latter couple naked in Angel's office, before adding, with disturbing Paul McCartney-style thumbs-up cheeriness, 'Good on ya, mate!'). Yet, at the centre of the episode is Lorne, unsure – despite its many attractions – of his place in the bewildering, neon-and-glitter, plasticfantastic world that the gang now find themselves a part of.

Angel spent most of the previous night fighting a Thraxis demon. Apparently the blood of this species burns. Many of Wolfram & Hart's clients have refused to come to this year's Halloween party, fearing that Angel would use the opportunity to kill them. Such parties usually begin with a ritual sacrifice – this year, however, is an exception. Angel initially plans to skip the party to watch ice hockey on TV. However, his team is losing so he reluctantly goes to the party. Fred says that she dressed as Raggedy Ann every Halloween for eight years. Wesley never really celebrated Halloween in England (where, until recently, the event was something of a nonentity). Spike notes disdainfully that in his day no self-respecting creature of the night even went out on All Hallow's Eve. He says that, instead, they left all that nonsense to the posers (see *Buffy*: 'Halloween', 'Fear Itself' and 'All the Way'). Lorne calls Harmony 'Harmonica' (see **39**, 'Disharmony') and notes that the entire fourth floor has a crush on her. Harmony tells Angel that morale within Wolfram & Hart sucks and that the staff, almost without exception, loathe him. Wolfram & Hart have a Psyche Component Storage Facility where Lorne's sleep is kept after its extraction. Fred notes that this isn't the only operation of its kind that the firm offers: Madeline Choux in Accounting has, apparently, had her ennui removed.

Soundtrack: Lorne sings a snatch of Thelma Houston's disco classic 'Don't Leave Me This Way', which features prominently during the episode. At the party, there's a lengthy and rather slammin' (albeit anonymous) techno track playing which Spike, with his positive mind-set, considers to be the best song ever written.

Critique: 'Moving *Angel* to Wednesday night has turned out to be one of the best scheduling moves of the season by any network,' noted *Variety*'s Josef Adalin.

Did You Know?: 'I asked David Boreanaz from *Angel* to be in it,' noted British singer Dido Armstrong concerning David's appearance in the video for her single 'White Flag'. 'I wanted someone dark and young. He's a lot of fun and was really up for it even though it was something he didn't have to do.'

Cast and Crew Comments: '[It's] a full-on romp, a lot of fun,' noted Jeff Bell concerning this episode. 'That's the [joy] of being on a show like *Angel*, that the tone can change not just from week-to-week, but scene-to-scene. We can have something terrible happen at a very funny moment, and we're trying to exploit those opportunities as much as possible.'

'What a ball that was,' Andy Hallett told *TV Zone*. 'The party was off the wall. I can honestly say I've never let loose on-camera as much as I did when we shot those scenes. Mercedes and I were dancing so hard that my mask started to peel off.'

94
The Cautionary Tale of Numero Cinco

US Transmission Date: 5 November 2003
UK Transmission Date: 17 February 2004

Writer: Jeffrey Bell
Director: Jeffrey Bell
Cast: Danny Mora (Numero Cinco), Bruno Gioiello (Security Guard),
Ed Cray (Homeless Murder Victim)[18]

When Angel is thrown through a plate-glass window by Wolfram & Hart's aged mail-delivery guy, Numero Cinco, it sets in motion a bizarre chain of events that culminates

---

[18] Uncredited.

in Angel fighting an Aztec Day of the Dead heart-sucking demon with Cinco's four undead Mexican wrestling brothers.

Dudes and Babes: Wolfram & Hart's mask-wearing mail-room employee (who had been in the background of several episodes earlier this season) is, in reality, Numero Cinco – a famous Mexican wrestler from a family of famous Mexican wrestlers.

A Little Learning is a Dangerous Thing: Spike tells Wesley he believes that Angel has lost his faith in the Shanshu prophecy (see **22**, 'To Shanshu in LA'; **92**, 'Hellbound'). Wes notes that the prophecy tells of an apocalyptic battle and a vampire with a soul who will play a major role in these events. There is also a suggestion that the vampire will then become human again. Spike wonders if heroically closing a Hellmouth could qualify (see *Buffy*: 'Chosen') though Wes notes that the specific battle itself is not identified. Nor, seemingly, is the *identity* of the vampire with a soul. However, Spike ultimately decides that the prophecy is probably nonsense, a fable designed to get vampires to play nice.

Denial, Thy Name is Angel: Discussing the on-going Wolfram & Hart situation with Gunn, Angel confesses that he is feeling a bit disconnected from what they are actually doing. Subsequently, Wesley notes that Angel seems to blame his melancholy on his new position. However, Wesley doesn't believe it's anything to do with the work. Rather, it's because Angel has lost hope that the work has any meaning. (There is a suggestion, from Angel himself, that the reason the demon who steals the hearts of heroes didn't take Angel's heart, despite having the opportunity to do so, was because of this. Wesley, however, suggests that the demon wants these hearts for sustenance – for the meat, not the metaphor. Gunn says that, as meat goes, Angel's heart is a dried-up chunk of beef jerky, something that Numero Cinco also points out later in the episode.) Angel declares that, as long as they keep saving lives, what does it matter if he believes in Shanshu or any other prophecy? Wesley replies that it matters a great deal. Hope, he believes, is the only thing that will stop Angel from becoming jaded and cynical like Numero Cinco.

The Conspiracy Starts at Home Time: Angel reminds Wesley of the dreaded 'The Father Will Kill The Son' prophecy (see **58**, 'Couplet'; **61**, 'Forgiving'). However, since Angel's deal with Wolfram & Hart to save Connor (see **88**, 'Home') effectively removed vast chunks of everyone's memories – bar Angel's – concerning the events of Seasons Three and Four in which Connor was a central player, Wesley has no idea what Angel is talking about (see also, **106**, 'Origin').

Work is a Four-Letter Word: Gunn notes that today Wolfram & Hart bankrupted a company that dumps raw waste into Santa Monica bay, banished a clan of pyro-warlocks into a Hell dimension and started a foster care programme for children whose parents have been killed by vampires. He believes that's a good day's work. Gunn knows that handling legal issues is nowhere near as heroic to Angel as doing the rescuing in person. But, Gunn notes, this is the first time in his life that he's anxious to get to work every day.

It's a Designer Label!: Lorne's cream suit and Gunn's stylish lawyer threads.

References: *Thunderbirds* also concerned five brothers who fought crime under a secret identity. There are allusions to *El Cid*, Chaka Khan's 'I'm Every Woman', the character of Wonder Woman, jazz pianist Herbie Hancock, *Pinocchio*, *Julius Caesar*, *The Matrix*, the nursery rhyme 'If Wishes Were Horses', OJ Simpson's celebrated lawyer Johnnie Cochran, prolific painter Grandma Moses and the crime novelist Agatha Christie. Also, the Greek myth of Achilles, the Get Out of Jail Free card from the board game *Monopoly* and the Bronze Star Medal.[19]

---

[19] This decoration, first awarded after 1941, is given to persons who, while serving with the US military, distinguished themselves by heroic or meritorious achievement while engaged in an action against the enemy.

Bitch!: Lorne is having difficulty working out which birthday card to send to a client, whom he describes as an ageing sexpot, celebrating a decade of turning 29. The woman has two children who are no longer little, a husband who seems to think that the extras trailer is a buffet table and, Lorne concludes, gravity really isn't doing her any favours. So, he has a simple question which he needs Fred's help with: Sexy Soccer Mama or Brainy Beauty? Fred suggests not sending a card at all, not mentioning the birthday, just sending flowers.

'West Hollywood?': When Spike tells Lorne about Angel's fight with Numero Cinco, Lorne says that it must have been quite a smackdown. 'There was *no* smacking,' says Angel, hurriedly.

Awesome!: All the stuff about the Devil's Robot.

'You May Remember Me From Such Films and TV Series As . . .': Danny Mora appeared in *Mr. Mom*, *Sliders*, *Road Ends* and *Chico and the Man*. Bruno Gioiello's CV includes *Jumbo Girl*, *Mickey Blue Eyes* and *The West Wing*. Ed Cray was in *Slave* and *Mr. Id*.

Behind the Camera: Jeffrey Bell made his name as a writer/producer for several years on *The X-Files* and, subsequently, *Alias*. Australian-born director of photography Ross Berryman had previously worked on *Timecop*, *Early Edition*, *Dead Calm*, *Strictly Ballroom*, *BMX Bandits* and *A Slice of Life*.

Not Exactly a Haven For the Bruthas: One of Aztec culture's most powerful warriors, Terzcatcatl forged a mystical talisman that allowed him to harness the power of the Sun God. He was discovered before he could use it and was sentenced to die on the Day of the Dead.[20] However, before he was executed, he had a shaman curse him to return from the grave every fifty years. On each rising the

---

[20] *Día de los Muertos*, a Mexican feast day on 31 October. Foods are traditionally prepared in honour of the dead.

demon eats the hearts of heroes to renew himself while he searches for a talisman, which has been passed down from champion to champion over the centuries. Terzcatcatl always rises in East LA. He murdered over a dozen people during his most recent killing spree; his victims include a Gulf War veteran, a woman who worked with a gang outreach programme and a firefighter who once rescued his entire crew. Fifty years ago Terzcatcatl was defeated by Los Hermanos Numeros – five Mexican wrestling brothers who, by night, fought demons. Numero Cinco, the sole survivor, lures Terzcatcatl to his brothers' graves hoping to be killed himself so that he can finally be reunited with them.

Cigarettes & Alcohol: Spike bemoans the fact that, in his non-corporeal state, he can't do any of the enjoyable things in life – drink, smoke or 'diddle my willy'.

Logic, Let Me Introduce You to This Window: When Lorne asks Cinco for his opinion as to which card he should send to his client, Fred is not even in the same corridor; she approaches them just as Lorne is finishing his question. Yet she tells Lorne that she heard what he said. Why is one of Wesley's staff using a computer to create a virtual image of the Aztec demon? We've previously seen that Angel is a very accomplished artist (see *Buffy*: 'Passion'; **10**, 'Parting Gifts'; **27**, 'Dear Boy'; **91**, 'Unleashed'). A drawing would surely be achieved much more quickly. How do details of Cinco's attack on Angel end up on the Internet within minutes of it happening? (This assumes that Lorne is talking literally as opposed to metaphorically when he says that he heard about it on the net.) Cinco's brothers all burst out of their graves. However, their bodies subsequently fade away – were they merely spirits? If so, can non-corporeal spirits do things like clawing their way through impacted earth and fighting heart-sucking demons? And what happened to the body of Cinco himself? Does grabbing a vampire and dragging him inside constitute an invitation into your home? It's non-verbal, but the thought probably counts. It seems that Angel is unsure about the amount to which his friends' memories have been altered by his deal with Wolfram & Hart – why else would he mention the Father/Son prophecy to Wesley? A modern-looking weight-bar is seen during the 1950s flashback along with what appears to be a 1970s vintage telephone. Were the Aztecs *all* cannibals, as Wesley seems to indicate when discussing Aztec culture with Gunn?

El Diablo Robotico!: During Cinco's tale of his brothers' glory days, he mentions a celebrated occasion when the Devil built a robot. The brothers seemingly fought and defeated the machine. Angel has not heard of this great victory. Cinco is saddened, noting that nobody remembers the good stuff these days. Subsequently, Angel asks Wesley if *he* knows anything about the Devil building a robot. 'El Diablo Robotico,' Wesley says, knowingly, leaving Angel to bemoan the fact that nobody ever tells him *anything*.

I Just *Love* Your Accent: Spike brilliantly describes the prophecy concerning what will happen to the vampire with a soul as 'that sandshoe thingumabob' (see **22**, 'To Shanshu in LA').

Motors: Another car from Angel's fleet of them is seen – a classic red convertible.

Quote/Unquote: Lorne: 'Fred, sweetie, you're sorta like a woman . . .'
    Angel: 'Is this blood?' Gunn: 'Yeah, but it's OK. It's yours.'
    Spike, to Angel: 'The geriatric community will be soiling their nappies when they hear you're on the case.'

Notes: 'You were going to drag me into your quest for the Aztec demon.' Just what *is* this nonsense disguised as an episode of *Angel*? Whatever it is, it's the worst *Angel* story in about three years. 'The Cautionary Tale of Numero Cinco' loses any chance it had of being taken seriously when one realises that the episode, basically, exists to give the title character the chance to feel connected to his mission again. A long-winded and painfully obvious series of banal sequences follow, most of which focus on the concept of hope (both lost and found), but include such frequently bizarre characterisation and fragmented plot pieces that, after a while, the viewer simply waves a little white flag and switches off their brain completely. The episode's plus points are, thus, drowned beneath a welter of pointless ephemera and supposedly colourful characterisation. What can we say about 'The Cautionary Tale of Numero Cinco' in the context of the series' overall structure? Flawed, but interesting? Let's call it flawed and leave it at that in the expectation that a writer as talented as Jeff Bell couldn't possibly get it this badly wrong in so many ways a second time.

Spike notes that Angel was always a bit of a drama queen. Angel's fountain pen is filled with blood instead of ink, as demon law requires all signatures to be in blood. The volumes from the Wolfram & Hart repository which Wesley and Angel access are of the same type – blank until commanded to produce a specific text – that Wesley was introduced to by Sirk in **88**, 'Home' (see also **95**, 'Lineage'; **96**, 'Destiny'). The text that Wesley reads, the *Xiaochimayan Codex*, written in Cuauhtitlan pictograms, includes details on pre-Hispanic, specifically Meso-American, myths. Gunn knows that Angel isn't happy working at Wolfram & Hart especially considering all the bureaucracy and the fact that a lot of their employees want Angel and his friends dead. But, Gunn points out, in-house attacks *are* down thirty per cent. He considers that they've accomplished more in one month than they did with Angel Investigations in a year. The episode appears to take place on, or around, 31 October 2003. After his brothers' deaths (seemingly in October 1953), Cinco was recruited to work for Wolfram & Hart by a very young Holland Manners. Having buried his brothers behind San Gregorio, each year on the anniversary of their death, Cinco performs a ritual hoping that they will return.

Soundtrack: The episode's main theme is Calexico's Tex-Mex classic 'Güero Canelo'.

Critique: 'There are a few impressive moments, mainly early in the episode before it gets bogged down by tedious *Star Trek*isms,' noted David Darlington in *Shivers*. 'But it's all a bit risible and too damn up itself, so it comes as a relief when the episode finally meanders to a halt.'

Did You Know?: Underneath *Angel*'s monster make-up, action sequences and witty conceits, James Marsters insists that there is considerable depth to the show. 'Joss always aims so high in his themes,' he told Kate O'Hare. 'He's got two people striving to be good. How *do* you reform your life? We're all human beings. We all have regret . . . and we all want to believe that we can redeem ourselves.'

Cast and Crew Comments: 'When I came to Mutant Enemy where you're supposed to pitch emotionally based stories [I thought] it would be cool to do Mexican wrestling,' Jeff Bell told Bryan Cairns. 'Evidently, Joss has always had a soft spot for it as well. I tried to do it at *The X-Files*, so it's [been] six years in the making.'

Joss Whedon's Comments: Asked about the phenomenal impact of DVD sales relating to TV shows, Joss noted that: 'It creates a new revenue stream that studios are learning to exploit. I don't know if that will ever translate back to a show. They're all separate units of a big company. [But] it doesn't hurt. The *Angel* DVDs have been really popular, proving, besides the Nielsens, that we have a loyal fan base.'

95
Lineage

US Transmission Date: 12 November 2003
UK Transmission Date: 24 February 2004

Writer: Drew Goddard
Director: Jefferson Kibbee
Cast: Roy Dotrice (Roger Wyndam-Pryce), Treva Etienne (Emil)

Still feeling guilty about having failed to protect Fred during an undercover-operation-gone-wrong, Wesley's life is further complicated when his father turns up at Wolfram & Hart. A former member of the Council of Watchers, Roger Wyndam-Pryce has an interesting offer to make to his estranged son. Then some ninja cyborgs stage an attack on the building.

A Little Learning is a Dangerous Thing: At the age of six or seven, Wesley attempted to perform a resurrection spell on a bird that died after flying into his bedroom window. Luckily his father caught him before he could complete the spell, otherwise, Roger believes, the zombie bird would have pecked out Wesley's eyeballs.

Roger notes that the atrocities committed by Wolfram & Hart are well documented.

The Conspiracy Starts at Home Time: The cyborg assassin which infiltrates Wolfram & Hart was designed to look and act like Wesley's father. It seems to have been programmed with extensive background information about Wesley (including material such as personality profiles taken directly from the Watchers' Council files). Manipulating Wesley into letting him into Wolfram & Hart's secure vault, the cyborg takes the Staff of Devo'sin which is needed to extract Angel's free will from his body. Wesley rescues the situation by shooting Roger, still believing the cyborg actually to be his father. In death, the glamour that made the machine look like Roger is broken and its true nature is revealed.

Spike believes that he has become trapped at Wolfram & Hart for a nefarious purpose and that Eve is part of the reason for this. The amulet which made Spike as he is was originally given to Angel (see **88**, 'Home'). Spike says it's therefore reasonable to assume that The Senior Partners meant to make Angel a ghost. Eve replies with an interesting question: who said that the amulet was *ever* meant for Angel?

Denial, Thy Name is Angel: Could it be that Angel really is, as Eve suggests, worried about the next occasion that

Wesley will betray him while trying to do the right thing (see **59**, 'Loyalty')?

Denial, Thy Name is Wesley: Wesley's awkward relationship with his father had previously been mentioned in both **14**, 'I've Got You Under My Skin' and **41**, 'Belonging'. In **17**, 'Eternity', Angelus told Wesley that he had a massive inferiority complex where his father was concerned. In this episode we see that, despite the many positive changes Wesley has gone through – both emotionally and physically – during the past few years, this remains all too true. Just a few moments in the presence of Roger sees Wesley revert to a bumbling clown who is more likely to trip over his own feet than provide a brilliant solution. Just as he was when he first arrived in Sunnydale, in other words (see also **72**, 'Spin the Bottle'). Wes admits to Angel that he finds it difficult to think clearly when his father is around. Angel is sympathetic, noting that the complex relationship between fathers and sons can often be torture (see **15**, 'The Prodigal').

At the end of the episode, guilty over having killed the cyborg that he believed to be his father, Wesley calls his real father in England. Just as in **41**, 'Belonging', Mr Wyndam-Pryce seems abrasive and condescending towards his son during their conversation.

Work is a Four-Letter Word: Wesley explains to his father that Lorne runs the Wolfram & Hart Entertainment Division. Roger, sarcastically, notes he can understand why *that* would be important in the fight against ultimate evil. Gunn responds that Roger would be amazed how many horrible movies the company has stopped from reaching the general public.

It's a Designer Label!: Angel's tasteful grey jacket, Eve's crimson blouse and short skirt and Lorne's bright scarlet ensemble.

References: There are allusions to The Better Business Bureau, Dutch surrealist graphic artist Maurits Cornelis

Escher (1898–1972),[21] actor Louis Gossett Jr (*Roots, An Officer and a Gentleman*) and his performance in *Iron Eagle II*, the Harry Potter novels, British politician Sir Winston Churchill (1874–1965), Irish actor and singer Richard Harris (1930–2002), *The Bionic Woman* and *RoboCop*. Also, Oscar-winning actress Dame Judi Dench. Wesley's codeword to enter his secret vault is Elysium. In Greek mythology, this was a section of The Underworld – the final resting place of the souls of the righteous. The design of the cyborgs somewhat resembles the Raston Warrior Robots in *Doctor Who*. There are oblique dialogue references to one of the series' most regular allusions, *Apocalypse Now*,[22] and some visual allusions to another, *Die Hard*.

'West Hollywood?': When meeting Roger for the first time, Lorne notes that it's like Winston Churchill and a young Richard Harris had a beautiful love child. This, according to his sources, may not be as ridiculous as it sounds.

Awesome!: Spike being lost for words after Roger reminds him of the carnage Spike caused at their previous meeting. The only thing that Spike can think of to say is, 'So, how've you been?'

---

[21] Fred's description of the cyborg's interior resembling something Escher would have devised, except with electronics instead of geese, suggests that she's thinking specifically about Escher's celebrated 1938 woodcut *Day and Night*. Other famous Escher works include *Tower of Babel* (1928), *Castrovalva* (1930), *Reptiles* (1943), *Eye* (1946), *Relativity* (1953) and *Belvedere* (1958).

[22] The story of the making of Francis Ford Coppola's epic Vietnam odyssey, based on Joseph Conrad's novel *Heart of Darkness*, is almost as legendary as the actual movie itself. It took over a year to film on location in the Philippines, with a tornado and a near-fatal heart attack for it's leading actor, Martin Sheen, prolonging the shoot. This was followed by post-production of over two years before the movie finally emerged to critical and commercial acclaim in 1979. The story concerns US army assassin Captain Willard (Sheen) being sent up the Nung river into Cambodia to 'terminate, with extreme prejudice' the command of rogue Special Forces Colonel Kurtz (Marlon Brando). As Giles points out in *Buffy*: 'Restless', however, it's Willard's journey and the madness that he observes en route that are the main focus of the movie rather than the war itself. One of Joss Whedon's favourite films, *Apocalypse Now*, in addition to having been previously referenced or alluded to in several *Buffy* and *Angel* episodes (*Buffy*: 'Gingerbread', 'Restless', 'Him'; **11**, Somnambulist'; **43**, 'Through the Looking Glass'; **58**, 'Couplet'; **73**, 'Apocalypse Nowish'), was also one of the key influences on Whedon's sci-fi Western, *Firefly*.

'You May Remember Me From Such Films and TV Series As . . .': Born in London in 1923, Roy Dotrice played Zeus in *Hercules: The Legendary Journeys*, Father in *Beauty and the Beast* and the title role in *Dickens of London*. He provided voice work on the classic BBC documentary series *The Ascent of Man* and his CV also includes appearances in *LA Law*, *Space: 1999*, *Babylon 5*, *Hart to Hart*, *Picket Fences*, *Amadeus* and *The Equalizer* opposite his son-in-law Edward Woodward. Roy is the father of actress Michele Dotrice. Treva Etienne played Tony Sanders in *London's Burning* and appeared in *Eyes Wide Shut*, *Black Hawk Down* and *Pirates of the Caribbean*.

Sex and Drugs and Rock'n'Roll: When Angel is discussing with Fred how the cyborgs were created, Spike casually notes that sex taking place between robots and humans is much more common than most people think (a clear reference to his own dalliance with the Buffybot in *Buffy*: 'Intervention'). Then, thankfully, he shuts up.

Lorne tells Roger a seemingly very risqué story that concludes with him covered in cherries, the police pounding on the door and Judi Dench screaming 'that's way too much to pay for a pair of pants!'

Fred is given a course of antibiotics after being attacked by a cyborg as there is some concern about where the grappling hook that wounded her had previously been.

Logic, Let Me Introduce You to This Window: An army of cyborg demons, one of whom has assumed the identity of Wesley's father, infiltrate Wolfram & Hart. Why, exactly? Their purpose in wishing to obtain Angel's free will is never explained either in this or any subsequent episode. When did Fred become so proficient and knowledgeable concerning weaponry? Weren't the Council of Watchers' files and psychological profiles all blown up along with the actual Council itself (see *Buffy*: 'Never Leave Me')? Where do the cyborgs conceal the lethal chains and hooks that they carry? There's the changing memories question again – seemingly Wesley remembers that Cordelia was possessed by Jasmine and that she killed Lilah while under Jasmine's influence (see **78**, 'Calvary'). Yet he doesn't remember Connor? In **92**, 'Hellbound', Eve expressed her concern about Fred's department's spending. Here, she tells Fred to let The Senior Partners know if she needs more resources. This could, of course, be part of a clever agenda to play off the various departmental heads against each other. Angel's free will, apparently, looks like a big wobbly, smoky thing.

Quote/Unquote: Emil: 'You're making me so hot right now.' Fred: 'Wow, turned on by a woman holding an enormous gun? What a surprise.'

Fred, to Wesley: 'I wish I was your father, I'd tell you to grow up.' Roger: 'It doesn't work. I've tried.'

Spike: 'I killed my mom. Actually, I'd *already* killed her. Then she tried to shag me, so I had to . . .' Wesley: 'Thank you. I'm very comforted.'

Angel, on the same subject: 'I killed my *actual* dad. It's one of the first things I did when I became a vampire.' Wesley: 'I hardly see how that's the same situation.' Angel: 'Yeah, I really didn't think that one through.'

Notes: 'You never had any use for me as a child, and you can't bear the thought of me as an adult. Tell me, what is it that galls you? That I was never as good at the job as you, or that I might be better?' Displaying the bouncebackability for which Joss Whedon's shows have become so noted, following on from the dreadful previous episode, 'Lineage' is a little masterpiece of dramatic indulgence. It was less than five years ago that Alexis Denisof first stumbled into Sunnydale, an immediate target of hatred for many *Buffy* fans. How times change, and how fans' attitudes change with them. For much of the last three years, Wes has been one of the best of many excellent reasons to watch *Angel*. In the first episode in a while to focus primarily upon him, Denisof reminds us why Joss Whedon considers him to be one of the finest actors working in television today. 'Lineage' explores another *Angel* truism-as-metaphor – no matter how old you are, you will always be a child to your parents – in a cunning and well-structured piece of dramatic construction. As the oft-mentioned, but never previously seen, Machiavellian Roger Wyndam-Pryce, Roy Dotrice is terse, pithy and very sinister. It's easy to see where Wesley's inferiority complex came from. There are amusing, if brief, subplots involving Spike, Eve and Lorne and a number of terrific fight sequences. Atypically, there are also Big Concept ideas present concerning the weight of parental aspirations and the psychological pain of rejection and belittlement. And, key to it all, Denisof at his very best – funny and just a bit dangerous.

Wesley asks how his mother is and Roger replies that she's as sturdy as ever. Both Spike and Angel attempt to empathise with Wesley, noting that they, too, killed a parent (in *Buffy*: 'Lies My Parents Told Me' and **15**, 'The Prodigal' respectively). Spike always believed that, rather than being born, Wesley was grown in some sort of greenhouse for dandies. Roger notes that Wesley was head boy at the Watchers' Academy (see **72**, 'Spin the Bottle'), although he adds that the pickings were a bit slim that particular year. One of the texts that Wesley accesses is the *Saitama Codex*. Roger Wyndam-Pryce and Spike have previously met. In 1963 representatives from the Council of Watchers, including Wesley's father, discovered Spike slaughtering everyone in an orphanage in Vienna. Spike killed two of the men before escaping. (The fact that Spike and Drusilla had spent some time in Vienna had previously been disclosed in *Buffy*: 'Surprise'.) Roger tells Wesley that the Council is being reformed after it's destruction in *Buffy*: 'Never Leave Me' and alludes to the fact that many friends of his died in that explosion. (Technically, of course, *everything* that Roger tells Wesley is a lie although, as subsequently discovered in **99**, 'Damage', the Council *is*, indeed, in the process of being revived, albeit with Rupert Giles as its leader, as opposed to Mr Wyndam-Pryce.) Roger also notes that some on the Council consider Wesley's tenure as a Watcher to be their most embarrassing failure (see *Buffy*: 'Bad Girls', 'Consequences', 'Enemies', 'Graduation Day' Part 2; **99**, 'Damage'), a suggestion that appears to hurt Wesley a great deal. Again, whether this is actually true or not is, ultimately, left up to the viewer. Roger muses that, in his day, the Council fought vampires, werewolves and an occasional swamp man. Now he has to deal with protohuman, cybernetic chain-fighters. Wes notes that these are complicated times. The weapons dealer whom Wesley meets is Emil (previously mentioned in **69**, 'The House Always Wins'. Emil supplied the collapsible sword that Wes used with such hilariously euphemistic results in **72**, 'Spin the Bottle'). Emil's henchmen are named Dante and Phillipe. Wesley keeps valuable and dangerous items in a hidden vault behind his office.

When the power goes out, Spike yells, 'You'll never take me, Pavayne!' (a reference to **92**, 'Hellbound' – the events of which seem to have affected Spike more than he is willing to admit). Wesley tells his father that he chopped off his last girlfriend's head after she was stabbed in the neck by a Higher Power (see **78**, 'Calvary'; **79**, 'Salvage'). Eve and Angel discuss Wesley kidnapping Connor and handing him over to Holtz and the fact that Wesley has no memory of these events (see **59**, 'Loyalty'; **60**, 'Sleep Tight'; **88**, 'Home'; **106**, 'Origin'). Emil notes that his business depends on trust and that complaints are usually dealt with through killing, torture, beating and, sometimes, fire. Wesley tells Angel that a group of the cyborgs took out a demon cabal in Jakarta, while others destroyed the Tanmar Death Chamber.

Soundtrack: The sinister, atonal, Oriental-sounding score, like some of the dialogue, seems to have been influenced by *Apocalypse Now*.

Critique: The new *Angel* episodes are more self-contained and the stories are easier to follow, Robert Bianco noted. 'What hasn't altered, however, is Joss Whedon's ingenious mix of comedy and suspense; his fascination with the meanings of right, wrong and responsibility; and his ability to produce a ceaselessly entertaining hour of television.'

Describing *Angel* as one of 'TV's Top Five Most Daring Shows of 2003', *MSN Entertainment News* noted that: 'With *Buffy* retired, its spin-off can finally get the respect it's been deserving for the past four years. A lot went down for Angel and his crew in 2003, and in typical tradition, most of it was very dark . . . As long as The WB execs keep giving this show air time, Whedon and company will continue to turn out the smartest drama on network TV.'

Did You Know?: According to a story which appeared on the Hollywood gossip website, the *Daily Dish* in November 2003, David Boreanaz failed to find a buyer for his Mercedes. David tried to sell his top-of-the-range car on e-Bay during October, the report claimed. But buyers were seemingly put off by the $78,000 asking price. The report alleged that David had even offered to personally deliver the car and spend a day with the buyer.

Cast and Crew Comments: 'I was worried about Fred becoming a regular. My old roomie was a big *Buffy* fan and she said "I was on the website and people are not excited about a new character joining the show," ' Amy Acker told *Femme Fatales*. 'It was before I'd even started.' A Texas native, Acker was born in Dallas and initially trained to be a ballet dancer rather than an actress (see **57**, 'Waiting in the Wings'). 'Then I had knee surgery [and] decided to take an acting class.' Amy then enrolled at the Southern Methodist University to study Fine Arts. 'During my senior year this theatre company asked me to do Shakespeare [with them] for eight months, before I even graduated.'

Drew Goddard's Comments: 'There's no place I'd rather be,' Drew told his hometown newspaper, the *Los Alamos Monitor*. 'I mosey in to work at about 9.30, talk about vampires all day, leave about 7 [and get] paid for it. You couldn't find a better job.' Drew went on to explain that he and the show's other writers work on each episode, break the story and then write down every scene as a group. Each writer then takes turns writing a complete episode on their own. The process usually takes about two weeks from start to finish, he added, although at certain times, scripts could be needed in as short a time as three days.

96
Destiny

US Transmission Date: 19 November 2003
UK Transmission Date: 2 March 2004

Writers: David Fury, Steven S DeKnight
Director: Skip Schoolnik
Cast: Justin Connor (Jerry), Mark Kelly (Reese),
Aaron D Spears (Security Guard #1)[23]

A power surge caused by the arrival of a mysterious package recorporealises Spike. The same package also seems to send many of the staff at Wolfram & Hart insane. Reinvestigating the Shanshu prophecy, Angel is told of a magical cup. Drinking from this will, it is claimed, restore the prophesied ensouled vampire's humanity. But to *which* ensouled vampire does the prophecy refer?

The Conspiracy Starts at Home Time: A member of Wesley's department and an ex-Watcher, Rutherford Sirk began working for Wolfram & Hart some time before the Council was destroyed (see **88**, 'Home'). Having stolen the original transcript of the *Devandire Sibylline Codex*, Sirk convinces Angel and Spike that the answer to their destiny lies in Death Valley and arms the pair with newly translated verses from the prophecy of the Shanshu. This, it eventually becomes clear, is *all* part of an elaborate deception. The final scene of the episode reveals that Sirk (who has now disappeared) has been working for Eve. Meanwhile, Eve herself is involved (in both a physical and conspiratorial sense) with Lindsey McDonald (last seen – along with his *evil hand* – in **40**, 'Dead End').

A Little Learning is a Dangerous Thing: While talking to Angel about Wesley's belief that he had killed his father (see **95**, 'Lineage'), Spike says that if Wesley wants to experience true guilt he should try staking his mother when

---

[23] Uncredited.

she's coming on to him. Harmony overhears and mutters, '*That* explains a lot.' Spike notes, quickly, that this was a long time ago and his mother wasn't really herself.

Sirk tells Angel that Angel didn't read the Shanshu prophecy (see **22**, 'To Shanshu in LA'), he merely read a translation. Sirk likens this to the difference between the King James version of the Bible and the original text in Aramaic or Hebrew. Sirk elaborates on the historical context and subtlety of usage contained within the prophecy, noting that the flavour of the original meaning gets lost with each subsequent translation. He says that Angel may as well have read a twelve-year-old's book report on the subject. Sirk then reads the passages from the prophecy which is, seemingly, full of elaborate metaphors (Sirk sarcastically asks if he has to explain what metaphors are to Angel and Spike). Sirk describes how the vampire with a soul must drink from the Cup of Perpetual Torment. Angel asks if this is another metaphor but Sirk assures him that the cup itself is real.

Denial, Thy Names Are Angel and Spike: As they battle for the right to be the first to the mythical cup, the depths of Angel and Spike's mutual antipathy is revealed. Spike alleges that every time Angel looks at Spike he must see all of the dirty and wicked things that Spike has done and all of the lives that he's taken. Everything that Spike has become is Angel's fault, Spike concludes. Drusilla may have sired him but it was Angelus who made Spike a monster. Angel replies that he didn't make Spike what he is, he merely opened up the door and let the real Spike out. Spike argues that Angel never knew the *real* William, he was too busy trying to see his own reflection in Spike, praying that there was someone as disgusting as Angelus so he could live with himself. Spike, he proudly declares, is *nothing* like Angel (see *Buffy*: 'Dirty Girls'). Angel agrees, suggesting instead that Spike is *much less* than him, which is why Buffy never really loved Spike; because he wasn't Angel. Spike replies that perhaps this means that Buffy was thinking about Angel, all of those *many* times when she and Spike were enjoying sex. It's noticeable, however, that when Spike finally beats Angel he cannot bring himself to stake his grandsire, using the excuse that Buffy would be upset if he did.

It's a Designer Label!: Gunn's brown shirt, Harmony's very pretty light-blue skirt, Eve's red dress.

References: Allusions to *You've Got Mail*, *Chitty Chitty Bang Bang*, *Hong Kong Phooey*, *Monty Python's Flying Circus*, Howard Hawks's *His Girl Friday*, the Greek Myth of Pandora's Box, *The Music Man* (see **93**, 'Life of the Party'), *Looking for Mr Goodbar*, the King James Bible (first published in 1611), Matthew 18:9 ('thine eye offends me'), Sparks's 'This Town Ain't Big Enough for the Both of Us', and Superman. Sirk paraphrases the maxim 'it ain't over till the fat lady sings'. There are several visual references to *Indiana Jones and the Last Crusade*.

'West Hollywood?': In a scene full of sexual tension and overt S&M allusions, when they are first introduced, Angelus asks William if he has any idea what it's like to have only women as travelling companions. As he does this, Angelus holds William's arm in the sunlight, causing his skin to burn. Angelus says that he likes the ladies all right but, lately, he's been wondering what it would be like to share the slaughter of innocents with another man. He then deliberately extends his own arm into the sunlight and seems to enjoy the pain he experiences. He asks if William believes this makes him some kind of deviant. William, apparently anxious to prove that he's equal to the challenge, extends his hand into the sunlight again. Angelus believes that he and William are going to be good friends.

Awesome!: The lengthy and brutal Angel/Spike fight in the Opera House. The sequence in which Gunn and Eve are arguing and, in the background, a Wolfram & Hart employee is walking menacingly towards them with an axe. Just as the man is about to smash the window that separates him from his intended victims, someone dives on top of him leaving Gunn and Eve still bitching away at each other unaware of their close brush with death. Also, the hugely unexpected final scene. We'd all pretty much guessed that Eve had her own sinister agenda in play but not that it included Lindsey.

'You May Remember Me From Such Films and TV Series As . . .': Christian Kane played Wick Lobo on *Rescue 77* and Flyboy Leggat on *Fame LA*. He also appeared in *Just Married* and fronted his own country-rock band, Kane. Juliet Landau, despite appearances in films such as *The Grifters*, *Pump Up the Volume*, *Theodore Rex*, *Toolbox Murders* and *Citizens of Perpetual Indulgence*, and in TV series like *Parker Lewis Can't Lose* and *La Femme Nikita*, remains best known for her performance as Loretta King opposite her father, Martin, in Tim Burton's *Ed Wood*. Michael Halsey's impressive CV includes *Sabotage!*, *The Aqua Girls*, *Matlock*, *Blake's 7*, *Moonlighting*, *The Dukes of Hazzard*, *Fawlty Towers*, *It Ain't Half Hot Mum* and *Secret Army*.

Justin Connor appeared in *Resurrection Mary*, *Boomtown* and *Monk*. Mark Kelly was in *Swatters*, *CSI* and *She Spies*. Aaron D Spears appeared in *Cappuccino* and *Everybody Loves Raymond*.

Behind the Camera: Skip Schoolnik was the regular editor on *Buffy* along with over thirty films and TV movies including *Fighting for My Daughter*, *For Richer and Poorer*, *Purgatory*, *Popeye Doyle*, *Halloween II* and *Kung Fu: The Movie*.

LA-Speak: Gunn: 'I say you start by untyin' the brutha.'

Sex and Drugs and Rock'n'Roll: In addition to sharing a mutually abusive relationship with his sire Darla, Angelus was also sexually active with Drusilla around the time that William was first sired (however, see **108**, 'The Girl in Question'). It is implied in *Buffy*: 'Lie to Me', 'What's My Line', 'Passion' and several other episodes that this incestuous relationship lasted throughout the period until Angelus acquired his soul in 1898.

When Spike realises that he is corporeal, he immediately tells Angel that he needs to borrow Harmony. Harmony is, momentarily, aghast at the implication that she and Spike should have sex just because he's solid again. Spike simply flatters Harmony and she quickly informs Angel that she will be taking a long lunch as she and Spike head, giggling, towards a convenient office. During their subsequent intercourse, Harmony calls out Spike's name. Spike tells her not to talk and spoil the moment. However, he fails to notice Harmony's eyes bleeding. Harmony then morphs into her vampire face and sinks her teeth into his neck, telling Spike that he is using her. He doesn't want her, she continues, but his Slayer whore.

Logic, Let Me Introduce You to This Window: Sirk notes that the Cup of Perpetual Torment was first housed in the hidden city of Petra. It disappeared during the Crusades and resurfaced in the Vatican only to vanish once more during the third year of the Inquisition. (As this began in 1232, that would place the cup's disappearance in or around 1235.) From there it, somehow, found it's way to Nevada. Thus, once again, we have an example of a mythical artefact from the ancient world in the *Buffy*-universe being hidden on a continent known only to the indigenous population and, allegedly, a few lost Vikings, until its 'discovery' in 1492 (see also *Buffy*: 'The Harsh Light of Day', 'End of Days'). Who took the cup there? How did they know that they wouldn't fall off the end of the world? During the sequence with Angelus and William in the carriage, the bride whom Angelus has feasted upon opens and closes her eyes on several occasions. (To be fair, it's never made entirely clear in the dialogue between the two vampires whether she is supposed to be alive or dead.) William's hair looks very different to how it appeared in *Buffy*: 'Fool for Love', despite the events depicted here taking place mere hours after those previously seen. And, speaking of hair, what on earth is wrong with Harmony's in the opening scene? Since when did Fred *ever* call Gunn by his surname, as opposed to Charles, as she does twice here?

I Just *Love* Your Accent: When Harmony opens the package sent to Spike, there is a sudden flash of light from inside the box. Spike notes that this was 'a slap and a tickle'.

Motors: Spike steals Angel's Viper to drive to Death Valley (see **90**, 'Just Rewards'; **97**, 'Harm's Way').

Cruelty to Animals: When Spike drinks some of Angel's prepared blood, he asks if he's tasting otter (see **89**, 'Conviction').

Quote/Unquote: Spike, to Angel: 'Fighting for truth, justice and soccer moms? You still can't lay flesh on a cross without smelling like bacon, can ya?'

Angel: 'That's not a prize you're holding ... It's a burden. A cross. One you're going to have to bear till it burns you to ashes. Believe me. I know.'

Fred: 'God, what happened?' Angel: 'I fell down some stairs. Big stairs.'

Notes: 'You had a soul forced on you ... *I* fought for my soul. Almost did me in a dozen times over, but I kept fighting. Because it was the right thing to do.' It's the *Angel* version of *Monty Python's Holy Grail*: an epic quest saga full of stirring deeds, madcap chasing about – and running away – and not a little comedy. 'Destiny' also includes numerous flashbacks to the early days of William the Bloody Awful Poet's vampire existence, and a welcome return for Juliet Landau. Having spent three episodes providing little more than cameos, James Marsters is given the opportunity to remind viewers why he was brought on to *Angel* in the first place. Because he and Boreanaz together are *really funny*. Even when they're beating the tar out of each other. Perhaps, *especially* when they're beating the tar out of each other. 'Destiny' touches on some hardcore dramatic clichés (the bizarre *ménage à trois* that was Angel, Spike and Dru circa *Buffy* Season Two, for instance), but it does so with a knowing wink to the series' fans – don't worry about all this serious stuff, it seems to say, there's bound to be a cracking joke just around the corner. After all, no series blessed with Mercedes McNab's talents is going to be laughless for long. And the triple-bluff ending? Now, *that*'s a classic.

Angelus and Spike were first, formally, introduced by Drusilla at the Royal London Hotel, which is in England apparently, in 1880. (Presumably this meeting took place very soon after Drusilla first sired William – see *Buffy*: 'Fool for Love' – but shortly *before* William and Drusilla returned to William's home and William sired his mother Anne – see *Buffy*: 'Lies My Parents Told Me'.) Darla was not present at this historic meeting, having been sent for by The Master (see *Buffy*: 'The Harvest'). This indicates that The Master was still in London almost 120 years after he met Angel there (see **29**, 'Darla'). Angelus and William's first massacre together occurred soon afterwards at a wedding, during which Angelus horribly murdered a priest and beat the groom to death with his own arm – actions that *really* impressed the young William. During their time in London, Drusilla would routinely prowl the East End looking for street urchins to murder.

According to Gunn, both The White Room and The Conduit have vanished since the events of **92**, 'Hellbound'. They have been replaced by a howling abyss. Eve alleges that the existence of two ensouled vampires at the same time was never meant to happen and this is the likely cause of the cosmic disturbance. The solution, according to Sirk, is for either Angel or Spike to drink from the Cup of Perpetual Torment as written in the Shanshu Prophecies. This vessel is said to currently reside in Death Valley at an abandoned opera house, Columns, which was buried by an earthquake in 1938. Whichever vampire drinks from the cup is the one that the prophecy refers to and will have his past sins washed clean and become mortal. Except that, actually, the story is pure invention and the cup contains Mountain Dew (as Spike discovers when he finally drinks from it). The Senior Partners end the chaos by temporarily stabilising the universal equilibrium. They are said by Eve to be as furious about the whole mess as Angel and his friends are. Eve again mentions that she went to school in

Santa Cruz and refers to battling Id Monsters (both references to **93**, 'Life of the Party').

Soundtrack: An instrumental snatch of the Dead Kennedys' controversial 1981 single 'Too Drunk to F*ck' plays, loudly, as Spike drives Angel's Viper along Route 66 in a scene very reminiscent of the closing sequence of *Buffy*: 'Lover's Walk'.

Critique: 'The ending promises the season's first extended storyline,' noted *DreamWatch*'s K Stoddard Hayes. 'And it looks like it's going to be a knockout.'

Did You Know?: Alexis Denisof's absence from this episode was due to him being on his honeymoon with his new wife, Alyson Hannigan.

Cast and Crew Comments: 'The show's writers have tapped into my sarcastic streak,' Andy Hallett told Steve Eramo. 'Of all the regulars, Lorne probably feels the most comfortable being a wise-ass to Angel.'

Steven DeKnight's Comments: 'It's kind of a joke around here when I write a fight,' Steven told *Xposé*. 'It's a Steve DeKnight fight so it's going to be way over budget.' DeKnight noted that he had to take some scripted material out of 'Destiny' prior to shooting, but got away with some sequences that he thought would be deleted due to content. 'At the end, I was very specific – Angel and Spike were a bloody mess from the brutality of beating the hell out of each other.' Surprisingly perhaps, The WB allowed this to pass. 'They are usually extremely squeamish about showing blood.'

97
Harm's Way

US Transmission Date: 14 January 2004
UK Transmission Date: 9 March 2004

Writers: Elizabeth Craft, Sarah Fain
Director: Vern Gillium

Cast: Danielle Nicolet (Tamika), Jennifer Haworth (Brittany),
Stacy Reed (Charlotte), David Gangler (Dan),
Christopher Gehrmane (Rudy), Brendan Hines (Eli),
Bryce Mouer (Tobias Dupree), Olga Vilner (Vinji Leader),
Nick Jaine (Sahrvin Leader)

On the surface, she's the single It-Girl-About-Town, but
Harmony Kendall is having one of those days when
absolutely nothing goes right. She can't seem to connect
with anyone at work and then she wakes up in bed with a
dead guy next to her. As if that wasn't bad enough, her
firm now operates a zero-tolerance policy towards murder.

Dudes and Babes: Tamika has worked in the Wolfram &
Hart secretary pool for five years and has a typing speed
of eighty words per minute. She's also a vampire and has
become dangerously obsessed with Harmony ever since the
latter was selected as Angel's assistant after only four and
a half weeks on the job. When Tamika observes Harmony
talking to demon-rights advocate Tobias Dupree (who was
mediating a dispute between feuding demon clans for
Wolfram & Hart), Tamika takes the opportunity to frame
her perceived rival.

Eli worked for Wolfram & Hart's accounting department and became a victim of the company's recently
initiated zero-tolerance policy against murder when his
out-of-hours hobby (dismembering virgins) was discovered.

Spike tells Fred that he's grateful for all the hard work
she put in to try and recorporealise him and that he won't
forget her kindness towards him (see **103**, 'A Hole in the
World').

A Little Learning is a Dangerous Thing: Fred tells Angel
that her lab has upgraded the Wolfram & Hart weapons
scanner. He asks if it's foolproof and, while Fred isn't
willing to offer a total guarantee against some fool being
able to bypass it, she says that it *is* state of the art.

Denial, Thy Name is Fred: Harmony notes that Fred has
two good-looking guys after her. All of the office girls

think it's Knox and Gunn, she notes. However she knows
that it's really Knox and Wesley. Fred begins to confirm
this then gets rather flustered, though she does admit both
of them are hot. She's more interested in knowing why the
office girls are discussing who she's dating.

Denial, Thy Name is Harmony: Panicking after discovering
a dead man's body in her bed, Harmony comes to the
obvious conclusion: it's all Fred's fault since she was the
one who suggested that Harmony talk to the guy in the
first place.

The Conspiracy Starts at Home Time: The LA branch of
Wolfram & Hart was officially founded in 1791 although
there have been various allusions to the company existing,
in one form or another, since the dawn of time – in this,
and other, dimensions.

The detective who called Angel regarding Dupree's
murder was one Dave Griffin. Angel is told that Wolfram
& Hart actually *own* the LAPD, information which
surprises neither Gunn nor Wesley.

Love is a Four-Letter Word: When Spike sits next to
Harmony in the bar at the episode's end, she asks what
he's still doing in LA. She thought he would be chasing the
Slayer in Europe. Spike admits that he got as far as buying
a boat ticket for the trip, but then he thought about it. A
man simply cannot go out in a blaze of glory like he did,
saving the world, and then show up three months later, on
a cruise ship in the south of France. It's hard to top an exit
like that. Harmony assures Spike that girls really don't
care about stuff like that. Just one look at Spike and Buffy
will forget about how horribly he treated her in the past
and how he took her for granted. Spike denies that he ever
did that to Buffy, then realises that Harmony is referring
to his relationship with *her*. Spike expects that Buffy *would*
be happy enough to see him, but he believes that such a
journey would make his self-sacrifice worthless (which,
when you think about it, is a *really* egotistical conceit).
Harmony says that she knows what it's like not to matter,

but Spike points out she clearly mattered to someone: Tamika tried to frame her, ergo Harmony must have mattered a great deal to her. The realisation of this seems to delight Harmony.

It's a Designer Label!: Harmony's overall pink look and fluffy white coat. Also Fred's green miniskirt, Lorne's trenchcoat and dark-blue jacket and Wesley's black shirt.

References: Major multinational corporations with whom Wolfram & Hart have a close working relationship include Yoyodyne (from Thomas Pynchon's novel *The Crying of Lot 49*; it was also the name of the evil company in *The Adventures of Buckaroo Banzai*), Weyland-Yutami (from the *Alien* movies) and NewsCorp (20th-Century Fox's owners). Also, allusions to Fred's love of the Dixie Chicks (see **89**, 'Conviction'), Dobie Gray's 'The In Crowd', the painkiller Vicodin, Exodus 21 ('eye for an eye'), Revelation 6 (the Four Horsemen of the Apocalypse), Italian states-man Niccolò Machiavelli (1469–1527), Gilbert and Sul-livan (see **89**, 'Conviction') and perfume manufacturers Chanel. Stock footage of the Hollywood Sign, the entrance to the Santa Monica Yacht Club and a Beverly Hills street sign feature in the Wolfram & Hart video.

Bitch!: When it's suggested by one of the female lunchroom employees that Lorne is grooming Dan for promotion, Harmony adds that she believes Angel also grooms her. This, notes the woman, would explain Harmony's hair.

'West Hollywood?': Fred notes during her autopsy of Dupree that the size and depth of the bite marks on the victim indicate that he was killed by a female vampire. 'Or gay?' asks Harmony, desperately. Fred explains that it doesn't actually work that way.

Awesome!: The dreadfully inane Wolfram & Hart promo-tional video (and, particularly, Angel's stilted and self-conscious body language during it). Fred and Harmony bonding over cocktails. Harmony increasingly desperately dumping her colleagues into the maintenance closet as she seeks to prove her innocence. Gunn hilariously apologising to the demons for Angel's awful translation of their language. Harmony and Tamika's martial arts fight using chopsticks.

'You May Remember Me From Such Films and TV Series As . . .': Danielle Nicolet played Cheryl in *Shadow of Doubt* and Caryn in *3rd Rock from the Sun* and appeared in *The Prince*, *Stargate SG-1* and *Where Truth Lies*. Jennifer Haworth's movies include *Karma* and *Incorporated*. Stacy Reed appeared in *The Job* and *The West Wing*. Christopher Gehrmane's CV includes *Will & Grace*, *CSI* and *Las Vegas*. Brendan Hines appeared in *True Dreams*. Bryce Mouer played Lyle Jones in *Spyder Games*. Olga Vilner featured in *The Handler* and *NYPD Blue*. Nick Jaine was in *Judging Amy*.

LA-Speak: Harmony notes that both of the feuding demon clans think poodles are 'wicked bad luck'.

Cigarettes & Alcohol: Spike mentions that he's spent the last few days celebrating his non-ghost status (see **96**, 'Destiny'). When Fred asks if he's been experiencing any unexpected side effects, he replies that he *has* a bit of a hangover – however, that's probably due to the copious drinking he's been doing.

Sex and Drugs and Rock'n'Roll: Having told Harmony in the bar that he is an astronaut, Tobias Dupree returns with Harmony to her apartment apparently for the purpose of a night of wild and abandoned sex. However, Harmony has had the date-rape drug Rohypnol slipped into her drink by Tamika. Once Harmony is unconscious, Tamika breaks in and kills Dupree in an effort to frame Harmony and, ultimately, get her job.

Logic, Let Me Introduce You to This Window: The age-old question about how vampires can appear in photographs or on video must be asked yet again (see numerous episodes, particularly **24**, 'Are You Now or Have You Ever Been?'). Cameras and camcorders use mirrors as part of their focusing mechanism. If a vampire's senses are honed so acutely that they can appreciate otter's blood mixed with pig's blood (see **96**, 'Destiny'), why can't Harmony tell that she's drinking pig's blood tainted with human? Does the zero-tolerance policy operated by Wolfram & Hart also apply to humans who work there? If it does, how are those who break the rule disposed of? We know from **90**, 'Just Rewards' that Buffy is currently in Europe. In this episode Spike indicates that she's in the South of France. By **108**, 'The Girl in Question' we discover that she's actually living with Dawn and Andrew in Rome. It's never made entirely clear on which floor Fred's departmental lab is situated in relation to Angel's office and the lobby – most episodes suggest it's downstairs, although the direction in which Fred is heading after her conversation with Wesley in **89**, 'Conviction' indicates it may be upstairs. Either way, it appears to be in a completely different part of the building to the corridor containing the maintenance closet in which Harmony has already dumped Rudy and Lorne. So, given that, how does Harmony manage to get Fred from her lab to the closet to dump her in as well without anyone noticing?

Cruelty to Animals: Harmony tells Angel that she did a lot of research into the protocols of the feuding demon clans. Camel meat is considered a great delicacy by both. She believed that ordering a live camel from a catering company would be a great way to start the summit. Angel, as the host, would have the honour of slicing off the camel's hump and sticking a hot poker through its heart. The demon leaders would then rip the animal's carcass apart with their bare hands. Needless to say, Angel is unimpressed with her initiative. He tells Harmony that her job is to answer the telephone, make appointments and anticipate his needs which, he states, do not include a petting zoo in the lobby. As Harmony starts to cry, Fred suggests helpfully that she might consider a cheese platter or chips and dip instead. Subsequently, the caterer calls and offers a wildebeest as an alternative option. Harmony briefly considers this, then decides it's probably best to go with the chips.

Quote/Unquote: Harmony: 'Don't forget about Wesley. I get the vibe that he's totally crushing over Fred.' Brittany: 'Mr Wyndam-Pryce? Everyone knows he's ... muffins!'

Harmony, to Fred: 'I wish I were more like you. Except for the part about being all into science. And not having a lot up-front.'

Harmony, to the guy whose name she can't remember that she finds next to her in her bed: 'Apparently you and I ... you know. And, I'm sure I rocked your world and all. But I gotta go to work.'

Harmony, on Angel: 'He's not a helper, he's a chopper.'

Notes: 'Keep it simple, Harm, it suits you,' notes Spike in this witty vehicle for the considerable talents of Mercedes McNab. For so long a line-feed straight-woman in both *Buffy* and *Angel*, Harmony was, at last, beginning to blossom in her new environment. Under-appreciated and sycophantic in equal measure, Harmony was the developing star around which many of the season's best comedy moments were to be structured. Giving McNab an episode to shine in, therefore, seemed a logical and welcome move. A cunning metaphor for alcoholism ('drinking, that's my problem' notes Harmony at one point) and date-rape, 'Harm's Way' features some great sight-gags, including a wonderfully bad Wolfram & Hart in-house video, a gruesome ritual beheading and a glimpse of the company's in-house office gossip. (Fred's sleeping arrangements and Wesley's orientation are the talk of the staff coffee room it would seem.) There's also a somewhat uninteresting sub-plot about a demon clan turf war, but it's a desperate Harmony dumping unconscious body after unconscious body into the Wolfram & Hart maintenance closet as she seeks to uncover a sinister conspiracy against her that really sets this episode's comedic tone. McNab is also great in the final scene with James Marsters, which ties up one very obvious loose end outstanding from *Buffy*.

Angel's blood mug has the motto '#1 Boss' on it. Angel's team have been preparing a summit between two demon clans, the Vinjis and the Sahrvin, who have been feuding for five generations. The war apparently began when one of the demons used the wrong type of fork at a Sahrvin bonding ceremony. Wesley notes both clans are vicious and wonders why Wolfram & Hart don't let them wipe each other out. Gunn replies that if they manage to broker a peace, it will impress the demon world. Tobias Dupree, who was originally from San Francisco's Bay Area, was close to bringing the two sides together before he was killed. Both the clans, who are sticklers for etiquette, say that they will accept the sacrifice of a Wolfram & Hart employee if Angel cannot produce Dupree's killer. After his augmentation (see **89**, 'Conviction') Gunn is now fluent in several demon languages. Lorne's office is said to be a carb-free zone. Lorne's assistant is a personable, if somewhat highly strung, young man called Dan.

Harmony lives in a small apartment complex. One of her neighbours is an old lady called Ms Jackobi who ignores Harmony's cheerful greetings and owns a small yappy-type dog. In Harmony's bathroom, her mirror has 'Be Your Best' stencilled on it. Harmony attacks people from the right, whereas the person who killed Dupree attacked from the left. She tells Fred that she was very popular in high school but that since she became a vampire at graduation (see *Buffy*: 'Graduation Day' Part 2) she's had trouble connecting with people. She says that she has been clean of human blood for eight months. Tamika refers to Harmony's obsessive hobby of collecting ornamental unicorns (see *Buffy*: 'Real Me'). Harmony's fighting skills have improved greatly since she and Xander resorted to hair-pulling in *Buffy*: 'The Initiative'. Harmony's tick-list of things to do is:

- Big Demon summit
- Remind Security of summit
- Arrange transportation

- Return camel
- Confirm catering

Wolfram & Hart has a newly introduced policy prohibiting the drinking of human blood by any employee and they carry out random blood tests to ensure compliance. (These are the responsibility of the somewhat cheerless Rudy.) The company have a Non-Human Resources department. The Wolfram & Hart advertisement video boasts that the company owns the souls of various captains of industry and is owed the first-born of several female movie stars. It also mentions that the firm's offices are built on ground deconsecrated by the blood of mass murderer Matthias Pavayne (see **92**, 'Hellbound'). The company's phone extension for curses is 592. The vampire seen in the Wolfram & Hart company video is the one that Angel killed in the opening sequence of **89**, 'Conviction'. The video also features clips from **93**, 'Life of the Party' and **91**, 'Unleashed'.

Soundtrack: The song playing on Harmony's alarm radio is 'Hey Sailor!' by the Detroit Cobras.

Critique: 'The "lower decks" approach allows for a light-weight main plot,' wrote David Darlington. 'If the resolution seems ludicrously convenient, it's really only because it doesn't, actually, matter that much.'

Did You Know?: 'Ever since I was a little girl I wanted to be an actress,' Mercedes McNab told Steve Eramo. 'I used to stand in front of the mirror and imitate commercials.'

In an interview with *Zap2it.com*'s Kate O'Hare, Mercedes revealed that, when they were both acting on *Buffy*, she and James Marsters had a brief romantic fling. 'I went on a date with James,' she noted. 'We're just buddies. It didn't really go any further than that.'

David Boreanaz's Comments: 'Having James [Marsters] on the show, it's almost like *Butch Cassidy and the Sundance Kid* for our characters,' David Boreanaz told *DreamWatch*. 'We love and hate each other at the same time.'

Cast and Crew Comments: 'It's just Mercedes front-and-centre,' Jeff Bell told *Sci-Fi Wire*. 'It's really funny – the working girl happens to be an evil vampire trying to walk the straight and narrow … The story is told from Harmony's [point of view]. She's in pretty much every scene, so you're limited to how she perceives everybody. Mercedes did a great job.'

98
Soul Purpose

US Transmission Date: 21 January 2004
UK Transmission Date: 16 March 2004

Writer: Brent Fletcher
Director: David Boreanaz
Cast: Ciara Hughes (The Blue Fairy), Rob Evors (Man),
Jodi Harris (Woman), Carmen Nicole (Lana)

Angel has begun to feel the pressure of his constant flirtation with some of the greyer areas of moral certainty. And his dreams have taken a decidedly odd turn. Meanwhile, Spike has found a new best friend – a man who calls himself Doyle and who alleges that he gets visions from The Powers That Be with which to help the helpless.

Dreaming (As *Buffy* Often Proves) is Free: This episode features numerous dream sequences in which Angel subconsciously appears to question his destiny and – perhaps more importantly – his friends' hidden opinions about him. For example, Angel dreams that when Spike reached the Cup of Perpetual Torment (see **96**, 'Destiny'), instead of being a fake, the cup really *was* what it was alleged to be. All of Angel's life has been a lie, Spike suggests. Everything he has done, the many lives he's saved, his dreams of redemption – all of it has been for nothing, because the Shanshu prophecy was never about him. Angel then watches Spike drink from the cup and become human as he, himself, crumbles to dust. Later Angel finds Wesley in his room. Wesley helps Angel into bed and then suddenly stakes him, saying that Angel has become irrelevant and that Spike's arrival has made getting rid of Angel much easier. These dreams suggest that Angel harbours secret fears of inadequacy. He is, quite obviously, concerned that the Shanshu prophecy refers to Spike rather than to himself – perhaps for egotistical reasons, although his speech to Spike in **96**, 'Destiny', partially repeated in this episode, suggests that his motives are mostly pure. Wesley's cameo can be seen to reflect Angel's continuing uncertainty concerning Wesley's loyalty post-Connor. The fact that Wesley was so easily able to kill, as he believed, his own father (see **95**, 'Lineage') indicates that, should the situation require it, Wesley would have absolutely no hesitation in killing Angel too (see **11**, 'Somnambulist'; **14**, 'I've Got You Under My Skin'; **47**, 'That Old Gang of Mine'; **76**, 'Awakening'; **77** 'Soulless', among others). It's also worth remembering that, unconsciously, Angel may have held a similar impression of Wesley from long before the Connor fiasco. Remember that in Angel's Darla-induced dream in **25**, 'First Impressions', a sinister Wesley was there in the background hammering a nail into a coffin – almost certainly a coffin for Angel. Regardless of Wesley's self-sacrifice to bring Angel back from a watery grave (see **67**, 'Deep Down'), it's clear that Angel still doesn't entirely trust his best friend.

There is a scene of Fred operating on Angel. She pulls out a dead goldfish noting that it is Angel's soul. A dried walnut represents Angel's heart. Having removed everything that Angel has inside him, Fred gazes into a hollow abyss at Angel's core and believes that she can hear the ocean. Angel dreams that Spike and Buffy are also in his bed, having sex. Then, in what appears to be a movie screening room, Angel and his friends watch as LA is engulfed in a fiery apocalypse.

Perhaps the worst of Angel's dreams, from the viewpoint of his own ambitions, is when he sees the Blue Fairy make Spike human again after Spike has single-handedly ended Armageddon and turned the world into a beautiful, happily-ever-after, candy mountain place. Angel's most heartfelt wish is to achieve exactly this – something that he's never made any secret of (see **8**, 'I Will Remember You'; **22**, 'To Shanshu in LA', etc.). While everyone is congratulating Spike, Angel is left to take the place of Numero Cinco as the Wolfram & Hart mailman. This menial position, it appears, is the destiny for all champions who find that their heart is no longer in the mission (see **94**, 'The Cautionary Tale of Numero Cinco').

There is a lengthy sequence in a bar where Lorne plays honky-tonk piano, with Harmony as a waitress and Angel trying to sing to an audience of his friends. But he finds that he has no voice. Fred notes that she told Wesley and Gunn that Angel was empty. Gunn has yellowy cat eyes, an obvious reference to Gunn's connection to The Conduit (see **88**, 'Home'; **92**, 'Hellbound'). This also suggests that Angel has concerns about the level to which the augmentation of Gunn's mind has corrupted him. Lorne, on the other hand, constantly tries to alert Angel to the stain on the front of his shirt – which turns out to be the parasite creature causing the dreams. This subconscious image implies that, of all his friends, Lorne is the one whose opinions Angel trusts the most.

Angel finally realises that the parasite is on his chest. He squashes it but then sees Eve standing at the foot of his bed telling him that he has merely 'killed junior'. Carrying an engraved box, she tells Angel that she is not there and he is dreaming but that the dream is almost over. She then places a much larger parasite on Angel's bed. Angel then finds himself in a comfortable chair, sitting in the middle of a field with his friends. Wesley tells him that he can stay as long as he wants. But Angel realises that he isn't supposed to be there, despite his friends trying to persuade him that all he has to do is to stop caring. It's at this point that Spike arrives and rips the second parasite creature from Angel, waking him.

Dudes and Babes: Spike notes that one cannot throw a stone in this town without hitting some bimbo in trouble.

A Little Learning is a Dangerous Thing: Harmony says that if she hears about anything relating to The Senior Partners, she is supposed to tell Angel immediately. Also, if anything is delivered to Wolfram & Hart with runes written on it, she is requested to tell Angel. However, she has been asked *not* to try and read the runes herself as that can cause a fire.

Denial, Thy Name is Angel: Gunn and Wesley have very different ideas on how to deal with a warlock named Lucien Drake. Gunn tells Angel that Drake has at least a thousand followers, many of whom have sold their children in return for access to dark magicks. Wesley describes them as a fanatical religious fringe group stock-piling weapons. Gunn notes that the cult has alliances and connections; if Wolfram & Hart confront them directly, it could be bad for business. However, if Drake were to be eliminated, the cult would probably fight among themselves. Angel asks, therefore, if they are doing this because it's right or because it's cost effective. Wesley and Gunn concede that, actually, it's a bit of both. Wesley begins to say that, once again, they find themselves in something of a moral grey area, but Angel angrily asks if they can't get through a single day without having to compromise on their ideals yet again. Wesley favours a covert assassination attempt; Gunn wants 48 hours to organise a coup from within Drake's inner circle. As the discussion continues, Angel becomes agitated, suggesting that they should just kill them all – warlocks, minions – they're all evil so why not wipe them out and get back to the basics of good versus evil. Recovering his composure, Angel asks Gunn to arrange a meeting with his best Judas and see if a coup can be arranged. If Gunn has any hint that the plan will not succeed, then they'll go with Wesley's alternative.

The Conspiracy Starts at Home Time: Eve attempts to distract Wesley and Fred from finding out what is wrong with Angel by asking them to research various aspects of a stone relic covered with runic symbols.

Lies: Spike meets a man whom the viewers know to be Lindsey McDonald. However, he claims to be called Doyle. He wonders what Spike plans to do with his life now that he has it back. Spike has a destiny, Lindsey suggests, though he denies having anything to do with the Cup of Perpetual Torment. He only does, he continues, what 'they' tell him to do. Spike asks who they are. Lindsey replies that he is merely a drifter who was minding his own business until he was given the gift of vision by The Powers That Be; he sees people who are in trouble, people who need a champion. Spike suggests that this is more Angel's gig than his. Lindsey says that Angel isn't part of the plan anymore, he's working for the other side. Spike asks if he is supposed to jump every time that 'Doyle' gets a vision of someone in peril. Spike doesn't have to believe him, but, Lindsey wonders, if a young woman is murdered that night and Spike does nothing to stop it, can he live with himself?

After Spike has performed his first good deed (see **Work is a Four-Letter Word**), Lindsey notes that there are lots of people who need saving. He suggests that, in the past, Spike has merely flirted with doing what's right, mainly to impress women (specifically Buffy). However, tonight Spike did something good, which is an interesting contrast to Angel's failure to achieve a positive result from *his* first mission (see **1**, 'City Of').

Work is a Four-Letter Word: A young woman is attacked by a vampire in an alley. As the vampire prepares to kill her, Spike interrupts him. The vampire tells Spike to get lost and Spike replies, wistfully, that some people believe he already is. Spike then fights and kills the vampire, impaling it on a broken railing. The woman offers her thanks. Spike, however, is unsympathetic, noting that she's asking for trouble being alone in this particular neighbourhood. The woman, defensively, says that she was just trying to get home. 'Get a cab,' adds Spike, helpfully.

The Politics of Deception: Lindsey's body tattoos (previously glimpsed in **96**, 'Destiny') are designed to prevent

The Senior Partners from sensing his presence. Note that Eve's apartment has similar designs drawn on its walls, the implication being that while she and Lindsey are in there, her bosses can't see whatever skulduggery it is that they're up to. Their scheme specifically seems to involve undermining Angel while simultaneously boosting Spike's champion credentials. This, Eve suggests, will soon make The Senior Partners question whether they have backed the wrong horse. Their intention isn't to kill Angel, at least not yet, hence Lindsey faking a vision to tell Spike that Angel is in trouble. Later, Angel tells Eve that he doesn't believe The Senior Partners gave him the firm only to then turn him into a vegetable. Angel thinks that Eve is playing her own game and wonders what The Senior Partners will do to her when they find out about her extracurricular activities.

References: The inspiration for this episode may have come from an Alan Moore issue of *Superman* ('The Man Who Had Everything') which also features a parasitic creature producing hallucinations. Angel's dream contains visual and dialogue references to *Jaws* and an appearance by the Blue Fairy from *Pinocchio*. Harmony, perhaps inevitably, doesn't know the difference between Machiavelli (see **97**, 'Harm's Way') and Matchabelli perfume. She reads a copy of *Trendy* magazine. There are allusions to the Jesus and Mary Chain's 'The Living End', the biblical concept of Hades (the grave), Winston Churchill's 'finest hour' speech of 18 June 1940, John Schlesinger's *Marathon Man*, the 1980s TV series *Miami Vice* and the lead characters of Crockett and Tubbs (Don Johnson and Philip Michael Thomas), *1984*, *Gypsy* ('sing out, Louise'), 'My Country, 'tis of Thee' ('let freedom ring'), nuclear physicist Albert Einstein (see **35**, 'Happy Anniversary') and *The Wizard of Oz* (Angel telling his friends about his dream). Spike calls Wesley Mr Vader – his knowledge of the original *Star Wars* trilogy having previously been highlighted in *Buffy*: 'School Hard'. Note that when, in Angel's dream, Spike drinks from the cup, he becomes a quasi-Christlike figure, bathed in golden light and with his arms outstretched in the crucifix position.

Bitch!: In Angel's dream, when Fred extracts Angel's heart she notes that it really *is* a dried-up little walnut (see **94**, 'The Cautionary Tale of Numero Cinco').

'West Hollywood?': The strip club where Spike and Lindsey first meet is called the Peppermint Stick. Lindsey puts a glass down in front of Spike. 'Thanks, but [you're] not really my type, Mary,' says Spike, without taking his eyes from the stage.

Awesome!: Spike's slow-motion fight with two vampires. Plus, 'thank you, Bear!'

'You May Remember Me From Such Films and TV Series As . . .': Ciara Hughes appeared in *Cold Case*. Rob Evors was in *Six Feet Under*. Jodi Harris's CV includes *Legally Blonde*, *Bring It On* and *Beverley Hills 90210*. Carmen Nicole played Deborah McWhite in *The Yellow Truth*.

Behind the Camera: A former stuntman, Brent Fletcher worked on *The Watcher*, *Route 9*, *Suicide Kings* and *Clean Slate* before becoming production assistant on *Strange World*.

Cigarettes & Alcohol: In his new basement apartment, Spike has a fridge in which he keeps his bottles of beer – Brockmans.

Sex and Drugs and Rock'n'Roll: Wesley reads from a report which states that a vigilante killed two vampires at a gas station and then asked the women whom he had saved if they would like to accompany him, get a bottle of hooch and listen to some Sex Pistols records.

Logic, Let Me Introduce You to This Window: So, it was Lindsey, seemingly, who – at some point after the apocalyptic events of *Buffy*: 'Chosen' – climbed into a town-sized crater where once Sunnydale stood and retrieved the amulet that Spike used to save the world. The question of why he then sent the amulet to Angel, his sworn enemy, is covered at a later date (see **100**, 'You're Welcome'), but let's concentrate for the moment on his amazing powers of search and recovery. Talk about finding a needle in a haystack. Since when do Fred and Wesley do favours for either Eve or The Senior Partners? In Angel's dream Spike suggests that he's just a working-class bloke. What a class traitor (see *Buffy*: 'Fool for Love', 'Lies My Parents Told Me'). In the pre-title sequence, before Spike drinks from the Cup of Perpetual Torment, he holds it at such an angle that any contents would spill from it. Does eating ice cream too fast really produce pain equivalent to that of a vision from The Powers That Be? Fred's hairstyle changes between scenes. Wesley says that vampires don't get sick. It is unusual, but such things have happened before (see, for instance, *Buffy*: 'Graduation Day' Part 1).

Quote/Unquote: Fred, after Wesley asks if the Wolfram & Hart satellite has lethal capabilities which they could use to eliminate a target from the air: 'An orbital range microwave cannon. Focuses the satellite's communication signals into a pinpoint beam. It can raise the temperature of the targeted area a thousand degrees in five seconds . . . If we did that sort of thing.'

Harmony: 'I'm not allowed to talk to Accounting without Angel's approval. I accidentally authorised a few Bath-of-the-Month subscriptions.'

Spike: 'That's what you people do. You get reports, you sign cheques, you read memos. Here's to the corporate teat.'

Lindsey, to Eve: 'Good girls always get what they want.'

Notes: 'We didn't sell out. We're changing the system from the inside.' What exactly have we here? The best debut script on *Angel* since Tim Minear climbed on board, former stunt co-ordinator Brent Fletcher's 'Soul Purpose' is an episode about destiny and manipulation that is a brilliant intellectual parallelogram to **1**, 'City Of'. As Spike accepts a mysterious stranger's offer to help him become a hero worthy of fulfilling the ramifications of the Shanshu prophecy, an ailing Angel is plagued by increasingly horrible (though, occasionally, downright hilarious) hallucinations featuring his friends in starring roles. The dream sequences themselves include a medical one involving Fred – and a bear – which, unfortunately, goes on for about a minute too long to have the potential impact it deserved. Wesley's po-faced description of Spike saving a couple of girls from a vampire attack reminds the viewer, if any reminder were needed, that Alexis Denisof is, given the material, a comedy genius. There's also the welcome return of Christian Kane whose sinister little double act with Sarah Thompson is wonderfully played.

Spike accuses Lindsey of having sent him and Angel on a wild goose chase for the Cup of Perpetual Torment (see **96**, 'Destiny'). Lindsey admits to having sent Spike the box that made him corporeal, as well as recovering the amulet that Spike wore to save the world and delivering it to Angel (see *Buffy*: 'Chosen'; **89**, 'Conviction'). Lindsey tells Spike that Angel failed on his first mission in LA, a reference to Angel being unable to save Tina from the evil Russell Winters in **1**, 'City Of'. The Selminth parasite is a creature that attaches itself to the host's chest and injects its victim with an anaesthetic – to mask its presence – and various neurotoxins. These cause paralysis and hallucinations and eventually leave the victim in a permanent vegetative state. Lindsey arranges for Spike to live in a spartan basement apartment adjacent to a Korean Market. Wesley and Gunn used the Wolfram & Hart psychics to track Spike down. Gunn notes that Spike was planning a one-way trip the last time they saw each other (see **97**, 'Harm's Way'). The cake that the others present to Spike in Angel's dream features the motto WAY TO GO, SPIKE!

Soundtrack: In Angel's dream, when the Blue Fairy turns Spike human, his colleagues sing 'For He's a Jolly Good Fellow' while Angel slinks away. Later Lorne plays a short burst of 'My Darling Clementine'. The song playing at the Peppermint Stick when Spike meets Lindsey is 'Junk' by the Supersuckers.

Two audio clips of Sarah Michelle Gellar (taken from the *Buffy* episodes 'Bad Eggs' and 'The Prom') are used during Angel's dream when he sees Spike and Buffy having sex.

Did You Know?: Asked by Rob Francis about his musical tastes, James Marsters noted that 'I don't like bands [who] don't write their own music. Beyond that, if a group is expressing themselves, I love it. It's all magic. Country to punk rock, Chopin to Kurt Cobain. But it always all comes back to punk for me, because that was the last time that passion ruled the airwaves.' James, as readers may know, fronted his own The Clash and Nirvana-influenced rock band, Ghost of the Robot, as an outlet for his musical passion. Along with bandmates Aaron Anderson, Steven Sellars, Kevin McPherson and Charlie DeMars, James toured with the band extensively during 2003–04 when his *Buffy* and *Angel* filming duties allowed. Ghost of the Robot, via the Internet, released three singles: 'David Letterman', 'Valerie' and 'A New Man'; the album *Mad Brilliant* (which, purely co-incidentally, included a song called 'Angel') and an EP, *It's Nothing*. The full set goes for around £150 on e-Bay. The band split before they could release their final CD, *Gods of the Radio*, though several of the songs from its sessions were aired live during their 2004 European tour, including the saucy 'Bad', a tale of a one-night stand at a convention.

Cast and Crew Comments: 'I came in with some strong ideas and visuals that I wanted to do. I had a big meeting with Jeff Bell,' David Boreanaz said at The WB's winter press preview. 'A lot of the ideas got toned down, because I had to remind myself that I'm shooting *Angel* and not this crazy, cinematic, swooping thing.'

'Being directed by David was great,' James Marsters told Steven Eramo. 'The first thing we did was the opening teaser, which was a very complicated shot. I showed up on set and expected David to be the same easy-going guy we'd come to know and admire. I did not expect him to be such an accomplished director.'

Joss Whedon's Comments: 'I have to say I approached this whole concept of David directing with stark terror,' Joss Whedon confessed to *TV Zone*'s David Richardson. 'I've had editors direct, I've had cinematographers direct, I've had writers direct . . . [and] I've seen people I love, who are brilliant at their jobs, crash and burn.' However, Joss considered that, ultimately, Boreanaz had passed with flying colours. 'David directed as well as anybody we've had, and that's *embarrassing*!'

99
Damage

US Transmission Date: 28 January 2004
UK Transmission Date: 23 March 2004

Writers: Steven S DeKnight, Drew Goddard
Director: Jefferson Kibbe
Cast: Navi Rawat (Dana), Jasmine DiAngelo (Young Dana),
David Brouwer (Stock Boy), Kevin Quigley (Dr Rabinaw),
Alex S Alexander (Carol), Rebecca Metz (Young Nurse),
Michael Krawic (Vernon), Mesan Richardson (SWAT Team #1),
William Stanford Davis (Security Guard),
Mike Hungerford (Dock Worker), Debbie McLeod (Real Estate Agent),
Stan Klimecko (Walter)[24]

A deranged teenage girl with manifest superstrength bloodily escapes from an LA psychiatric ward, causing carnage in the process. However, as Angel and his friends quickly discover, far from being possessed by a demon, the girl – Dana – is actually a psychotic vampire Slayer. She has also attracted the attention of some old acquaintances of the gang.

Dreaming (As *Buffy* Often Proves) is Free: All Slayers have the ability to share dreams and memories with their predecessors and their potential successors (this was first established in the *Buffy the Vampire Slayer* movie and restated throughout *Buffy* in episodes such as 'Graduation Day' Part 2, 'This Year's Girl', 'Lessons' and 'Beneath You').

Work is a Four-Letter Word: Gunn frequently settles his legal cases on the golf course. This was, apparently,

---

[24] Uncredited.

another of the optional extras he was given during his augmentation. One of his partners appears to be the LA District Attorney.

Dudes and Babes: When Dana was ten, her mother and father were murdered and she was kidnapped by a man later identified as Walter Kindal. (Kindal himself was killed by police ten years later during an attempted liquor-store robbery.) After months of torture, Dana escaped and was found wandering in the street. She has spent the subsequent fifteen years in a near-catatonic state, until a few months ago (around the time that the small Californian town of Sunnydale mysteriously vanished into a big hole in the desert) when she suddenly became alert, began speaking in tongues and displaying almost superhuman strength. An error in her medication enables her to escape from the secure institution in which she is confined.

A Little Learning is a Dangerous Thing: When she faces Spike, Dana appears to be possessed by the memories of both Slayers that Spike previously killed – the Chinese girl during the Boxer Rebellion in 1900 and Nikki Wood in New York in 1977 (see *Buffy*: 'Fool for Love'). Spike tells Dana that he once dated someone who wasn't all there (a reference to Drusilla's demented psychic abilities).

The Conspiracy Starts at Home Time: Wesley calls Giles when Dana's true status is discovered. Angel is told that Giles is sending his top guy to deal with the situation. This turns out to be Andrew Wells (see *Buffy*: 'Storyteller').

It was Dana's nurse, Carol, who first contacted Wolfram & Hart. She has a cousin who works as a paralegal secretary for the firm.

'West Hollywood?': When Andrew sees Spike in the flesh he is deliriously happy that Spike is alive ... and 'more beautiful than ever'. Later, Andrew tells Spike that Spike isn't the only one who's been through a life-changing experience. Giles has been training Andrew. He's faster, stronger and 82 per cent more manly than the last time they met (see *Buffy*: 'Chosen'). The latter is, definitely, still open to debate (although, see **108**, 'The Girl in Question').

Denial, Thy Name is Andrew: When Andrew embraces Spike, an amused Angel asks if they know each other. Andrew says proudly that he and Spike saved the world together. Well, OK, Buffy *helped*, but it was mostly down to them.

References: The opening sequence is visually influenced by *The Ring*. Spike waking up to discover that his hands have been removed echoes a sequence in *Scream and Scream Again*. Allusions to the Playstation video game *Parasite Eve*, *The West Wing*, British model and actress Twiggy, Ken Kesey's *One Flew Over the Cuckoo's Nest*, *The Exorcist* (see **14**, 'I've Got You Under My Skin'), Exodus 13 ('a pillar of fire'), *The Masque of the Red Death* and Roseanne Barr's former husband Tom Arnold.

Geek-Speak: Andrew makes two references to *The Lord of the Rings* and also expresses great admiration for Spike's pectorals which he compares to those of Aragorn himself, Viggo Mortensen. He alludes to the character of Lieutenant Uhura from *Star Trek*, Yoda from *The Empire Strikes Back*, *Mean Streets*, the Mock Turtles' 'Can You Dig It?' and *X-Men* (specifically, the film's crappy third act).

Bitch!: Firstly Angel and Spike and then Spike and Andrew spending virtually the entire episode engaged in caustic one-liners.

Awesome!: Andrew's mispronunciation of the word vampire rubbing off on Angel. Andrew calling Fred 'attractive slender woman' and his girly scream when finding the docker's body. Dana's false memories, with Spike in the role of her abuser. Spike being thrown out of an upper storey window by Dana, and his sarcastic reply to Angel's question of what he's doing (Spike says that he thought he'd see what it feels like to bounce off the pavement and that it's pretty much what he expected). The stunningly profound final scene about the art of killing and the loss of innocence with Boreanaz and Marsters acting their little cotton socks off.

'You May Remember Me From Such Films and TV Series As . . .': Tom Lenk appeared in *Six Feet Under*, *Boogie Nights* and *Popular*. Navi Rawat was in *Jack the Dog*, *The OC*, *24* and *Roswell*. Kevin Quigley's CV includes *Swamp Thing*, *Murder She Wrote* and *Miami Vice*. Alex S Alexander appeared in *Hip, Edgy, Sexy, Cool* and *3rd Rock from the Sun*. Michael Krawic was in *Cliché*, *As Virgins Fall*, *Charlotte Sometimes*, *CSI*, *Chicago Hope*, *Mulholland Falls*, *Star Trek: Deep Space Nine* and *Walker, Texas Ranger*. Mesan Richardson appeared in *The District*. William Stanford Davis's CV includes *Subway Café*, *Primary Colors* and *The Shield*. Mike Hungerford's movies include *The Goldfish*. Debbie McLeod appeared in *The Bell Jar*, *The Guilt*, *JAG* and *Silk Stalkings*. Stan Klimecko was in *Pandora's Box*.

Sex and Drugs and Rock'n'Roll: Among the medications used to keep Dana pacified are diazepam, lithium and Thorazine.

Logic, Let Me Introduce You to This Window: The answer to the opening crossword clue, in case you're wondering, is 'Sweetly'. There's a marked lack of blood on Dana's hospital gown despite her having hacked off an orderly's head with an autopsy saw. Given the timescale established in this episode, Dana is approximately 25 years old. Firstly, she certainly doesn't look it. Secondly, isn't that a wee bit old for a Slayer to be called – even with the new situation regarding multiple Slayers? All of those previously seen have been teenagers. Fred still believes that there can only be one Slayer at a time. Angel, too, seemed surprised by Andrew's revelation that what Willow did in *Buffy*: 'Chosen' has created an entire army of Slayers. This seems very odd. Angel has certainly been in touch with Buffy, or someone very close to her, since Sunnydale's destruction (he knew she was in Europe in **90**, 'Just Rewards', for example). Why, therefore, wouldn't she have told him about this really important development, particularly as it has a significant bearing on her own immediate future. Would any drugs remain useful after approximately fifteen years stored in a tin box? More importantly, would the needle of a syringe held in the same conditions be rust-free? Angel asks Wesley to contact their informants in the police department to obtain Dana's last-known whereabouts. What informants? Wolfram & Hart *own* the LAPD according to **97**, 'Harm's Way'.

I Just *Love* Your Accent: Andrew's lunch bag has a Union Jack on it. Spike uses the term 'sack of hammers' to describe Dana's insanity, just as he once did to describe Drusilla in *Buffy*: 'Selfless'. This sounds like a plausible cockney slang expression for madness; however, neither *Cassell's Rhyming Slang* dictionary nor *The Oxford Dictionary of Slang* feature the phrase.

There Can Be Only One, Usually . . .: This episode takes place approximately six months after the events of *Buffy*: 'Chosen'. Andrew describes the origin story of the first Slayer and the Shadow Men (see *Buffy*: 'Get it Done'). It is noted that from then on, at any one time there could be hundreds, perhaps thousands, of potential Slayers in each generation, all experiencing vivid dreams of past Slayers and waiting to be called. But only one can be chosen. Or, very occasionally, *two* (see *Buffy*: 'What's My Line?' Part 1, 'Faith, Hope and Trick'). However, all that changed when Willow performed the ritual that empowered all potential Slayers.

Where Did They Go From There?: Andrew notes that after Sunnydale was destroyed, Rupert Giles, together with a number of key Sunnydale alumni – including Andrew himself and, perhaps, Robin Wood – has reactivated the Council of Watchers. They have sent out their representatives to find as many of the new Slayers as possible and provide them with whatever they need. Xander is currently in Africa. Willow and Kennedy are in Brazil – nominally São Paulo, though every time Andrew rings them they're actually in Rio. Meanwhile, Buffy is living in Rome, where Dawn is attending school. Buffy was apparently rounding up Slayers in Europe and decided that she liked it there, though Andrew thinks she probably just needed a break from California. He doesn't believe that Buffy knows Spike is alive and is curious as to why Spike hasn't contacted her yet. When coming to take Dana away from Angel, Andrew is accompanied by twelve Slayers. It appears that Buffy and her friends no longer trust Angel after his move to Wolfram & Hart (see **103**, 'A Hole in the World'; **108**, 'The Girl in Question').

Quote/Unquote: Angel, to Gunn: 'I liked you better when you just wanted to hit people.' And, to Spike: 'Shouldn't you be out in the streets protecting the city from people like you?'

Angel, asks Dr Rabinaw about Dana's escape: 'Let's go over it again, in case you left out any details.' Spike: 'What he said. But with a bit more of a threat at the end.'

Angel, on Spike: 'Sorry. He's . . . is "pathological idiot" an actual condition?'

Andrew, to Angel: 'I've got twelve vampire Slayers behind me, and not one of them has ever dated you.'

Notes: 'She's one of us now. She's a monster.' One of the most violently bloody episodes of *Angel*, 'Damage' pitches its dramatic tent in a field full of abuse monsters and forgoes the series' traditional examination of redemption in favour of what was rapidly becoming the fifth season's main conceptual and artistic concern: in a world of grey uncertainties, who can afford monochrome ideals on notions of right and wrong? Stunningly directed by Jefferson Kibbee, with amazing stuntwork, 'Damage' has many caustic things to say about the world that Angel and his friends seem now to be a willing part of. The arrival in LA of a mercifully still somewhat inept Andrew Wells, aside from moments of comedy heaven (let's face it, Tom Lenk and James Marsters as a double act works on so many levels), allows for a shade of introspection in the episode's central themes. Angel's placement in the belly of Wolfram

& Hart's beast has not gone down at all well with his former friends from Sunnydale. It's great that Andrew is given a scene to talk about how Buffy, Xander, Willow, Giles and Dawn are doing, and there are witty allusions to 'Fool for Love' and 'Storyteller' thrown into a literate and tight script to keep the continuity fans happy. But it's where Angel, Wesley and the gang are *now* that's the really important issue being discussed here. Symbolically, the stripping of Spike's trademark leather coat from his back by an enraged Dana is a pointed metaphor for the changes that have happened in the *Buffy*verse since Sunnydale left the map. What remains is, one suspects, the show that Joss Whedon always wanted *Angel* to be, unsure of its place in the new world order. Dark and nefarious. And utterly brilliant.

From what we can glean via Fred's emergency call, the shamanistic procedure used to reattach Spike's severed hands appears similar to the one used on Lindsey McDonald in **40**, 'Dead End'. Although, in Spike's case, he doesn't seem to have got an 'evil hand' as a result. Wesley notes that manifestations of multiple personalities often accompany demonic possession. When Wesley provides some rather incisive comments during Andrew's potted history of the Slayer mythology, Andrew notes that perhaps Giles may have been wrong about Wesley, much to Wesley's obvious annoyance (see *Buffy*: 'Bad Girls', 'Consequences', 'Enemies', 'Choices', 'The Prom' and 'Graduation Day'). Lorne hires a psychic named Vernon to help look for clues at Dana's former home. Dr Rabinaw videotaped his sessions with Dana intending to write a book about her. Andrew has been seeing a therapist since the traumatic events of *Buffy*: 'Chosen'.

Soundtrack: The excellent, riff-orientated 'Blood, Milk and Sky' by White Zombie plays as Dana emerges from the store after killing the security guard.

Did You Know?: 'Everything I know about this profession, I've learned during my time spent on the set with my fellow actors,' Andy Hallett confided to *TV Zone*. He was especially fulsome in his praise of Alexis Denisof. 'He's so focused and dedicated to his craft,' noted Hallett. 'I turn to Alexis for guidance on just about everything from memorising my lines to turning them into a real conversation.'

Cast and Crew Comments: 'I went in for an audition,' Amy Acker related when asked by *Femme Fatales* how she got her role on *Angel*. 'They'd been looking for someone since November [2000]. I had an audition in February [and] Joss wrote a scene for me, J and Alexis,' (see the *Angel* Season Three DVD extras). 'We did the scene, The WB saw the audition and I got a phone call asking if I'd like to become a regular.'

Joss Whedon's Comments: 'The idea of the show was redemption and what it takes to win back a life when you've misused yours terribly,' Joss told Kate O'Hare. *Angel*, Whedon continued, was important because it demonstrates how adults face up to what they have done in life and, ultimately, how to overcome the worst aspects of it. 'Plus, awesome fights. If I have any message for America, it's that you can solve problems through fisticuffs.'

100
You're Welcome

US Transmission Date: 4 February 2004
UK Transmission Date: 30 March 2004

Writers: David Fury
Director: David Fury

After the discovery of another tragic consequence of Wolfram & Hart's negotiations with evil, Angel has had enough of his new life and threatens to resign his position. He does this just as Cordelia Chase emerges from a year in a coma with a vision from The Powers That Be and a mission, seemingly, to save Angel from himself. She is successful in this endeavour and Angel is delighted to have his friend back. But Cordy is walking a very different road . . .

The Politics of Deception: Lindsey pretends to have a vision of demon-possessed Cordelia in an attempt to get Spike to kill her. Fortunately, this doesn't work.

A Little Learning is a Dangerous Thing: Wesley identifies the tattooed symbols that Lindsey wears as protection runes derived from the Enochian alphabet.[25] The symbols are used to mask the wearer from detection.

Cordelia notes that when she said she and Wesley should bypass Wesley's research department and look for information on the symbols themselves like they used to in the old days, that was a completely stupid idea and she asks why Wesley listened to her. Wes admits that he did so because he misses both the research sessions and, indeed, Cordy herself. (It is worth remembering, of course, that Wesley and Cordy were, however briefly, once involved in a relationship; see *Buffy*: 'The Prom', 'Graduation Day'.)

Denial, Thy Name is Angel: Angel admits that he is lost without Cordelia's guidance.

The Conspiracy Starts at Home Time: The extent of Lindsey and Eve's full plan is revealed. Insanely jealous that Angel was simply *given* all that Lindsey had worked so hard for during his time at Wolfram & Hart, Lindsey is seeking revenge on both Angel and The Senior Partners. Thus, he has manipulated and undermined Angel's self-confidence (see **96**, 'Destiny'; **98**, 'Soul Purpose'), while, at the same time making The Senior Partners question if they had picked the correct vampire with a soul to fulfil the Shanshu prophecy in the way that they want it to be fulfilled. Lindsey implies that The Senior Partners may soon be too old to continue their present activities. He is

---

[25] The Enochian alphabet was created in the sixteenth century: Dr John Dee (1527–1608), mystic, geographer and astrologer to the court of Queen Mary, and his associate, Sir Edward Kelly (1555–97), claimed that the Enochian language was translated for them by angels.

able to penetrate Wolfram & Hart's security, protected by his tattoos (and by the fact that just about everyone who may have recognised him from his time at the company was killed by The Beast in **74**, 'Habeas Corpses').

Work is a Four-Letter Word: Spike plays video games as therapy to improve the motorskills of his recently reattached hands (see **99**, 'Damage').

It's a Designer Label!: Cordelia notes that if Eve attempts to get out of her chair during interrogation she will feed Eve her Manolo Blahnik shoes – which, she continues, are *stunning*. Check out, also, Eve's insanely tight split-skirt.

References: Irish actor Colin Farrell (*The Recruit*, *Tigerland*, *Phone Booth*), *One Foot in the Grave*, *Eurotrash*, the Nintendo video game *Donkey Kong*, cookery icon Betty Crocker – star of the long-running radio show *The Betty Crocker School of the Air*, Downy's April Fresh and *Urban Cowboy*.

Bitch!: Cordy and Eve (whom Cordy dubs Lilah Junior) – a battle royal for the Premiership title of Queen Bee'atch.

The Charisma Show: Cordy tells Spike she has heard that he isn't evil anymore which fact, she considers, makes his still having that particular hairstyle rather silly.

Awesome!: Cordy thinks that Angel has made a deal with the devil in taking over Wolfram & Hart. Angel suggests that she's being melodramatic just as a satanic-looking demon with horns and a tail shakes Angel's hand and tells him that he's looking forward to their game of racquetball on Thursday (see **109**, 'Power Play'). Also Lindsey's Bondian adventures in the basement and his epic verbal and physical battle with a re-empowered Angel. Angel telling Harmony to guard Eve; if she tries to leave Harmony has Angel's permission to eat her. Harmony's surprise and delight at this and her subsequent disappointment that Eve, in fact, doesn't try anything, despite Harmony begging her to do so.

'You May Remember Me From Such Films and TV Series As . . .': A former cheerleader with the San Diego Chargers, the great Charisma Carpenter began her acting career in *Baywatch*, playing Hobie's girlfriend Wendie. Aaron Spelling personally auditioned her for the 'über-vixen-bitch' Ashley Green in NBC's *Malibu Shores*. She also played Beth Sullivan in the *Josh Kirby: Time Warrior* TV movies and appeared in a legendary advert for Spree sweets ('It's a kick in the mouth!'). Subsequent to the seven years she spent playing the much-loved Cordelia Chase firstly on *Buffy* and then on *Angel*, she starred as the eponymous Jane Grant in *See Jane Date* and appeared in *Charmed*.

Mark Colson featured in *Alias*, *Gilmore Girls* and *Grounded For Life*.

Not Exactly a Haven For the Demons: When Wesley performs the ritual to remove Lindsey's tattoos and to open a portal to The Senior Partners, the rite requires the use of a demon's arterial blood. Since Lorne is the only demon around at the time, he's required to provide some. Lorne is somewhat distressed at this, bemoaning the fact that such rituals never need the urine of a demon, something which he had plenty of to spare – indeed, he comments that he's just about to produce some when Gunn pulls out a nasty-looking knife to take his blood.

The Price of Getting Caught: Although Angel is unable to bring himself to accept Cordelia's suggestion and torture Eve for information, Harmony has no such qualms. Eve tells Angel that a Code Seven warning has been sent to all Wolfram & Hart employees except for the executive staff, telling them to evacuate the building. This is done because of the imminent release of a failsafe stored in the building's basement and designed to destroy Angel if The Senior Partners believe that he could no longer be controlled. She doesn't know exactly what the failsafe is except that it's huge and alive. Angel and Cordelia confront Lindsey who displays magically-enhanced strength and combat skills (which, he says, he learned in Nepal) to fight Angel, while

Cordelia works to prevent the failsafe from activating. Cordelia successfully shuts down the failsafe and a spell created by Wesley removes the tattoos from Lindsey. The Senior Partners promptly discover his whereabouts and Lindsey is sucked, screaming, into a spatial vortex (see **105**, 'Underneath').

Cigarettes & Alcohol: Angel and his friends plan to celebrate their success in averting the crisis at a pub called the Cat and Fiddle.

Sex and Drugs and Rock'n'Roll: When she learns about Angel's sexual encounter with Eve (see **93**, 'Life of the Party'), Cordelia says that she didn't think he could possibly do worse than Darla (see **37**, 'Reprise'). Cordelia and Angel discuss what might have been had they actually managed to get together on that night when she ascended and he was sent to the depths (see **66**, 'Tomorrow').

Logic, Let Me Introduce You to This Window: In a coma since the events of **83**, 'Inside Out', Cordelia supposedly wakes to warn Angel that she has been sent a vision from The Powers That Be of Lindsey's sinister plans. The final scene of the episode, however, suggests that in reality she never woke up at all, dying in her sleep. That renders her presence in this entire episode unexplained. So, what was it, a mass hallucination? Cordelia remembers every detail of the events of Season Four – including Connor. She was seemingly unaffected by the memory-altering spell (see **88**, 'Home'). As she was already in a coma at that stage, it does make sense that she would not have her memories affected. Couldn't Wolfram & Hart afford a private room for Cordelia? If the tattoos that he wears are designed to protect Lindsey from being detected by, as Wesley suggests, higher powers, seers or mystics, then how can Cordelia receive a vision from The Powers That Be which features Lindsey's tattoos prominently?

I Just *Love* Your Accent: Spike calls Angel a gormless tit, much to Angel's distress.

Quote/Unquote: Angel: 'With these resources, there's no one we can't save.' Cordelia: 'Except, maybe, yourself.'

Harmony, when Angel points out that Eve is talking and she can stop punching her: 'Already? Well, *that* sucks.'

Angel: 'I'm not gonna risk anybody I care about.' Spike: 'I'll go.' Angel: 'OK.'

Lindsey to Angel: 'You used to have fire in your heart. Now all you got in there is that big honkin' sword. How's that feel, champ?'

Notes: 'Spike's a hero and you're CEO of Hell Incorporated? What freakin' Bizzaroworld did I wake up in?!' We've waited a long time for this moment. No matter how good it's been since she left the show – and *Angel* has frequently been excellent during this period – there is absolutely no doubt that Charisma Carpenter *completes Angel*. That this was the last time we ever saw her on the show that she graced for four years was *no* cause for celebration. Cordy, frankly, *rocks* in this episode, whether it's in a brilliant scene with Angel discussing Doyle's sacrifice, a touching moment with Wesley concerning Lilah's death or as part of a side-splitting deal-with-the-devil sight-gag, she's always there, on the button, turning fine moments into great ones with a touch of elegance and class. Replete with an epic zombie fight, more sinister Lindsey and Eve games and something of a Bondian masterplan, 'You're Welcome' reminds us of something very important. That, aesthetic changes aside (see the previous episode's denouement for a further example), *Angel* remained, at heart – and at *soul* for that matter – a series about the differences between good and evil. And, in the episode's series-defining climactic battle, again, about the concept and the need for redemption in all aspects of the show. A great episode, then, and a fine farewell to a truly great character. Like Doyle, Cordy leaves, with a kiss, to do the right thing even if it isn't the *easy* thing. We shan't see the likes of her again. More's the pity.

Angel and his friends' latest client is a black arts dealer named Greenway who, while facing a racketeering charge, slaughtered a group of five nuns and then escaped through a portal into another dimension. This has cost Wolfram & Hart something in the region of $10 million. The slave of Archduke Sebassis has been found hiding in one of the photocopiers at Wolfram & Hart, living on toner. Seemingly, it took advantage of the confusion in 93, 'Life of the Party' to escape from its master. Cordelia apologises to Wesley for killing Lilah while possessed (see 78, 'Calvary') and she remembers, bitterly, that the last time she saw Harmony her former best friend tried to kill her (see 39, 'Disharmony'). She also watches the Angel Investigations promotional video that she made with Doyle in 9, 'Hero' and discusses with Angel Doyle's magnificent self-sacrifice and how he passed his visions on to her. Lindsey tells Spike that he, too, once had his hand cut off (see 22, 'To Shanshu in LA'). Angel reminds Lindsey that, when they first met, he threw Lindsey's client out of the window (1, 'City Of'). According to Spike demons who are evil have a different taste – more astringent, with an oaky tinge – to those who are not.

Ratings: According to a delighted WB press release, on 8 February, the 100th episode of *Angel* outperformed *The West Wing*, *King of Queens* and *Becker* in its time slot to rank third among persons aged 12 to 34 and among men aged 12 to 34. The series also defeated both CBS and NBC in the female 12 to 34-year-old demographic and in female teens. *Angel*, it was announced, had also posted year-to-year gains in all 12 to 34 and teen demographics as well as among adults 18 to 34 and men 18 to 34 (up a whopping 27 per cent from the previous year). Five days later, they cancelled the show.

Did You Know?: Charisma Carpenter's next assignment after filming her final *Angel* episode was a very tasteful series of photos for *Playboy* – she was the cover star of their June 2004 edition. Needless to say, the issue has since become something of a prized item among *Angel*'s male fans, with a handful of signed copies going for over $200 on e-Bay. In an accompanying article in which she was asked a series of intimate questions, Charisma revealed that: of all the women she appeared with on *Buffy* and *Angel*, Stephanie Romanov was the one that she would most like to film a girl-on-girl scene with; the music she listens to during sex includes the Rolling Stones and Ben Harper; Viggo Mortensen reminds Charisma of her husband; and that she once had sex at an Oscar party in the bathroom. Naughty!

Hitting the Century: On 4 December 2003, the cast and crew of *Angel* gathered on Stage 5 at Paramount Pictures, the home of the massive Wolfram & Hart set, to blow out the candles on a white and blood-red cake bearing the inscription 'Angel 100'.

Cast and Crew Comments: According to *TV Zone*, despite some 'remaining tensions' over the exact circumstances of her departure the previous year, Charisma Carpenter was happy with her return to *Angel*: 'The day was lovely. Joss wrote me a note and left flowers in my trailer expressing his gratitude for my return and that it meant a lot to him. The story was probably one of the sweetest they'd ever told.'

Charisma's return affected several of her former colleagues. 'It was a beautiful thing to have Charisma on the set once more and feel her energy,' an emotional David Boreanaz told Steven Eramo. 'I missed that and to get back into that groove was just a blast.'

David Fury's Comments: Asked by the *Northwestern Chronicle* about his feelings on the general quality of television writing today, David Fury noted an admiration for a number of long-running series including *The Sopranos*, *The West Wing* and *Six Feet Under*, along with newer shows like *Curb Your Enthusiasm* and *World Poker Tour* on the Travel Channel. His favourite books include *Seabiscuit*, *The Kite Runner*, Anne Lamott's *Bird by Bird* and Richard Greenberg's stageplay *Take Me Out*. As well as listening to the White Stripes and Ennio Morricone, David also said that his favourite movies included *Lost in*

Translation, *Kill Bill*, *Casablanca* and *Citizen Kane*. When asked what advice he would give to aspiring TV writers, David replied that a key ingredient is to hone your sense of humour. 'Nothing is more valuable than a writer who can write funny dialogue, be it for shows like *The Shield*, *Gilmore Girls* or *ER*. Lots of people can learn the craft of writing, but coming up with the funny [things] will get you hired, guaranteed.'

Joss Whedon's Comments: 'It's very much an opportunity for us to sum up [and say] "Good Lord, we've been doing this for a while" without being sly and post-modern and winking at the audience,' Whedon said of 'You're Welcome' at The WB's Winter Press Tour. 'We're using it as a milestone. Because Cordelia was there at the beginning, she can come and say, "Where are you now?" '

101
Why We Fight

US Transmission Date: 11 February 2004
UK Transmission Date: 6 April 2004

Writers: Steven S DeKnight, Drew Goddard
Director: Terrence O'Hara
Cast: Eyal Podell (Sam Lawson), Lindsey Ginter (Navy Officer),
Scott Klace (Civilian), Roy Werner (Heinreich),
Bradley Snedeker (Tyler), Mikey Day (O'Shea), Matt Goodwin (Hodge),
Camden Toy (The Prince of Lies), Bart McCarthy (Nostroyev),
Nick Spano (Spinelli), Joel Polis (Captain Franklin)[26]

1943: Angel is persuaded to join the US war effort as one of Uncle Sam's secret weapons against the Nazis when a captured U-Boat goes missing in hostile waters. Over sixty years later, the consequences of some of his actions in the dim and distant past come back to haunt him and his friends in a suitably, and morally, ambiguous way.

---

[26] Uncredited.

Dudes and Babes: Ensign Sam Lawson was part of a volunteer force that captured a wolf pack U-Boat for US Military Intelligence in 1943. The mission went sour when the submarine's cargo – some of the nastiest vampires in Europe (including, inevitably, Spike) – escaped and started killing the crew. Angel, given the mission of saving the boat, befriended Lawson.

Denial, Thy Name is Angel: After a German prisoner stabbed Lawson, who was the only person on board who could successfully repair the damaged vessel's engines, Angel was forced to make Lawson into a vampire so that the ship could be brought home and the other crew members could live. Angel told Lawson that this was the only occasion after he reacquired his soul in 1898 that he ever made anyone a vampire. When the boat was operational again, Angel forced Lawson (along with Spike) to leave, giving him eight hours to swim the approximate twenty miles to shore before the sun came up and killed him. Lawson has spent the subsequent sixty years living as a vampire. However, he suggests that he has gained no enjoyment from his killing ways. Although Angel is somewhat sceptical, it is more than possible that the tiniest fragment of Angel's soul was passed to Lawson when Angel sired him and it is for this reason that Lawson finds himself neither one thing nor the other. Lost, without a purpose, he has monitored Angel's life once each decade or so – he mentions that the last time he saw Angel, the vampire was living in a sewer and eating rats; see *Buffy*: 'Becoming' Part 1; **81**, 'Orpheus'. Lawson penetrates Wolfram & Hart's security and threatens to kill Fred, Wesley and Gunn before Angel gives him the closure that he has, perhaps, been searching for.

A Little Learning is a Dangerous Thing: Gunn reminds his colleagues that The White Room is empty (see **96**, 'Destiny') and that their link to The Senior Partners has vanished (see **100**, 'You're Welcome'). It is, therefore, hard getting information. Just as he is about to suggest some legal scheme to rectify this situation, Gunn suffers from an apparent loss of his recently acquired knowledge.

The Conspiracy Starts at Home Time: Gunn tells Angel there is no news yet as to the whereabouts of Lindsey. However, going by company precedent, Gunn believes that Lindsey should be boiling in his own filth by now (see **105**, 'Underneath'). Eve has also disappeared (she vanished swearing vengeance on Angel and his friends).

Work is a Four-Letter Word: In 1943, Angel was living in a New York apartment when he received a visit from members of the military and the intelligence services. Though reluctant, he was recruited (through persuasion and, you know, *threats*) to rescue a captured U-Boat with American submariners on board. Angel was, apparently, tracked down by a new agency called Demon Research Initiative (a possible forerunner of The Initiative? See *Buffy*: 'The Initiative') who knew a great deal about him – including the status of his soul. After the mission, once the submarine reached US coastal waters, Angel swam ashore in Maine and stayed underground until after the war to avoid being used by the government again. (He eventually turned up in a seedy Los Angeles hotel in 1952, see **24**, 'Are You Now or Have You Ever Been?')

References: 'My hat's off to the movie *U-571* and *Submarines for Dummies*, which were my main resources,' noted Steven DeKnight shortly after the episode aired. The title comes from a series of seven information films made by Frank Capra for the US War Department during the period 1942–45. [27] Conceptually, 'Why We Fight' is a visual mixture of *Das Boot*, *Miracleman* and those flashback episodes – like 'Apocrypha' and 'Triangle' – that *The X-Files* used to do so successfully. Sam Lawson was the

---

[27] Major Capra was assigned to the Office of War Information and ordered by the Chief of Staff, General George Marshall, to 'make a series of documented, factual-information films that will explain to our boys in the Army why we are fighting'. Capra's subsequent films were influenced by Leni Riefenstahl's *Triumph of the Will* (1936), a movie which, Capra noted, 'fired no gun, dropped no bombs. But as a psychological weapon aimed at destroying the will to resist, it was just as lethal.' Immediately after the war, Capra made his masterpiece, *It's a Wonderful Life*, which can be considered a critcal summation of many of the themes that his *Why We Fight* series articulated.

name of a character (played by Cliff Robertson) in Robert Aldrich's World War II drama *Too Late the Hero*. Also, German naval commander Admiral Karl Dönitz (1891– 1980) and Nazi propaganda minister Dr Joseph Goebbels (1897–1945), the Milton Bradley board game Jenga, *Apollo 13* ('she's a good boat'), the Nautilus (Captain Nemo's vessel from Jules Verne's *20,000 Leagues Under the Sea* and *The Mystery Island*),[28] *The Godfather*, the traditional Russian folk melody 'Coachman, Spare Your Horses', Popeye the Sailor Man, Pierre Choderlos de Laclos's *Les Liaisons Dangereuses* ('revenge is best served cold'), the Marvel Superhero Captain America and his human alter ego Steve Rogers (see **16**, 'The Ring').

'West Hollywood?': Nostroyev claims to have once been the lover of Rasputin.[29]

'You May Remember Me From Such Films and TV Series As …': Israeli-born Eyal Podell played Roland in *Charmed* and appeared in *The Chaos Factor*, *Behind Enemy Lines*, *Ally McBeal*, *The West Wing* and *Deep Blue Sea*. Lindsey Ginter's CV includes *Pearl Harbor*, *Mercury Rising*, *Gattaca* and *The X-Files*. Scott Klace was in *24*, *Enterprise* and *The District*. Roy Werner appeared in *Live From Baghdad*, *Firestorm Rising*, *Providence* and *Silk Stalkings*. Bradley Snedeker featured in *Navy NCIS*.

Aside from several notable appearances as monsters in various *Buffy* episodes, Camden Toy also appeared in *My Chorus*. Bart McCarthy's CV includes *Memorial Day*, *Malcolm in the Middle* and *Star Trek: Deep Space Nine*. Nick Spano played Donnie Stevens in *Even Stevens* and appeared in *Body Shots* and *7th Heaven*. Joel Polis was in *Swallow*, *Serial Killer*, *The Thing* and *Roseanne*.

---

[28] In real life, six ships from the US Navy have been named the USS *Nautilus* – the last two being submarines.

[29] Grigori Yefimovtich Rasputin (1871–1916), a self-styled Holy Man who held a sinister influence over the decadent Romanov court of Tsar Nicholas II and was assassinated by members of the Russian establishment. Played by Christopher Lee in Hammer's *Rasputin – The Mad Monk*. Also, according to Boney M, a cat that really was gone.

Behind the Camera: Terrence O'Hara directed the movie *Darkroom* and episodes of *Smallville*, *Dark Angel*, *Brimstone*, *The Pretender*, *Star Trek: Voyager* and *The X-Files*.

Not Exactly a Haven For the Demons: Spike's bunk-mates on the submarine were the Russian vampire Nostroyev and the ancient Prince of Lies, both of whom were, like Spike, captured by the SS in 1943. The Nazis' plan was to use mind control on vampires to create an army of super-soldiers against the Allies. The former Scourge of Siberia and Butcher of Alexandria Palace, Nostroyev was killed by Angel when he refused to follow orders. Angel also killed the Prince of Lies when he attacked a German prisoner after discovering that the Nazis were planning to tamper with his brain.

Cigarettes & Alcohol: Lorne plans to spend his evening at the fashionable LA night spot the Skybar (see **42**, 'Over the Rainbow'), which, he notes, is full of frat-boys and TV executives these days.

Logic, Let Me Introduce You to This Window: That's a remarkably spacious U-Boat they've got there. Anyone who has visited the surviving U-Boat (U-995) at the German naval military museum in Laboe can testify to just how narrow and cramped conditions are on board. When Angel sires Sam Lawson, the sailor almost instantly becomes a vampire. Previously, it had been established that the process takes at least one night before the vampire rises (see, for instance, **32**, 'Reunion'). The 1943 Angel seems much more self-confident and heroic than one would expect from someone who has lived in virtual isolation for forty years. There's very little water in the torpedo tube when Angel emerges from it. No one could get from the forward end of a submarine to the aft without going through the control room – there just isn't an alternative route. Electric power availability for the lights has nothing to do with whether the motors are working. During the 1943 flashback Spike uses the word 'groovy' a good decade and a half before it properly entered the vocabulary.[30] If Spike was being taken from Madrid to a lab in Germany, why is he being transported by sea? Why did Spike have his hair dyed black in 1943?[31]

Continuity: In *Buffy*: 'Angel', Darla suggests that Angel hasn't fed on a human in a hundred years. We already know that wasn't true (see **81**, 'Orpheus'). Here we discover that Angel had another dark secret to go along with the shot doughnut-shop clerk whom he drank from in the mid-1970s. In *Buffy*: 'School Hard', Spike says that he hasn't seen Angel in 'an age'. This episode doesn't, necessarily, contradict that statement. As far as we know, Angel and Spike have seen each other on just this one occasion in the almost one hundred years since Angel left Darla, Spike and Dru in China in 1900. (*Buffy*: 'Angel' and **29**, 'Darla' suggest that Angel and Darla met some time shortly after this, in Budapest, but there's no indication that Spike was party to this.) Even for vampires, 55 years could be said to constitute an age.

I Just *Love* Your Accent: In 1943, Spike sang a brief (and very tuneless) snatch of the then-British national anthem, 'God Save the King'.

Quote/Unquote: Angel: 'You're a Nazi?' Spike: 'No, I just *ate* one.'

Spike: 'Sneaky bastards, the SS. Don't ever go to a "free virgin blood party". Turns out, it's probably a trap!'

Lawson: 'You don't win a war by doing whatever it takes. You win by doing what's right.'

---

[30] The first recorded use of 'groovy', surprisingly, occurred as early as 1941. However, in those days it was very much a New Orleans jazz term – meaning 'playing with inspiration' (from the grooves on a record). During the late 1950s, the US Beatnik movement adopted it as a descriptive term for something or someone being attractive, fashionable or exciting.

[31] A question worth asking: what did Spike do for the rest of the war once he reached land? This author is sure that there are fan-fiction writers out there busy working on scenarios in which William the Bloody strides, magnificently, through the carnage of Monte Cassino or Arnhem.

Notes: 'We used to live in simple times,' notes Sam Lawson near the end of this conceptually fascinating piece of revenge tragedy. 'Why We Fight' is *Angel's* attempt to stretch its backstory away from clichés and obvious dramatic situations and into something more insightful and a shade more daring and complex. Lawson, sired by Angel during the Second World War to save a vital mission, turns up at Wolfram & Hart seeking vengeance. Or, perhaps, closure – the script is somewhat ambiguous on this point. In fact it's somewhat ambiguous on several points which, amazingly, actually works in the episode's favour. In a story about the ends of an action usually (but *not* always) justifying the means, Lawson's tragic personal story is the counterbalance to a cleverly weighted piece of outrageous conceit: to wit, a black-haired Spike, captured by the SS as part of a Nazi *meisterplan* to enslave an army of supersoldier vampires. There's fun and games to be had when Angel allows himself to be used by the State Department and become a superhero too. Underpinning the aesthetics, however, is a deeply ambitious, if not wholly successful, story concerning right versus need. Shaded with several of the show's key metaphors, 'Why We Fight' reminds us that *Angel* has always striven to reflect the pain of redemption as well as the pleasure. In that respect, although not a patch on some of the surrounding episodes, it maintains many of the running themes of this season. And though, conceptually, it uses a sledgehammer to crack a nut, any episode of American television which features, even vaguely, an anti-war message – in these days of compromise and sycophancy towards the White House's bombastic international agenda – has to be applauded for its bravery.

Wes has five or six hours of spell detailing to do. Gunn suggests he and Wesley study the portal incantations from last Monday's Mithroc retreat. Fred notes that she will have to do the Trask Experiment again as Knox made something of a hash of the first attempt. Wesley agrees, rather too quickly, that Knox is rather unreliable. The headline of the 1943 copy of the *New York Journal* glimpsed in Angel's apartment says ALLIES STRIKE BACK![32]

Soundtrack: There's a nice contrast between the authentic period music used in Angel's apartment in 1943 and the eerie, metallic score that dominates most of the U-Boat sequences.

Did You Know?: In the original shooting script for this episode, the two men who come to Angel's apartment in 1943 to persuade him to undertake the mission are identified as Commander Petrie and Mr Fury – references to DeKnight and Goddard's former *Buffy* colleagues Doug Petrie and David Fury. However, neither name is mentioned in the episode itself or in the credits.

Cast and Crew Comments: 'As an actor I've learned over the years when to shut my mouth, and I should've done that here,' James Marsters told *TV Zone*. 'I made the mistake of saying "Would Spike have blond hair back then? From what I understand, he started bleaching it during the 70s and the punk period." Well, that launched a whole wave of meetings and I wound up wearing a wig. Every close up was more about the wig than my acting. That said, it actually turned out to be a very good episode.'

Where Were You?: On Friday 13 February 2004, *Angel*'s fans – who just ten days earlier had been celebrating the series' 100th episode – received a very nasty surprise. 'Like some of the great series that are leaving the air this year, including *Frasier* and *Friends*, the cast, crew, writers and producers of *Angel* deserve to be able to wrap up the series in a way befitting a classic television series and that is why we went to Joss to let him know that this would be the last

---

[32] Given the approximate dating of the episode, it's fair to assume that the headline refers to either the conclusion of the allied North Africa campaign with the capture of Tunis in May 1943, or the joint invasion of Sicily two months later. The other major allied victories of 1943 – the apocalyptic massacres of Stalingrad and Kursk – didn't involve British or American forces at all, received little publicity in the West at the time and their massive significance to the overall victory only became clear much later.

year of the series on The WB,' noted an official press release from the network. The statement went on to suggest that the network had discussed continuing the *Angel* legacy with 'special movie events next year'.

'J [August Richards] called,' Andy Hallett told *Dream-Watch*. 'Joss and the other producers had come down to the set to tell everyone we'd been cancelled. Then my other line rang and it was a reporter asking me what I thought about it. I said, "Let me call you back – I'm just hearing about it myself." '[33]

The decision, as many commentators noted, mystified not only fans but also the producers of *Angel*'s lead-in show *Smallville*. As *TV Zone* noted, 'to judge by The WB's statement, the network's main reason for dropping *Angel* seems to be that it's a quality show that's been doing quite well.'

Joss Whedon responded to the news with a mixture of humour and passionate anger. '*Angel* is as strong as it's ever been. Except that it's dead,' he noted. 'I'm heartbroken. I can't speak for The WB's reasoning, and this would probably be a bad time for me to comment on any of the shows they're NOT cancelling,' he added. 'But they provided a home for both *Buffy* and *Angel* that otherwise would not have existed and I'm grateful for that.'

Joss Whedon's Comments: Joss subsequently posted more thoughts onto the Posting Board. 'We had no idea this was coming,' he noted. 'When *Buffy* ended, I was tapped out

---

[33] The actual scene being filmed at the time the cancellation was announced to the cast and crew – according to Hallett – was 'in the basement where a demon is torturing Gunn' which indicated that **106**, 'Origin' and not **105**, 'Underneath' – as often stated – was the episode in production during that fateful President's Day weekend. As a personal observation, this author was in Los Angeles having a very good time at the annual Gallifrey One convention in Van Nuys. I was on an autograph panel when someone thrust a copy of The WB's statement into my hands. With horrible irony, an hour later I was scheduled to moderate a fan panel called 'The Future of *Angel*'. That this event subsequently turned into a joyous affirmation of why the series was great and how we would all remember it was, largely, down to the audience – many of whom are named in the acknowledgements of this book. (The rest of the night, in the bar, commiserating with Danny Strong, BBCi's Rob Francis and various other friends and fans is a more blurry and discombobulated series of memories.)

and ready to send it off. When *Firefly* got the axe, I went into a state of denial so huge it may end in a movie. But, *Angel* . . . we really were starting to feel like we were on top – and then we strode right into the Pit of Snakes and Lava. You wanna know how I feel? Watch [*Buffy* episode] "The Body".'

Despite some fans' hopes having been raised by The WB mentioning the possibility of future TV movies, Joss was noncommittal – if not openly hostile – to this rather obvious crumb being thrown in Mutant Enemy's direction. 'I actually hope my actors and writers are all too busy,'[34] he noted.

102
Smile Time

US Transmission Date: 18 February 2004
UK Transmission Date: 13 April 2004

Writers: Ben Edlund, Joss Whedon
Director: Ben Edlund
Cast: David Fury (Gregor Framkin), Ridge Canipe (Tommy),
Jenny Vaughn Campbell (Tommy's Mother), Abigail Mavity (Hannah),
Brad Abrell (Puppet Voice), Leslie Carrara (Puppet Voice),
Donna Kimball (Puppet Voice), Drew Massey (Puppet Angel),
Victor Yerrid (Polo)

Several children in the LA area are hospitalised, apparently due to the malign influence of an early morning puppet TV show *Smile Time*. Angel investigates, then wishes that he hadn't when he's hexed and finds himself muppetised.

Puppet Dudes and Babes: Polo, Groofus, 'Ratio Hornblower and The Little Girl are a quartet of very nasty

---

[34] Speaking at the annual Saturn Awards shortly afterwards, Joss claimed that continued reports about *Angel* TV movies were simply rumours perpetuated by over-eager fans. 'There are no definite plans to do anything besides finish out the season as well and as hard as we can,' he told the audience. This view was echoed by David Boreanaz who told *TV Guide*, 'the only way I would do any kind of loose-end wrapping up would be if they decided to do something on a different, higher level, like a film'.

demons disguised as the puppet cast of the popular children's TV show *Smile Time*. They take over an entertainment venue and use it to wreak havoc on the unsuspecting viewing public. Having signed a contract with *Smile Time* creator Gregor Framkin when his show's ratings dipped (reducing Framkin himself to a helpless puppet), the demons use a hidden carrier wave that turns the TV into a two-way conduit to target individual children, while maintaining a cloak to prevent other viewers from seeing what is happening. Once a child is lured to the television, Polo drains the child's life essence – pure innocence, a very valuable commodity in the lower planes – and transfers it to the Nest Egg, a large repository kept in a secret room at the show's studio. This isn't the first time that they've pulled a similar stunt, observes Gunn, drawing his colleagues' attention to the last few seasons of *Happy Days* as a prime example.

Dudes and Babes: Nina's sister and niece are still seemingly unaware of her werewolf personality (see **91**, 'Unleashed'). Each month, when she's going to spend three days at Wolfram & Hart, she claims to her family that she'll be camping in the desert. Nina thinks that her sister, Jill, believes that Nina is turning into a new-agey, moon-worshipping wicca-type person. Angel wonders if telling Jill the truth would be less embarrassing for Nina.

A Little Learning is a Dangerous Thing: Groofus says that he's working on a great new educational song informing children about the differences between an analogy and a metaphor.

Wesley believes that Angel's puppet-transformation could be a hex or a powerful warding magic. Lorne offers an alternative explanation – some type of puppet cancer, much to Angel's annoyance. When Angel says he wants Wolfram & Hart on a state of red alert with the helicopters and the tear gas, Lorne reminds him that *Smile Time* is the number one show in its particular time slot – children across Southern California love it. Wolfram & Hart, therefore, would be ill-advised to declare a jihad on the studio that makes it.

Denial, Thy Names Are Angel and Wesley: In Wesley's office, Angel tells Wes that Nina invited him to breakfast after she had spent her night in the cage. Wes asks what Angel's answer was. Angel admits he changed the subject and locked her up. It wasn't just breakfast, he continues, noting that he and Nina have a platonic thing going on and that he was somewhat mystified by her sudden wish to take things further. Wes asks if Angel is blind; there are signals – odourless, invisible but unmistakable. Like the ones that Nina has been casting Angel's way for months. Angel is sure he would have noticed. Wesley assures his friend that this observation doesn't merely come from him, it is confirmed by those who really know – Fred, Harmony, the girls in transcription. Harmony apparently put it somewhat more bluntly asking why would a chick who's coming to spend three nights in a jail cell dress like it's her first date? Angel realises that the ladies are correct. He flusters that he doesn't have time for such a relationship at the moment. Besides, there's the 'one moment of perfect happiness' scenario. That would turn him back into Angelus and *nobody* wants that. Wes calms Angel and tells him that 99 per cent of the best relationships in recorded history had to make do with just acceptable happiness. Wes notes that Angel is hiding behind his gypsy curse, which is wrong when there's a beautiful, engaging, if occasionally hirsute, young woman who actually wants him. Angel is dismissive. He can be charming and funny and emotionally useful. More often than not, however, he is the guy in a dark corner with the blood habit and two hundred years of psychic baggage. 'Get over it!' shouts Wesley. Angel asks Wes why he is yelling at him. Wes becomes more reflective, telling Angel that if there's a woman whom one finds attractive and who doesn't view one as an entirely sexless shoulder to lean on, Angel has to do something about it. Angel looks at Wesley quizzically and asks 'Who are we talking about here?'

The Conspiracy Starts at Home Time: Gunn visits Dr Sparrow who gave him his brain upgrade (see **89**,

'Conviction'), fearing that the process is reversing itself. Sparrow confirms this and speculates that if Gunn's revised powers are fading, it must be because The Senior Partners want it that way. Sparrow may be able to help. He currently has a lot of money tied up in a shipment that's become stalled at customs. Gunn asks if it's drugs, but Sparrow assures him that, actually, it's an ancient curio which he hopes to turn a handsome profit on. If he were to give Gunn a permanent upgrade, Gunn could cut through all of his red-tape problems with regard to this item. Gunn is reluctant but, desperate to have his new knowledge restored, eventually agrees. You just *know* that this isn't going to end well (see **103**, 'A Hole in the World'; **104**, 'Shells'; **105**, 'Underneath').

It's a Designer Label!: Fred's purple miniskirt, Lorne's nasty orange shirt. Nina's cream top and extremely tight green combat pants.

References: *Smile Time* is based, not particularly subtly but very amusingly, on Jim Henson's legendary PBS children's show *Sesame Street*. There are allusions to *Spider-Man* ('proportionate excitability of a puppet'), Papa Smurf, Gepetto the wood carver from *Pinocchio*, Daniel Keyes's award-winning novella *Flowers for Algernon*, Cliff Robertson (see **101**, 'Why We Fight') and his Oscar-winning performance in *Charly*, Merlin the Magician and the Joker from *Batman*.

Awesome!: Angel and Wesley's beautiful heart-to-heart (see **Denial, Thy Names Are Angel and Wesley**). The revelation of Puppet-Angel to Wesley, Gunn, Fred and Lorne and their reaction to it. Puppet-Angel hiding, in shame and panic, under the desk from Nina. Puppet-Angel's fight in the corridor and the elevator with Spike (and winning). Werewolf-Nina attacking Puppet-Angel ('Bad Nina!') just after he's been at his most self-confessional. That hilarious shot, a parody of the final part of the title sequence, of Puppet-Angel with his sword walking into battle, followed by Gunn, Fred and Wesley. The final scene – Fred and Wesley kissing.

'You May Remember Me From Such Films and TV Series As . . .': Ridge Canipe appeared in *Cold Case*. Jenny Vaughn Campbell's CV includes *Macon County Jail* and *Presidio Med*. Abigail Mavity played Kaitlin in *100 Mile Rule* and also appeared in *When Billie Beat Bobby*, *Summerland* and *Touched By An Angel*.

Behind the Camera: Brad Abrell provided voice and puppeteer work on *Men in Black* and its sequel and *SpongeBob SquarePants*. Leslie Carrara was the voice of Spamela Hamderson on *Muppets Tonight!* Donna Kimball's CV includes acting roles in *Catch Me if You Can*, *Tracey Takes On* . . . and *Solaris*. Drew Massey is a puppeteer whose work can be seen in *Cats & Dogs*, *The Flintstones*, *Muppets From Space* and *Doctor Doolittle*. He also played Count Blah in *Greg The Bunny* where his co-star was Victor Yerrid (as the voice of Tardy Turtle). Yerrid was also a puppeteer on *Bear in the Big Blue House*.

Cigarettes & Alcohol: Polo drinks Jack Daniel's from a *Smile Time* mug while discussing the Angel problem with his fellow puppets.

Sex and Drugs and Rock'n'Roll: Knox gives Fred a Valentine card, which she declines. We later learn that they have dated on a few occasions but that Fred is more interested in Wesley.

Nina tells Angel that he has a lot going on in his life and the last thing he probably needs to deal with is a crush from monster girl, a charity case whom he was nice enough to help. When Angel reveals that he's now a puppet, Nina wonders why Angel cares about what others think? He is, after all, a bona fide hero. And, while hoping she doesn't sound like an art school cliché, the vampire thing he had going for him is, she believes, sexy.

Logic, Let Me Introduce You to This Window: The report that Fred receives states that eleven children, aged between five and eight, have collapsed in recent weeks and remain unconscious. She later says there have been only seven cases. Who, exactly, was the man with the towel over his head in the 'Don't Room'? Framkin, presumably, though annoyingly this point is never clarified within the episode itself. If it *was* Framkin then why has he got the towel draped over his head? Either Nina was expecting Angel to have shrunk to a height of three feet when he visited her cell or she has a nasty habit of looking at men in the crotch area. In the scene where Angel walks down the corridor and encounters the janitor, the first shot shows the janitor reaching Angel. In the next, he is still approaching.

Motors: Spike has crashed one of Angel's cars and is hoping to borrow another.

Quote/Unquote: Fred: 'Oh my God, Angel, you're . . . cute!'
   Angel, to Nina: 'I'm made of felt. And my nose comes off.'
   Framkin, to Lorne and Gunn: 'I bring joy and laughter to children. You bring tax exemptions to nasty corporations and acquittals to the clearly guilty.'
   Polo: 'We eat babies' lives.' Groofus: '*And* uphold a certain standard of quality edutainment.'

Notes: 'I'm gonna tear you a new puppet-hole, bitch!' Ben Edlund's hilarious pastiche puppet theatre juggles comedic set-pieces (Spike's fight with Puppet-Angel, for example, which genuinely has to be seen to be believed), dramatic revelation (Gunn's sudden loss of his upgraded mental powers) and brilliant characterisation (Angel and Wesley's argument about relationships). The central idea of a demonic variant of *Sesame Street* is clever enough in its own right to wrap an episode around. But there's also an interesting subplot concerning the return of Werewolf-Nina (from **91**, 'Unleashed'), some fabulous TV industry jokes and a nice turn by David Fury as the apparent puppet master. These surface impressions, however, merely give readers a hint at the depth of creativity going on in this superb episode. Even ignoring the perceptive allegories in the script concerning how we are frequently, as humans, controlled by exterior forces, 'Smile Time' is a story about loss – with each of the characters discovering an aspect of themselves that is in danger of coming adrift. All this, plus ten seconds of gratuitous soft-core nudity! Inventive, witty and delightfully silly, how ironic it should be that 'Smile Time' was broadcast in the US during the same week that it was announced *Angel* was being cancelled. One of the cleverest and most imaginative series of the last decade cancelled at a time when it was receiving some of its best-ever ratings. The WB, however, *were* happy to renew moderately amusing but, ultimately, rather insubstantial genre product such as *Charmed* and *Smallville*, and undemanding middle-American slush such as *7th Heaven* and *Everwood*. There's no justice.

This episode takes place one week after Valentine's Day and on a full moon four months after Nina's werewolf attack (see **91**, 'Unleashed'). Fred's current address is 511 Windwood Circle. Wesley has a dartboard in his office (his prowess at darts had previously been demonstrated in **19**, 'Sanctuary' and **23**, 'Judgment') and the hand-drawn Unique Media map of Los Angeles previously seen in the Hyperion in **59**, 'Loyalty'. Gunn suggests that every contract signed with the lower plane is filed with the Library of Demonic Congress. Lorne loves the little marshmallows traditionally served with hot chocolate, which is something he has in common with Spike (see *Buffy*: 'Lover's Walk'). Lorne says that he knows most of the TV showrunners in town. The *Smile Time* show broadcasts each morning from 7.00 to 7.30 on KTCE, Channel 12. Gregor Framkin's story was a real rags-to-riches tale. He started making puppets in his garage with a glue gun and a couple of old couches. The patient whom Dr Sparrow sees before Gunn is being given X-ray vision.

Soundtrack: The several songs that the *Smile Time* puppets sing, including 'The *Smile Time* Theme', 'Courage and Pluck', 'There's a Little Bit of Math in Everything' and the episode's key song, 'Self-Esteem is For Everybody', were all written by Joss Whedon.

Critique: 'Smile Time' was inventive, scary and lots of fun, considered the *Beacon Journal*'s RD Heldenfels who also noted that it included some odd choices, including the portrayal of Angel as a bit of a goof with women. 'But it's still guaranteed to be one of the high points of TV this week. I wish the show wouldn't end.'

There were many appalling ironies in the timing of *Angel*'s cancellation, noted Kevin Williamson in the *Calgary Sun*, not the least of which was that the decision was taken to end this smart, stylish entertainment during the same week that the reality-romance genre's revolting answer to dwarf-tossing, *The Littlest Groom*, began. 'But the worst of them all is that *Angel*, which took a few years to find its footing, is enjoying its best, most confident season to date,' continued Williamson, who went on to note that what distinguished *Angel* was a subversive sense of humour, a respect for its audience's intelligence and the use of its genre as a metaphor.

In *Xposé* magazine's 2004 *Angel* Special, 'Smile Time' was voted by the readership as their favourite episode of the series, narrowly beating **57**, 'Waiting in the Wings'; **18**, 'Five by Five' and **103**, 'A Hole in the World'.

Did You Know?: At the time this episode was made, Jenny Mollen was dating writer/producer Drew Goddard.

Cast and Crew Comments: Unsurprisingly, 'Smile Time' is a favourite episode of many of the cast and crew. Describing the shooting as a riot, Alexis Denisof noted: 'I'm sure the editors had a nightmare trying to cut around our smirks and giggles.'

'I thought I wasn't going to be able to do it without laughing,' Jenny Mollen told Bryan Cairns concerning her initial scene with the Angel puppet. 'Luckily, I was there early that day and got to see Amy and Alexis take forever with their scenes with the puppet. They kept crying, they were laughing so hard so I got it out of my system.'

Cancellation Blues: 'When we heard the news, we were coming off 'Smile Time' and we were shocked because we thought we were doing really good shows,' noted Steven

DeKnight. 'On the other hand, we saw the writing on the wall. Our numbers are up but not significantly enough. Plus, The WB is really excited about *Dark Shadows* and nobody thought they'd do two vampire shows.'[35] When asked by *Xposé* if he had any parting thoughts for disappointed *Angel* fans, DeKnight mused: 'For all the people contributing to the 'Save *Angel*' campaign, save your money because the show is over. The machinery is being dismantled as we speak. And, thank you for your support.'

The 'Save *Angel*' Campaign: Within hours of the cancellation announcement, the inevitable 'Save *Angel*' campaign was launched by outraged fans. This quickly raised thousands of dollars to pay for newspaper ads begging WB executives to rethink their decision and a truck-mounted billboard that drove around Los Angeles for some weeks afterwards with the slogan '*Angel*: We'll follow him to hell . . . Or another network.' The group also organised postcard campaigns, rallies and protests outside The WB's headquarters. Ultimately, although they failed in their main objective, the 'Save *Angel*' campaign's organisers raised over $13,000, which they presented to Joss Whedon on 11 May 2004. The money was then passed on to the International Red Cross Foundation.

Joss Whedon's Comments: Asked by *Science Fiction Weekly* whether there was any likelihood of Sarah Michelle Gellar appearing in *Angel* during any of the final episodes, a somewhat exasperated Joss noted: 'Last year she said that she would be interested in coming on the show. This year, she said it felt too soon.'

---

[35] So, whatever happened to John Wells's remake of the 1960s horror-soap *Dark Shadows* – the commissioning of which, many people believe, encouraged The WB to cancel *Angel*? According to *TV Guide*'s Matt Roush there were said to be serious problems with the pilot – not least the fact that its director Rob Bowman (*The X-Files*) left the project halfway through. 'While The WB argue that *Angel*'s cancellation had nothing to do with *Dark Shadows*' development, I have no problem connecting those dots,' concluded Roush.

103
A Hole in the World

US Transmission Date: 25 February 2004
UK Transmission Date: 20 April 2004

Writer: Joss Whedon
Director: Joss Whedon
Cast: John Duff (Delivery Man), Jeremy Glazer (Lawyer),
Kevin Grevioux (Delivery Man)[36]

A stone sarcophagus from a time pre-dating even The Senior Partners arrives at Wolfram & Hart. While opening it, Fred swallows a deadly mystical pathogen. Spike and Angel rush to England in an effort to find a cure before Winifred is killed by a malevolent ancient entity, Illyria, dead for millions of years but now incubating within their friend. But, to save Fred, they must endanger thousands of lives. Is this too great a price?

Dudes and Really Old Babes: Fred's deputy in the Practical Science division, Knox, is revealed in this episode to be, in reality, a fanatical disciple of Illyria. Having (briefly) dated Fred, Knox chose her to be the vessel for the predestined reincarnation of his god. Millions of years ago, well before humans first appeared, The Old Ones governed the world. One of these pure-bred demons was Illyria, a fierce warrior both feared and beloved by those whom she ruled and whose kingdom was situated in the area that is now LA. Illyria was eventually defeated by a cabal of her fellow demons and her essence was placed in a sarcophagus within The Deeper Well, a prison for the dead souls of The Old Ones. Recently the sarcophagus has disappeared, part of an eons-old plan for the demon's escape perpetuated by her acolytes. It was brought to LA, where it was detained by customs. Gunn was manipulated into having the relic released (see **102**, 'Smile Time') and it subsequently arrived at Fred's lab. An iris in the sarcophagus spread a parasitic

---

[36] Uncredited.

agent which infected Fred, liquefied her organs, hardened her skin, hollowed her out using the shell of her body to gestate the lifeforce within, and, ultimately, killed her. Angel and Spike learn that it *is* possible for Illyria to be drawn back into The Deeper Well. However, doing so would become the mystical equivalent of an airborne pathogen – infecting every person between Los Angeles and the Cotswolds, and hundreds of thousands would die. Moments after Fred's death, she is reborn, as Illyria. The demon occupies Fred's body, although she now has violently dark-blue hair and eyes.

A Little Learning is a Dangerous Thing: The guardian of The Deeper Well is Drogyn. He knows Angel and regards him, cautiously, as an ally. Drogyn dislikes being asked questions because he cannot lie (see **109**, 'Power Play'). The Deeper Well houses a seemingly infinite number of sarcophagi and extends through the earth's core. Hence, Drogyn failed to notice that one was missing for some months.

Who's the Hardest?: Spike and Angel spend the episode involved in a heated theoretical argument over who would win in a fight between cavemen and astronauts. Ostensibly merely another example of their mutual loathing, this actually turns into a fascinating discussion on many different levels and spreads to other members of staff. Spike believes that the cavemen would hold the upper hand because of their primal, savage instinct. Angel suggests that the human race has evolved. Spike argues that they've evolved into a bunch of namby-pamby, self-analysing w**kers who could never hope to overcome pure aggression. Angel disagrees, saying there are other factors to take into account such as teamwork and superstition and fear just as Wesley asks why they have been yelling at each other for forty minutes. He then thinks about the question for a moment and asks if the astronauts have weapons.

Later, Spike is angry when he's summoned by Angel to discuss his future. Spike notes that Harmony pulled him out of a very promising poker game in the Accounts

Receivable department where, he adds, all the guys agree that astronauts don't stand a chance against cavemen. Subsequently, Fred and Lorne discuss the question. Fred notes that cavemen have fire, the astronauts should, therefore, have some kind of weapon. The final reference is when a delirious Fred tells Wesley that, of course, the cavemen will win every time.

Denial, Thy Name is Angel: Angel implies, to Spike, that he is desperate to save Fred, not only because she is their friend, but also because he was unable to save Cordelia in a similar situation (see **83**, 'Inside Out'; **100**, 'You're Welcome').

The Conspiracy Starts at Home Time: Knox tells Gunn, much to the latter's distress, that it was Gunn's signature on the customs form he signed in exchange for his legal upgrade that allowed the deadly sarcophagus into the building (see **104**, 'Shells').

LA is a Two-Letter Word: Before leaving Texas to attend school in LA, Fred teased her parents that she *could* stay home, meet a nice boy, get married, live in her room and have babies who would sleep in her dresser drawer. Mr Burkle, actually, didn't see a downside to that plan, noting that he, himself, lived in a drawer until he was three and it didn't stunt him. Fred reminds her father that she is going to the city of angels. Mr Burkle replies that if she should actually meet an angel there, he'll eat the dogs. LA, he continues, is full of junkies and spoilt movie actors (see **49**, 'Fredless').

It's a Designer Label!: Wesley's Bondian poloneck.

References: Allusions to the mathematician Mitchell Feigenbaum and Chaos Theory, *Romeo and Juliet* ('get a balcony, you two'), boxer Jake LaMotta, 'My Blue Heaven' ('And baby makes three'), Debarge's 'Rhythm of the Night', Carmen Miranda, *Anywhere But Here*, I Timothy 6:12 (see also **9**, 'Hero'), Walt Disney (who is alleged to have had himself cryogenically frozen when he died) and James Bond. The passage that Wesley reads to the dying Fred is from Frances Hodgson Burnett's *The Little Princess*. Christmas Land, containing Christmas Town, was one of the magical realms, accessible through a tree, in Tim Burton's *The Nightmare Before Christmas*. Wesley paraphrases the Rolling Stones' 'Time is On My Side'. Spike alludes to the popular conundrum 'when is a door not a door?' There are visual references to *Sleepy Hollow* and *The Lord of the Rings*. Gunn's dialogue concerning the house of pain could be an oblique allusion to various House of Mystery graphic representations of the Dionysiac Greco-Roman sex cults of the first and second centuries AD. [37]

Bitch!: When called upon to hear Eve sing, Lorne notes that Fred once told him, after a perfectly sinful amount of Chinese food and apropos of absolutely nothing, that she believed a lot of people would choose to be Lorne's particular shade of green. Lorne therefore continues that if he hears one note that suggests that Eve had any involvement, his colleagues won't even have time to kill Eve. Additionally, if she sings anything by Diane Warren this will *also* result in her death. After reading her, Lorne decides that Eve had nothing to do with what's happening to Fred. Nevertheless, he pointedly tells Eve that she has a very nasty future awaiting her (see **110**, 'Not Fade Away').

Irritated by Drogyn's ask-me-no-questions stance, Spike notes that Illyria's demon essence has been freed and asks why Drogyn believes he and Angel have travelled to The Deeper Well. He then continues with a string of several other questions for the man who cannot lie culminating in asking who is Manchester United's goalkeeper? (Spike's support of this famous, if in some areas somewhat unloved, English football team had previously been mentioned in *Buffy*: 'Becoming' Part 1. In this regard, Spike, a

---

[37] Such House of Mystery paintings usually depict hedonistic initiation ceremonies with devotees of the *Bacchae*, and other Euripidian forms of sado-erotic pleasure, abandoning themselves in erotic dancing. All are presided over by Diké, the Greek goddess of justice and punishment.

Londoner, is somewhat typical of Manchester United fans generally – most of whom live *anywhere* but Manchester. In answer to his question concerning the goalie, at the time the episode was made it was American Tim Howard.)

Spike is shocked when Angel suggests that Spike likes stabbing Angel. Spike *much* prefers hitting Angel with blunt instruments apparently.

The Odd Couple: Angel believes that Spike hanging around Wolfram & Hart isn't working for either of them. Spike sarcastically asks if Angel is suggesting they should annoy other people. Spike then alleges that Angel simply can't take the competition. Angel denies this, believing that Lindsey brought Spike back as a spirit bound to Wolfram & Hart deliberately. Spike says that he isn't attached to Wolfram & Hart, he simply doesn't have anywhere else to go. The company has offices in every major city in the world (and some beyond) so Angel offers Spike the resources to go anywhere – cars, gadgets, an expense account. Spike can fight the good fight in style. And, if possible, in Outer Mongolia.

Awesome!: The pointedly metaphorical cavemen-versus-astronauts debate. Fred coughing up blood and collapsing in Lorne's arms. Wesley shooting the employee who merely suggests that, surely, the whole company can't be working Ms Burkle's case. And then, Wes asking his secretary to send in anyone *else* who isn't working on finding a solution for Fred. The painful, emotional and almost voyeuristic final sequences of Wesley watching a scared, but brave, Fred weaken and then, heartbreakingly, die.

'You May Remember Me From Such Films and TV Series As . . .': Jennifer Griffin appeared in *Snoops*, *Six Feet Under*, *Born Into Exile*, *Vanilla Sky*, *A Perfect World*, *MacGyver* and *Hotel Lobby*. Mississippi-born Gary Grubbs is one of those great character actors who seem to have been in *everything*. His CV includes *The Astronaut's Wife*, *Will & Grace*, *The X-Files*, *JFK* (as Al Oser), *Foxfire*, *Silkwood*, *Caroline in the City*, *The A-Team*, *The Dukes of*

Hazzard, *M*A*S*H*, *The Rockford Files* and *Charlie's Angels*. John Duff appeared in *The Rundown*. Jeremy Glazer was in *ER*. Kevin Grevioux's movies include *Underworld* (on which he was also associate producer), *Planet of the Apes*, *Charlie's Angels* and *Batman Forever*. Glasgow-born Alec Newman appeared in *Judge John Deed*, *Murder Rooms* and *Tru Calling*.

Sex and Drugs and Rock'n'Roll: Gunn jokes with Wesley that he and Fred are getting back together. Then, with Wesley looking shattered, he admits that he is simply messing with Wesley's head. Gunn assures Wesley that the developing relationship between Wes and Fred is fine with him. What he and Fred had has been over for a long time and he knows how Wes feels about her. However, he does add that if Wesley ever hurts her, he will kill him like a chicken.

Logic, Let Me Introduce You to This Window: Spike says that he has never flown in an aeroplane before. That must mean he's done a *lot* of boat travelling in his time. Knox knew all about the significance of the sarcophagus. Why, therefore, is he so outwardly dismissive upon the item's arrival? Who, exactly, is he putting on this act *for*? When Richard Wilkins ascended to full demon status (see *Buffy*: 'Graduation Day' Part 2), he changed into a giant snake. This, it is implied, is a pure-bred demon's natural form (see the illustration of Illyria that Wesley finds). Illyria, on the other hand, seems to have no difficulty occupying the body of a human (however, see **107**, 'Time Bomb'). It is stated that Illyria's kingdom of a million years ago was where Los Angeles is now. A million years ago, that would have been somewhere in the middle of the ocean. The Conduit was gone and The White Room had turned into a howling abyss the last time that Gunn visited it (see **96**, 'Destiny'), a fact which Gunn repeated as recently as the previous episode. Now, both are back with no reference as to where they vanished to, or why.

I Just *Love* Your Accent: Spike suggests that he and Angel should hit London's West End and take in a show after they save Fred. Angel notes that he's never seen *Les Misérables*. Spike has and wasn't impressed, implying that halfway through the first act Angel will be considering drinking humans again.

Spike uses one of his favourite British swearwords, 'bollocks' (see *Buffy*: 'The Yoko Factor', 'Real Me', 'Fool for Love', 'Tabula Rasa', 'Wrecked', 'Him', 'Touched'). Additionally, he gives Drogyn the same crude two-fingered up-yours gesture that he once gave to Xander in *Buffy*: 'Hush'.[38]

Quote/Unquote: Spike: 'Not *this* girl. Not *this* day.'

Gunn: 'You want someone else's life for hers? You can have mine.' Conduit: 'I already do.'

Fred: 'I haven't had this many big strapping men by my bedside since that night with the varsity lacrosse team.' And: 'I walk with heroes.'

Spike: 'I figure there's a bloke, somewhere around New Zealand, standing on a bridge like this, looking back at us. There's a hole in the world . . . We ought to've known.'

Notes: 'Deals are for the devil.' Joss Whedon's bittersweet requiem for Fred Burkle is a lyrical, poetic and achingly sad teleplay which deals with both major universal themes and small-scale, very human, emotions. It is charged, *beautifully* acted by one of the finest ensemble casts on television and features moments of spellbinding drama, extreme sadness and impressive wit. There's Angel and Spike's theoretical bitching session which, by the climax, has turned into an impossible quest for a helpless friend. There's Wesley's reaction to a suggestion, made by a hapless lackey, that the whole company can't be working on Ms Burkle's case. There's Gunn's further, surreal adventures in The White Room. 'A Hole in the World', in short, is a work of class, talent and considerable integrity

---

[38] Amusingly, this gesture continues to turn up on lists of 'Obscure Cultural References' on some *Buffy* Internet sites. The probable rationale is that the first historical use of the gesture is often alleged to have been by British – mostly Welsh – longbowmen as an insult to French archers during the battle of Agincourt (1415). However, several sources suggest this is an urban myth.

in a television landscape frequently devoid of both and drowning, instead, in a sea of wilful compromise and lowest-common-denominator lack of ambition. *Angel*'s cancellation obviously upset its many fans – this author included – but it also should make the blood boil of anyone with a love of imaginative, bold drama. Television's loss, in this particular case, is no one's gain.

Angel and Spike once fought together in St Petersburg where they decapitated some adversaries with a length of wire. Angel remembers that he has flown in a helicopter before (see **89**, 'Conviction') though he appears to suffer from vertigo. Wesley's secretary is called Jennifer. The first book that he reads while in Fred's bedroom is *The Dread Host's Compendium of Immortal Leeches*. Fred originally left Texas to take a graduate physics course at UCLA (see **41**, 'Belonging'). When she first arrived in LA, she stayed with a friend called Bethany. She'd had a stuffed rabbit named Feigenbaum since childhood and once ordered a seemingly rather expensive commemorative plate off e-Bay. She tells her father that she loves him like she loves pancakes. In the opening scene Fred uses the Angel Investigations' flame thrower (see **52**, 'Quickening'; **54**, 'Dad'). Fred and Angel both allude to Angel saving Fred from the monsters of Pylea (see **43**, 'Through the Looking Glass'). The entire Wolfram & Hart staff (except, seemingly, Angel) know all about Wesley and Fred's flowering relationship. Gunn has a team conducting a search for Lindsey (see **100**, 'You're Welcome'; **105**, 'Underneath'). He encounters The Conduit who appears as Gunn himself in The White Room. The Conduit can take whatever shape Gunn's mind decides it should. Gunn has several toy robots in his office. Spike says that he's had experience of fighting mummies, almost none of whom were as pretty as Fred. Wolfram & Hart's aeroplanes can get from LA to England in just four hours (a normal 747 takes approximately ten hours to complete the same journey). When Lorne gives Eve a clear reading, Angel points out that Lorne has been wrong before (Lorne previously failed to detect Dr Royce was evil in **91**, 'Unleashed' and that Angel was really Angelus in **78**, 'Calvary'). Ancient Relics is situated two floors below Practical Science within Wolfram & Hart.

Soundtrack: Gunn sings 'Three Little Maids from School' from Gilbert and Sullivan's *The Mikado* (when Wesley catches him in the act, he pretends he was actually singing something from the gangsta rap *oeuvre*). Lorne sings a couple of lines from the Country standard 'You Are My Sunshine'. At the point when Fred joins in, Lorne realises something is terribly wrong with her. Eve sings a brief snatch of 'LA Song' – written by David Greenwalt and previously performed by Lindsey at Caritas in **40**, 'Dead End'.

Critique: 'If there is a fault with 'A Hole in the World', it's simply that it's too . . . ordinary,' wrote David Richardson. 'It stands or falls on whether you believe that a show's only lead female has been killed off.'

Did You Know?: *Angel* received some suitable acknowledgements for it's achievements at the 30th Annual Saturn Awards as presented by the Academy of Science Fiction, Fantasy & Horror Films. The show was named joint winner of Best Network Television Show with *CSI: Crime Scene Investigation*. Awards were also given to David Boreanaz, Amy Acker and James Marsters.

Cast and Crew Comments: Asked to nominate his favourite moment of his time on *Angel*, James Marsters quickly pointed to 'that scene in "A Hole in the World" where Spike and Angel are arguing about cavemen and astronauts. Joss let David and me go to town with that scene. Joss's dialogue is so sweet in the mouth and easy to memorise.'

Joss Whedon's Comments: 'It's not pretty being the guy who followed the puppet episode,' noted Joss in a WB statement concerning 'A Hole in the World'. However, he declared that he was excited by the episode coming, as it did, 'from the piece of the brain labelled "the heart" '.

104
Shells

US Transmission Date: 3 March 2004
UK Transmission Date: 27 April 2004

Writer: Steven S DeKnight
Director: Steven S DeKnight

Blue-haired Old One Illyria is now in full control of Fred's body. But death doesn't have to be the end, reasons Angel. With this in mind, her friends try everything to find a way to bring Fred back. But Wesley, for one, quickly realises that this is futile.

Dudes and Babes: Illyria maintains some of Fred's memories (or electrical spasms as she, rather unpoetically, refers to them). She is also able to uncannily duplicate Fred's voice. Wesley describes Illyria as the infection that consumed Fred and destroyed her soul in the fires of resurrection. Knox notes that Illyria is beyond flesh, beyond perfection. He claims that he truly loved Fred – she had a warmth that took you in and held you until everything cold and distant melted away. That's precisely why Knox chose Fred to be the vessel for Illyria's rebirth – because she was the only one worthy of such a role.

A Little Learning is a Dangerous Thing: During their flight home, Angel and Spike discuss the permanence, or otherwise, of death in their world, citing the examples of vampires generally, Buffy and Spike himself who all died but returned to life. Death doesn't have to be the end, Angel notes. Rules can be broken. All one has to do is to push hard enough.

Denial, Thy Name is Gunn: Learning from Dr Sparrow that Fred's soul burned up when Illyria entered her body, and cannot be restored, Charles can't bring himself to confess to Angel or Wesley his role in Fred's death. Ultimately, Wesley discovers the nature of Gunn's bargain with Sparrow. Wesley notes that no gift from Wolfram & Hart is ever free. Gunn pleads that all he did was to sign a piece of paper and that he didn't believe it would affect anyone – certainly not Fred. Wesley understands Gunn not wanting to lose his new powers; that, he can forgive. On the other hand, Gunn knew, almost instantly, what was happening to Fred and who was responsible yet he said nothing. Stabbing Gunn with a scalpel, Wesley notes he is somewhat less forgiving about *that*.

Denial, Thy Name is Wesley: Subsequently, Wesley tells Angel what he did. Angel doesn't recall seeing 'Stab Gunn' on that morning's agenda. Wesley argues that he avoided any major organs and that Gunn will *probably* survive (see **105**, 'Underneath').

The Conspiracy Starts at Home Time: Illyria is aware of the Wolf, the Ram and the Hart (see **43**, 'Through the Looking Glass'). However, she notes that in her time they were weak, barely above the vampire. Wesley learns that Illyria is searching for her temple, the Vahla La'nesh, which was built under what is now Los Angeles. This is only accessible by a mystical gateway and is home to Illyria's Army of Doom. The gateway was locked by the embryonic Wolfram & Hart, though Knox has obtained a skeleton key. Illyria passes through the gateway, only to find that her temple and her army have long been destroyed. A crushed Illyria asks Wesley to help her adjust to living in this world. He accepts on the sole condition she refrain from killing people.

Work is a Four-Letter Word: Spike declines Angel's offer to send him away (see **103**, 'A Hole in the World'), opting to stay with Wolfram & Hart in tribute to the sacrifice that Fred made.

It's a Designer Label!: Only one thing to mention here: Illyria's spiffy new threads (as Spike describes them) – a red leather catsuit (*very Avengers*).

References: On board the Wolfram & Hart aeroplane, Spike looks at a miniature bottle of Jack Daniel's and performs a hilarious variant on *Father Ted*'s perception sketch ('here's a drink, but it's *very far away*'). There are allusions to R.E.M's 'It's The End of the World As We Know It (And I Feel Fine)', Eddie Izzard's *Circle* ('opposable thumbs'), *The Merchant of Venice* ('a pound of flesh'), the Californian supermarket chain Ralph's, escapologist Harry Houdini (see **4**, 'I Fall to Pieces'), *The Black Adder* ('huzzah!'), *The Addams Family* ('Showtime'), Frankenstein and Felix the Cat's nemesis Poindexter. Gunn alludes to the three incarnations of the DC superhero The Flash (Jay Garrick, Barry Allen and Wally West). Knox's cellphone had a Rick Springfield screensaver which, Harmony believes, opens up a whole new set of questions. The term 'smoke and mirrors' – meaning to obscure reality by the use of tricks – has its origin in Mayan religious ceremonies. During these, priests would use fire and mirrors made from polished iron pyrite crystals to establish a required ambience of wonder among the audience.

Bitch!: In Gunn's office, a bloodied Knox is bound to a chair with duct tape. Harmony asks Gunn if he's going to torture Knox. Gunn admits that he's considering it and Harm eagerly offers to help.

Awesome!: Illyria throwing Angel through two sets of windows. Harmony telling Wesley that the girl of his dreams loved him and that's more than most people ever get. The cheese sandwich/cellphone discussion. 'You didn't *feel her die.*' An emotional Gunn, in hospital, telling Harmony that it's all his fault. Wesley coldly shooting Knox while Angel is in the middle of a somewhat pretentious speech about how he will fight Illyria for Knox's life if required. And, subsequently, Angel angrily asking Wes if he was even *listening*. Illyria's disdain for the combined efforts of Angel, Spike and Wesley to bring her down – 'unimpressive'! The final montage.

Cigarettes & Alcohol: Returning from England, Spike laments that he can't manage to get drunk on miniature bottles of alcohol. Harmony remembers the occasion she and Fred went for a drink (see **97**, 'Harm's Way'). Feeling responsible for his inability to read Knox's intentions, a disillusioned Lorne retreats to his office and gets drunk.

Sex and Drugs and Rock'n'Roll: Knox tells Illyria that he has loved her from the moment that he first saw her, when he was eleven, pressed between the pages of a forbidden text. Knox would stare at her image for hours locked in his room. His mum thought that he was looking at porn.

Logic, Let Me Introduce You to This Window: Illyria asks Knox if he is her Qua'ha'xahn. Knox notes that he is her priest, servant and guide to the world. He has taken her sacraments and placed them close to his heart according to the ancient ways. Illyria is dismissive noting that her last Qua'ha'xahn was taller. But Illyria is from a time before humans even existed (see *Buffy*: 'The Harvest'; **103**, 'A Hole in the World'; **107**, 'Time Bomb'). She then says that she believed humans would have long died out by now. Even the most liberal estimates concerning evolution place the dawn of mankind as considerably more recently than a million years ago. Does Angel's strict no murder (and, presumably, attempted murder) policy (see **97**, 'Harm's Way') extend to Wesley shooting Knox and stabbing Gunn? The footage of the Wolfram & Hart plane returning from England is a different plane to that seen in the previous episode.

Quote/Unquote: Angel: 'It's the soul that matters.' Spike: 'Trust us. We're kind of experts.'

Illyria: 'My world is gone.' Wesley: 'Now you know how I feel.'

Angel: 'What did you get out of the doctor?' Spike: 'Screams. Various fluids.'

Illyria: 'Your breed is fragile. How is it they came to control this world?' Knox: 'Opposable thumbs. Fire. Television.'

Notes: 'Everything she was is gone. Forever.' A stirring pre-title sequence begins this episode which features outstanding performances from all the regulars. A journey into the concept of self and a story about consequences which features a neat role reversal with a story arc from *Angel*'s fourth season, 'Shells' displays a willingness to experiment with unexpected dramatic conceits. So, for instance, it's Harmony who delivers genuinely insightful wisdom to a heartbroken Wesley. Angel rings Giles and is given another lesson in the different roads that the Sunnydale *alumni* are now travelling compared to him and his friends. And, magnificently, there's Spike – the voice of articulate reason one moment, then doing a cunning variant on *Father Ted*'s perception sketch the next. Perhaps inevitably, after the pain and heartache of the previous episode, 'Shells' comes over as something of a mild anti-climax, oddly structured and with a very downbeat ending. Yet it still contains magical, thrilling set-piece moments, unexpected twists and brilliant dialogue that remind the viewer why we *care* so much for this underrated, under-appreciated show. *Angel*'s story in a nutshell.

Angel calls Rupert Giles in England in the hope of getting Willow to restore Fred's soul. Spike notes that Willow has raised the dead before (see *Buffy*: 'Bargaining' Part 1). Giles refuses to help (apparently because Angel is still working for Wolfram & Hart; see **99**, 'Damage'), adding that Willow is currently in the Himalayas and, anyway, not on this astral plane (see *Buffy*: 'Who Are You?'). Illyria is able to slow down time. Angel combats this effect using a crystal from her sarcophagus. Wesley notes that atmospheric displacement generally accompanies teleportation. Lorne has a framed photo of a gorgeous Rickenbacker 330 guitar in his office. [39]

Soundtrack: The song played over the final montage is 'A Place Called Home' by Kim Richey.

Did You Know?: Jonathan Woodward met his future wife on the *Angel* set. 'Carrie was David's costume designer,'

---

[39] One of the most desirable rock'n'roll icons in the world, as used by the likes of George Harrison, John Lennon, Pete Townshend, Roger McGuinn, Paul Weller, Johnny Marr, Peter Buck, Noel Gallagher, etc.

Jonathan told Bryan Cairns. 'We got through the season and no one knew we were dating. We kept it quiet until the wrap party.' However, Jonathan does have one bad memory of his time, not only on *Angel* but also on both *Buffy* and *Firefly* in which he made guest appearances. 'It's a bit of a touchy subject. Every time I got killed on one of Joss's shows, the show ends up getting cancelled shortly afterwards.'

Cast and Crew Comments: Asked whether he had any idea of the phenomenon his character would become, James Marsters told *Science Fiction Weekly* that, 'I'm still resistant to think about that because, in general, celebrity will destroy your soul. If you concentrate too much on how popular you are, it just trips with your head.'

105
Underneath

US Transmission Date: 13 April 2004
UK Transmission Date: 4 May 2004

Writers: Sarah Fain, Elizabeth Craft
Director: Skip Schoolnik
Cast: Nicholl Hiren (Trish), Christian Boewe (Zach),
Jared Poe (Bartender)[40]

While Wesley and Illyria debate the nature of humanity, and some other metaphysical stuff, Angel and Spike find Eve in hiding and seek answers about The Senior Partners' part in their ongoing troubles. With Gunn, the pair enter a Wolfram & Hart holding dimension to save Lindsey McDonald from a personal Hell. But, again, there is a huge price to be paid by Angel and his friends.

Dreaming (As *Buffy* Often Proves) is Free: Wesley dreams of himself sitting in a chair with Fred by his side. She asks him to tell her a joke. Wesley obliges, describing how two

---
[40] Uncredited.

men walk into a bar – the first orders a Scotch and soda. The second remembers something he'd forgotten, and it doubles him over with pain. He falls to the floor and looks back at the first man, but he doesn't call out to him. They're not that close (it loses a lot of the humour in translation, obviously). Fred tells Wesley that she always knows where he is and Wes acknowledges this as his particular skill. Fred notes that this is only the first layer – doesn't Wesley want to see how deep she goes? Wesley suddenly awakes to find himself sitting in the same chair. Illyria notes he called her names meant to hurt feelings that she no longer possesses and then spent hours making noise with his nose. Wesley called her a twit. He says that he was having a nightmare and doesn't suppose that Illyria has ever experienced such a thing. She replies that, in her time, nightmares walked the earth skewering victims in plain sight, laying their fears and worst desires out for everyone to see. Now, she believes, nightmares are trapped inside the heads of humans, pitiful echoes of themselves. She idly wonders whom they angered to merit such a terrible fate. Wesley asks if she finds this world disappointing and Illyria admits that she does. Wesley concedes that he's not all that fond of it himself. Illyria asks him the same question that he asked her in **104**, 'Shells' – in that case 'Why don't you leave?'

Dudes and Babes: Tall, broad and immaculately dressed, Marcus Hamilton is Eve's replacement as Angel's liaison with The Senior Partners. Eve is revealed to be an immortal (see **89**, 'Conviction'), created by The Partners specifically to act as their liaison to Angel. She continues to insist that she is only ever given information on a need-to-know basis. Once Marcus catches up with her, Eve signs a contract which transfers all of her connections to The Partners, as well as her immortality and certain other privileges, to him. The Partners feel that Eve has become too easily distracted from her duties by falling in love with Lindsey.

A Little Learning is a Dangerous Thing: Lindsey spent years researching The Senior Partners and their nefarious skulduggery. Eve also notes that he *really* hates Angel and probably knows more about Angel than Angel does himself. She adds that it's perfectly possible The Senior Partners took Lindsey (see **100**, 'You're Welcome') at least partly to stop him and Angel having any sort of meaningful discussion that might concern them and their agenda. Later, Lindsey tells Angel that the world is a cesspool, full of selfish and greedy beasts. The apocalypse that Angel has been preparing for has already begun without Angel even realising it. Everything that's happened to Angel, Lindsey suggests, has occurred simply to distract him from seeing the big picture. Meanwhile, the world keeps sliding towards entropy and degradation and what does Angel do? He sits in his chair and signs cheques, just as The Senior Partners planned it. The war is here, Angel is told, and he is already two soldiers down.

Denial, Thy Name is Gunn: Angel visits Gunn, still in bed after being stabbed by Wesley. The Senior Partners have found Eve and seem to have sent something to assassinate her. Angel needs to know if he has any jurisdiction to protect her. Angel reminds Gunn that he paid a high price for what's in his brain and Angel would like him to use the knowledge he gained to do some good. Gunn replies that there is a provision in Angel's Wolfram & Hart contract that allows him, as CEO, to invoke a custody order on any wayward employee. Gunn notes this is not, usually, used for protection, but it should suffice. Angel tells Gunn he understands how badly Charles feels concerning his part in what happened to Fred and, indeed, that he *should*. For the rest of his life it should wake Gunn up in the middle of the night, and it probably will because, essentially, he is a good man. Gunn admits that he knew when he signed the form for Dr Sparrow that there would be consequences. Angel understands, noting that you never run out of chances when searching for atonement. But you *have* to take those chances. You cannot hide in a hospital room and pretend that it will all go away, because it never will.

The Conspiracy Starts at Home Time: Spike claims there are thousands of different kinds of Hell, although he can only name three – Fire Hell, Ice Hell and Upside-Down Hell. Angel says that he doesn't particularly care if Lindsey is in Toy-Poodles-On-Parade Hell, he has information that Angel needs. Gunn assumed there must have been a precedent for what happened to Lindsey and, ultimately, found one. The Senior Partners once had a problem with a man in the Tokyo division. Gunn believes that Lindsey probably got the idea for the stealth tattoos by studying this man. He was sent to a Wolfram & Hart holding dimension while The Senior Partners decided what to do with him, a location where, Gunn believes, Lindsey will also be.

In the holding dimension, Lindsey's fantasy life includes a wife named Trish and a young son, Zach – both, in reality, his warders.

Work is a Four-Letter Word: Spike now considers himself a (very loosely) affiliated member of Angel's team. He asks what they are called, hoping it's not Scoobies, the name which Xander coined for Buffy's team of helpers (see *Buffy*: 'What's My Line?' Part 1). Angel notes that they don't have a name. Spike is pleased to hear it. This is for the best, he notes, as Angel would want to call them 'Angel's Avengers' or something equally inane. Angel rather likes the sound of that.

It's a Designer Label!: Harmony, Lorne and Angel all comment on how well dressed Marcus is.

References: The entire realisation of the holding dimension is a visual steal from *The Truman Show*. Lindsey paraphrases the Ramones' 'I Don't Wanna Go Down to the Basement'. Allusions to the ABC reality show *The Bachelorette* and the couple who became media celebrities on it, Trish and Ryan, Lerner and Loewe's stage musical *Brigadoon*, Rupert Holmes's 'Escape (The Pina Colada Song)', *Knight Rider*, *Leave it to Beaver* ('cut the act, Ward, June's gone'), *Hamlet*, *The Terminator* (see **50**, 'Billy'; **74**, 'Habeas Corpses'), the Smurfs (see **102**, 'Smile Time'), Mr Green Jeans (see **90**, 'Just Rewards'), the weak

Tom Hanks vehicle *The 'burbs*, Thomas Guide maps, *Batman* and the character of Chicken Little who, according to the folk-tale, believed the sky was falling. 'You're soaking in it' was the catchphrase of Madge the Manicurist, the advertising face of Colgate-Palmolive during the 60s and 70s. There are conceptual references to *Groundhog Day* and visual ones to *The French Connection*, *The Matrix* and *Two Days in the Valley*.

Awesome!: Spike's curiously poetic wisdom in the face of Angel's depression over Fred. The first, dramatic appearance of Adam Baldwin, kicking in the door to Eve's apartment. The contrast between maudlin Lorne and, subsequently, scared-but-funny Lorne. Eve, Lorne and Harmony's hilarious reaction to Hamilton's murder of a Wolfram & Hart security man (see *Buffy*: 'Tabula Rasa' for a similar sight-gag). Machine-gun-massacre-a-go-go.

'You May Remember Me From Such Films and TV Series As . . .': Adam Baldwin is probably best known to readers as the violently antisocial Jayne Cobb in *Firefly*. His impressive CV also includes appearances in *Betrayal*, *The X-Files*, *Jackpot*, *The Patriot*, *Full Metal Jacket*, *From the Earth to the Moon*, *Poison Ivy*, *The Cape*, *Independence Day* and *Stargate SG-1*. Nicholl Hiren was in *Boomtown* and *Monk*. Christian Boewe played Montgomery Krolak in *Daddio*. Jared Poe appeared in *The X-Files*.

Not Exactly a Haven For the Bruthas: The heavily armed warders of Wolfram & Hart's temporary holding dimension act as the wives, children, neighbours, work colleagues and other assorted people who occupy the small-town Americana suburban façade of this particular Hell. Prisoners in this dimension are identified by an amulet which causes the wearer to believe that the fantasy life they lead is, in fact, reality and erases any memory of their previous lives. If the amulet is removed and not placed, immediately, on a new inmate, the warders will kill anyone not wearing an amulet. Angel, Spike and Gunn remove Lindsey from the dimension, but can only escape when

Gunn, seeking redemption for his betrayal of his friends, places the amulet around his own neck to take Lindsey's place. The actual physical punishment of the prisoners is carried out by The Wrath, a demon whose torture chamber is situated in the basement. It subjects the prisoners – sent to the basement on some minor errand – to bloodcurdling torture which ends with the removal of the victim's heart. Unable to die in this place, the victim instantly grows a new heart and returns to the fantasy life upstairs – until the next day when they must, again, visit the basement.

Cigarettes & Alcohol: Spike brings a can of beer and a briefcase to his first official meeting with Angel. Wesley, meanwhile, has been spending his time since **104**, 'Shells' drinking whisky and occasionally dreaming about Fred.

In the bar Lorne gets very maudlin. He thinks it's pathetic that he's become too scared and sad to tell people the truth when he reads their futures, so he just says what they want to hear instead. He believes that the term Happy Hour should be banned from the English language because there's *nothing* happy about this, or any other, hour. He started drinking, he notes, the moment that he found out a girl he loved was going to die. Every time he gets to the bottom of the glass, he hopes that last drop is going to take him the distance. But it never does.

Logic, Let Me Introduce You to This Window: If Cordelia's hospital care was being taken care of by Wolfram & Hart, like Gunn's, then why does he get a private room when she didn't? The punishment basement of Lindsey's home in the holding dimension is a redressed set from *Buffy* – it's Buffy's basement seen in several episodes in Season Seven (it's a wonder Spike didn't recognise it as he actually *lived* there for some months). This is Spike's *first day* as a loosely affiliated member of Angel's team. Yet when he sees the meeting agenda that Angel has prepared, he asks why he is always assigned to reconnaissance and never gets a decently flash gig like save the girl, or steal the emerald with the girl.

Motors: Angel, Spike and Gunn take the company's Camaro SS convertible on their rescue mission to find Lindsey. The car, it appears, can navigate itself towards (and through) the dimensional portal. The Chevrolet Camaro was introduced by General Motors in 1967 as competition for the popular Ford Mustang.

Cruelty to Animals: Illyria mentions a number of alternate dimensions, one of which is filled with nothing but shrimp. Anya had previously alluded to this curious realm in *Buffy*: 'Superstar', while its mirror-dimension, the world *without* shrimp, was spoken of – also by Anya – in *Buffy*: 'Triangle'.

Quote/Unquote: Angel, on Wolfram & Hart: 'Bad things always happen here.' Spike: 'Hate to break it to you, mate, but bad things always happen *everywhere*.'

Angel: 'The thing about atonement is you never run out of chances. But you gotta take them.'

Gunn, electing to remain in the holding dimension: 'This is where I belong.'

Illyria, to Wesley: 'Your world is so small and yet you box yourselves in rooms even smaller.'

Notes: 'It's been here all along. Underneath. You're just too stupid to see it.' What a truly astonishing piece of work. 'Underneath' is a forty-minute tone-poem which, with some clarity, philosophises on the proper nature of Hell – both personal and conceptual. Fain and Craft's lyrical script is marbled with poetic imagery. It's often hilariously funny too, but with some brutal action set-pieces included. Highlights include the revelation that Spike is a *Knight Rider* fan and Illyria's gorgeous litany of alternate dimensions. There's also the brilliantly handled introduction of the dryly amusing Marcus Hamilton. 'Underneath' reminds viewers that the foundations this series is built upon are its characters, and they're all at their finest here with Harmony, Lorne, Gunn and Wesley given moments of dramatic insight amid the laughs and the outrageous fight sequences. Spike and Angel discuss Hell as a concept and time as an abstract, a scene that goes right to the very heart of what *Angel* is all about. Another quite brilliant episode from, it bears repeating, the best television series to be cancelled this year.

Angel remembers his Hell is a Place on Earth conversation with Holland Manners (see **37**, 'Reprise'). On his meeting agendas Angel uses bullet points, which Spike considers classy. Angel and Spike are not affected by the sunlight in the holding dimension (similarly, the suns of Pylea weren't deadly to Angel, see **42**, 'Over the Rainbow'). Harmony notes that it's tough getting an accurate time of arrival on alternate dimension travel, though she assures Lorne that she *has* tried. The bartender who serves Lorne is named Carlos. Lorne reads his future, which, he claims, includes a June wedding. As they attempt to escape from the pursuing Marcus, Lorne assures Eve that she will like Canada, which, he notes, is full of deserters.[41] Illyria says that, as an Old One, she walked intangible worlds of smoke and half-truths, torment and unnamable beauty: opaline towers as high as small moons; glaciers that rippled with insensate lust; and one world with nothing but shrimp – though she quickly tired of that one.

Soundtrack: The demon barman sings a couplet from 'Lady' (a song covered by both Kenny Rogers and Lionel Ritchie). Listen also to the wonderfully cheesy, 50s romantic-comedy-type music that accompanies the sequences of Lindsey's fantasy life.

Did You Know?: Is it true that Christian Kane based his performance of Lindsey on his own attorney? In an interview with BBCi's Rob Francis, Christian confirmed that it was. 'His name is Bernard Kahil. He's in Nashville and does all the music stuff for me. A lot of the stuff I did on *Angel* was based on Bernard, they call him "Bernie the Attorney".'

---

[41] Canada, along with Europe, was a favourite sanctuary during the late 1960s and early 70s for many young Americans who didn't fancy getting themselves drafted and killed in the Mekong Delta in Vietnam.

Cast and Crew Comments: 'The person who made me laugh most was Andy Hallett,' Adam Baldwin told *DreamWatch*. 'He's so gregarious and outgoing. The cast were all very professional and funny, it looked like a family atmosphere on set.'

For Sarah Thompson, the pairing of Eve with Lindsey McDonald was an unexpected bonus. Christian Kane and Sarah have mutual friends and had known each other for some time prior to working together. '[The scene] where you find out Lindsey is Eve's boyfriend wasn't shot at the same time as the rest of that episode,' Sarah told *Xposé*. 'We did it about a week later. I remember walking into my trailer one morning and finding an envelope marked "Confidential". I'd never worked on a series before where things were so hush-hush. Even the rest of the cast didn't know.'

106
Origin

US Transmission Date: 20 April 2004
UK Transmission Date: 11 May 2004

Writer: Drew Goddard
Director: Terrence O'Hara
Cast: Adrienne Brett Evans (Connor's Mother),
Jim Abele (Connor's Father)

As Angel's friends come to terms with the loss of another soldier, a concerned couple, Lawrence and Colleen Riley, arrive at Wolfram & Hart's offices. Their son has been the target of a recent attempt on his life, but it was the superstrength he displayed that has them concerned. Wesley introduces Angel to the young man whose name is Connor.

Dudes and Babes: Wesley and Angel observe Illyria in Fred's lab. Wesley notes she is either counting oxygen molecules, analysing the Petri dish that she just put into her mouth or sleeping. He genuinely can't tell which.

A Little Learning is a Dangerous Thing: The Rileys tell Wesley that their son was collecting the mail when a van deliberately crashed into him in an apparent hit-and-run incident. Connor, however, survived with barely a scratch on him. The police concluded that it was probably pure luck; however, an officer later told them that their son may be different. He referred them to Wolfram & Hart.

Denial, Thy Name is Angel: At first Angel is highly reluctant to involve Connor in his life again but, having saved his adoptive parents from a demon attack, he soon changes his mind.

The Conspiracy Starts at Home Time: Kith'arn demons are the minions of the warlock Cyvus Vail. They attack Connor's parents in order to send a message to Angel concerning his son. Vail is a powerful leader in the demon community, with metaphorical tendrils throughout the LA area. He specialises in memory restructuring and reality shifts and headed the team – including some of the most powerful sorcerers on the West Coast – which created a new life for Connor and altered everyone's memories of him (see **88**, 'Home'). Vail considers the memories he fashioned for Connor to be some of his finest work and he was handsomely paid for the job, Lorne noting that Vail could buy Bolivia for the fee he received from Wolfram & Hart. Vail's knowledge of Angel's deal with The Senior Partners gives him the upper hand in the bargain he strikes with the vampire. Connor will fulfil the ancient prophecy (see **61**, 'Forgiving') and kill Sahjhan – an old enemy of Vail's – when the demon is released from the urn in which Angel once trapped him. If this is achieved, Vail will leave Connor's family alone and will not reveal to Connor, or to Angel's friends, the truth about the events that he has wiped from their memories.

Lies: An Orlon Window is a spell – contained within a glass cube – that allows warlocks to see the altered past as it once was. Vail tells Angel that if the Window breaks near someone whose memories have been altered, the original memories will be returned.

In the Wolfram & Hart archives (see **54**, 'Dad'), Illyria notes that humans all seem concerned with names, dates and times. Wesley tells her that reality was changed. Illyria does not appear to understand, saying that Wesley is a summation of his recollections. Each change is simply a point of experience – we are more than just memories, Wesley asserts. Illyria suggests that Fred changed the moment that her memories did. Wesley asks if Illyria can see what Fred's memories were before they were changed, but she says that they are gone. At this point, Wesley finds the Vail contract with Angel's signature on it and believes that Angel has betrayed his friends. Illyria asks if this changes Wesley's view of Fred. Is she, Illyria wonders, still the person that Wesley thought she was? None of us are, replies a horrified Wesley.

At Vail's home, Wesley angrily confronts Angel and suggests that Angel changed the world deliberately. Angel admits that Connor is his son. Wesley then asks if Angel traded Fred's life for Connor's. Wesley picks up the Orlon Window as Angel tells him that destroying it will not bring Fred back. Wesley puts that assertion to the test and, in a blinding flash, all of his memories concerning Connor are restored. Illyria also regains Fred's wiped memories although, as she subsequently notes, there are now two sets of recollections in her mind – those that actually happened and those that were fabricated. It is hard for Illyria to tell which is which. Wesley suggests that she try to push reality from her mind and focus on the other memories. They were, after all created for a reason. To hide from the truth? asks Illyria. No, Wesley replies. To endure it. (There is a visual implication – confirmed in **110**, 'Not Fade Away' – that when the Orlon Window was broken Connor, too, regained his memories of his past life and it is the feral warrior buried deep within him that kills Sahjhan rather than the cheerful, bright and pacifist young man Connor has become.)

Denial, Thy Name is Sahjhan: In the middle of their fight to the death, a confident Sahjhan tells Connor that the prophecy predicting his own death at Connor's hands is turning out to be somewhat overrated. He suggests that the good hiding he is in the process of giving Connor makes a fine case for the entire concept of free will.

Work is a Four-Letter Word: Angel puts Spike in charge of testing Illyria's skills. Spike tells Illyria that they need to establish some immediate ground rules. Firstly, Illyria should refrain from punching Spike in the face. Secondly, when Spike punches *Illyria* in the face, she should tell him how it feels so he can write her observations on his clipboard. Thirdly she shouldn't, under any circumstances, *touch* his clipboard. Illyria notes that she enjoys hurting Spike and subsequently asks Angel if she can keep Spike as a pet.

Spike establishes that Illyria can hit like a truck, selectively alter the flow of time (see **104**, 'Shells') and, possibly, talk to plants.

References: There are allusions to Mack trucks, the barbecue restaurant chain Tony Roma's, *Pulp Fiction*, *Aladdin*, *The History of Ali Baba and the 40 Thieves* ('open sesame, or whatever'), and horror novelist Anne Rice (see *Buffy*: 'School Hard'). Wesley asks Angel if the Orlon Windows was his thirty pieces of silver, referring to the money paid to Judas Iscariot for his betrayal of Christ (Matthew 26:15).

Bitch!: Connor wonders if everyone at Wolfram & Hart is a superhero. Angel says that they're mostly paralegals and secretaries and that life in the firm is pretty boring, really. As he says this Spike comes flying through the Operational Training and Research room doors with his clipboard being flung after him. Spike gets to his feet calling Illyria a filthy harlot and storms back into the room saying that he is going to tear her neck out.

Awesome!: Marcus's description of the young Connor as a raging psychopath. Illyria standing on Spike's head. Wesley smashing the Orlon Window. The Wrath giving a confused Gunn a lightbulb for the oven. The wonderful

Angel/Connor scenes. Connor decapitating Sahjhan. Connor trying to persuade a reluctant Angel to lighten up.

'You May Remember Me From Such Films and TV Series As . . .': Vincent Kartheiser's movies include *Dandelion*, *The Unsaid*, the classic *Crime + Punishment in Suburbia*, *Another Day in Paradise* and *Heaven Sent*. Jack Conley often gets meaty detective-type roles in movies such as *Payback*, *Mercury Rising*, *LA Confidential* and *Get Shorty*. He played Cain in *Buffy* and also appeared in *Collateral Damage*, *Traffic*, *Apollo 11* and *Apollo 13*, *NYPD Blue*, *Dark Skies*, *Shade*, *Without a Trace*, *CSI* and *Kindred: The Embraced*.

Dennis Christopher's movies include *Mind Rage*, *Skeletons*, *Bad English I: Tales of a Son of a Brit*, *Doppelgänger*, *The Disco Years*, *Jake Speed*, *Chariots of Fire* (as Charles Paddock), Fellini's *Roma*, *Breaking Away*, *A Sinful Life* and *Alien Predator*. On TV he guest-starred in *Moonlighting*, *Hooperman*, *Roswell*, *Freakylinks* and *Star Trek: Deep Space Nine*. Adrienne Brett Evans appeared in *Home Improvements* and *The Nanny*. Jim Abele's CV includes *Student Affairs*, *24*, *Caroline in the City* and *Wimps*.

LA-Speak: Connor: 'Dude, you're starting to freak me out.'

Not Exactly a Haven For the Bruthas: In the holding dimension, Gunn continues to be the subject of outrageously gruesome torture when Marcus Hamilton appears and offers Gunn a deal with The Senior Partners. Gunn, nobly, refuses to have anything to do with such an offer.

Cigarettes & Alcohol: Illyria observes that Wesley reeks of frustration. Spike notes that the smell is, actually, Scotch. Twelve-year-old Lagavulin, in fact, which he considers a very good choice.

Sex and Drugs and Rock'n'Roll: When Wesley notes that he had a disagreement with Angel, Spike suggests he keep in mind that Angel can't get laid without going crazy. This, Spike considers, makes dealing with Angel very funny.

Marcus tells Angel to be clear about the new order subsequent to his replacing Eve. Marcus is *not* a little girl and he and Angel will, most definitely, not be making love on the couch anytime soon (see **93**, 'Life of the Party').

Connor asks if Angel has a girlfriend. Angel replies that he can't afford to. Connor believes this must be lonely and Angel replies, somewhat defensively, that he keeps busy.

Connor is introduced to Illyria and tells her that he likes her attire. She observes that he is lusting after her. Connor explains that it's probably just the outfit but that he's always had a thing for older women. 'They were supposed to fix that,' mutters an annoyed Angel (see **64**, 'A New World'; **73**, 'Apocalypse Nowish'; **84**, 'Shiny Happy People').

Logic, Let Me Introduce You to This Window: Why does Angel put Spike, of all people, in charge of studying Illyria's strengths and weaknesses? Unless, of course, it's purely for sadistic reasons or his own amusement. Actually, come to think of it, a combination of both is *almost certainly* the reason. It has to be mentioned yet again that Wesley can clearly remember Angel's previous battles with Sahjhan, noting that Angel nearly died during the last one (see **61**, 'Forgiving'). Despite this, until the Orlon Window is smashed, he's unable to remember Connor's – more than significant – role in those events. The implication seems to be that, in the revised timeline, events still happened more or less as they did before, just without Connor being a part of them. Therefore Darla still came back and still killed herself but for a different reason than saving her unborn son; Holtz still jumped through the dimensional portal to Quor-Toth; Wesley still turned to the dark side, but for a different reason than his guilt over betraying Angel by kidnapping his son. And, presumably, it was someone else who copulated with Cordelia to produce Jasmine. It would be a brave production, however, that would have attempted to address some of these anomalies because the entire concept is the kind of thing that looks good on paper but, when you start to pick at it, the whole thing can come to pieces in your hands like wet cardboard. For instance, what other issue would temporarily ensoul Darla to the extent that she achieves a motherly redemption through self-sacrifice?

Isn't it a bit remiss of Angel to have misplaced the urn in which Sahjhan was trapped? It's also unexplained exactly how the urn got into Vail's possession. Angel was unable to beat Sahjhan in single combat without the aid of a magical urn yet here, Connor destroys the demon with almost arrogant ease. Wolfram & Hart didn't hide the details of their secret contract with Vail very well if Wesley is able to find it from a brief search through the archives. Maybe they *wanted* him to discover the truth? How did the Orlon Window get from Vail's hand to Wesley's – on the other side of the room – in the time that it takes Angel to turn around?

Motors: Connor's father drives a Honda SUV.

Quote/Unquote: Angel, to Wesley: 'I need you here, working, not drinking yourself into a coma, chasing ghosts. Fred's dead, Wes. You're still alive. Start acting like it.'

Connor: 'Do you spend all your time making out with other vampires? Like in Anne Rice novels?' Angel: 'No. I used to.'

Sahjhan: 'Thank you, mortal, for releasing me from my cursed prison. In gratitude, I grant you three wishes.' Connor: 'Really?' Sahjhan: 'Nah, I'm just messin' with ya.'

Notes: 'You gotta do what you can to protect your family. I learned that from my father.' Seemingly the first episode into full production after the decision to cancel *Angel* was taken, 'Origin' takes the opportunity to tie up a couple of necessary loose ends from the series' past. To wit: whatever did happen to Connor and to Sahjhan? The first thing to say is that Vincent Kartheiser is *great* in this – playing, admittedly, a much lighter version of Connor. Drew Goddard's script explains how much of the team's memories were altered by the deal that Angel made with

Wolfram & Hart in **88**, 'Home', and Wesley's discovery of his missing memories is heartbreakingly played – complete with a series of flashback images to the major events of Seasons Three and Four. It also gives Illyria a cunning pair of double-act moments, firstly with Spike and then, later, with Wes. Add in the graphic presentation of Gunn in Hell and we have another episode full of moments to keep the series' audience entertained and, more importantly, informed.

When Connor tells Angel that Angel breaking the spine of one of the demons who attacked his parents was the coolest thing he's ever seen, Angel notes that, really, it wasn't much. He begins to relate a story concerning an occasion in France, presumably, when, as Angelus, he was engaged in some deranged display of manic ultraviolence. Angel assures Connor that his father is in good hands – or claws, actually – with the Wolfram & Hart doctors. Connor is currently attending Stanford University (much to Angel's obvious pride, see **110**, 'Not Fade Away'). Sahjhan mentions Connor's life in Quor-Toth (see **60**, 'Sleep Tight'). The false memories that Vail created for Connor include one in which he was lost in a department store at the age of five. The vending machine in Wolfram & Hart's lobby sells dried scorpions. The Operational Training and Research room, in which Spike attempts to test Illyria, is equipped with automated training devices. Vail tells Angel that he is not the sort of man Angel wants as an enemy (see **109**, 'Power Play'; **110**, 'Not Fade Away').

Did You Know?: The Directors Guild of America's two-year campaign against late scripts has led to significant improvements in the on-time delivery of episodic television scripts, according to a piece in the *Hollywood Reporter*. *Angel* was one of several series highlighted that had made 'significant improvements' during the past year. Others included *24*, *Alias*, *ER* and *The West Wing*. 'This has been a real effort on everyone's part, and the improved data reflects that, by jointly addressing this problem, the DGA, the networks and the studios were able to effect significant change in less than two years,' noted DGA spokesman Rod Holcomb. It wasn't all good news for The WB, however, three of their shows – *Charmed*, *Gilmore Girls* and *Everwood* – were among the most frequent offenders in delivering scripts late.

Cast and Crew Comments: Asked if he had any plans to follow his pal David Boreanaz into directing, James Marsters noted that he was actually more interested in producing. 'As I see how things work in television, the things that interest me [are] larger arcs of characters [and] deciding what the story is that we're going to tell and how we tell it.'

107
Time Bomb

US Transmission Date: 27 April 2004
UK Transmission Date: 18 May 2004

Writer: Ben Edlund
Director: Vern Gillum
Cast: Jaime Bergman (Amanda), Jeff Yagher (Fell Leader),
Nick Gilhool (Fell Brother #1)

A daring rescue, a cunning plan, a demon pact and an ambiguous prophecy are all elements in the latest case for Angel's team at Wolfram & Hart. But while Angel and co. have the allegiances of blue-haired former Fred-type-woman, Illyria, to discuss, Marcus Hamilton, the firm's new liaison, is offering some of the staff temptations of almost biblical proportions.

Dudes and Babes: Illyria's power eventually proves too much to be contained in Fred's body. The sudden release of this energy bounces Illyria back and forth through time, causing her to repeat several events including an apparent attack by Wesley using a mutari generator. Believing this to be an attempt on her life, Illyria rapidly kills Spike, Wes,

Lorne and Angel, before being drawn back in time once more into an argument she recently had with Angel. During this, while grappling with Angel, she timeslips once more, this time taking an anomalous Angel in her wake. Eventually Illyria's power cannot be contained any longer and she is destroyed, but the resultant explosion sends Angel back to the recent past. He is able to use his knowledge of the future to prevent the deaths of his friends and himself. He also convinces Illyria that she should allow Wesley to use the mutari generator to siphon off enough of her growing power. Illyria agrees and, as a consequence, survives, although she is no longer able to alter the flow of time or to jump between dimensions.

A Little Learning is a Dangerous Thing: In his office, Wesley holds one of the archive source books and asks for all pre-Christian works dealing with the demon age, specifically for any mentions of The Old Ones.

The mutari generator, Wesley notes, creates a pinhole to an infinite extradimensional space, a negatively charged pocket universe. That *should* draw off Illyria's radiant essence. Angel asks whether it will *kill* her. Wesley confirms that it will. But ultimately he's lying and the device is used to save, rather than destroy, Illyria.

The Conspiracy Starts at Home Time: Gunn's latest clients are demons known as The Fell Brethren, who have contracted Wolfram & Hart to negotiate the sale of an unborn child. The child's mother is named Amanda. Her husband was brain-damaged after suffering an accident on a job. The baby, Gunn is assured, will be pampered, worshipped and fed a diet of berries, panda meat and consecrated urine. Gunn subsequently discovers that The Brethren intend to perform a ritual sacrifice, called the Gordabach, on the baby's thirteenth birthday. Angel ultimately, and much to Gunn's shock, allows the contracts to be signed giving the baby to The Brethren (see **110**, 'Not Fade Away').

Work is a Four-Letter Word: Hamilton holds Angel's department liable for damages caused by Illyria's rampages in the holding dimension. These include eleven torture units, two troop carriers, an ice-cream truck, eight beautifully maintained lawns and dozens of employees rendered useless to the company.

References: The title is also the name of Grant McKee and Ros Franey's exposé of the Guildford Four miscarriage of justice. Allusions to *The Poseidon Adventure*, *The Last of Sheila*, Hugh Hefner's *Penthouse*, tae kwon do, the Hindu god Shiva,[42] Babe the Blue Ox from the Paul Bunyan tales, Revelation 20 (the thousand-year war between good and evil), Hitchcock's *Vertigo*, *Star Trek* (the reference to mind-melding), *Batman*, the Shangri-Las' 'Leader of the Pack', cult leader Jim Jones,[43] *Fit Pregnancy* magazine, *Planet of the Apes* and the Dalai Lama (see **18**, 'Five by Five'). Lorne's '10-4, good buddy, copy that' are phrases commonly used in CB radio. Spike alludes to the popular maxim 'he that has the most toys, wins'.

Bitch!: Illyria notes that, when she was young, humanity was the muck at her feet. The Old Ones called what would eventually become mankind 'the ooze that eats itself'. She does concede, however, that the ooze was pretty at night – it sparkled; it also stank.

Awesome!: Spike asks what sort of damage they are looking at if Illyria goes all Chernobyl on them. Wesley gives a conservative guess of several city blocks. When Angel asks for an unconservative guess, Wesley suggests that Rand McNally would have to redraw their maps. Angel asks Lorne to go undercover, complete with shades and walkie-talkie, to keep an eye on Illyria. Hilarity, inevitably, ensues. A manic Wesley apologising to Gunn for stabbing him. The final scene, with Angel coldly

---

[42] The third deity of the Hindu triad, the Trimurti. Shiva is The Destroyer, the god of death and regeneration.

[43] In November 1978, 913 followers of Revd Jim Jones's People's Temple committed mass suicide at Jonestown, Guyana, by drinking cyanide-laced fruit juice. Jones (who claimed to be a reincarnation of Jesus Christ) had recently ordered the murder of a US Congressman investigating his cult.

informing Gunn that the baby belongs to The Fell. There's also some great self-deprecating humour when Wesley tells Gunn that Illyria still thinks she's God-King of the universe. Gunn wonders if Wesley means that she's like a TV star. No, nothing that bad, notes Wes. She's a bit more violent, though.

'You May Remember Me From Such Films and TV Series As . . .': Born in Salt Lake City in 1975, Jaime Bergman was the January 1999 *Playboy* Playmate of the Month. She married David Boreanaz in 2000 and the couple have a son, Jaden Rayne. Jaime's acting credits include *Any Given Sunday*, *Dark Wolf*, *Virgins*, *Gone in Sixty Seconds*, *Shasta McNasty* and – her most famous role – BJ Cummings in the comedy series *Son of the Beach*. Jeff Yagher appeared in *Live Shot*, *The Red Coat*, *Doogie Howser MD*, *Shag*, *No Secrets*, *V*, *21 Jump Street* and *Star Trek: Voyager*. Nick Gilhool was in *Sticky Fingers*, *See Jane Date* and *Dead Poets Society*.

Not Exactly a Haven For the Bruthas: Having tortured Gunn each day for two weeks, always culminating in the removal of Gunn's heart, The Wrath finds that Illyria has entered his realm. Removing the amulet that identifies Gunn as a prisoner in Wolfram & Hart's holding dimension, Illyria rescues Charles and leaves the amulet around the neck of The Wrath, forcing it to cut out it's own heart.

Logic, Let Me Introduce You to This Window: There is no Brazilian form of ninjutsu. Spike is probably referring to capoeira, a Brazilian martial art which combines elements of acrobatics and dance. If the amulet makes the wearer forget everything about their past life then how does The Wrath remember to cut out its own heart? Why, exactly, does Illyria rescue Gunn? The answer she gives to Wesley and Angel – that Gunn has meaning and value to them – makes no earthly sense.

Quote/Unquote: Marcus: 'Curing cancer, Mr Wyndam-Pryce?' Wesley: 'Wouldn't be cost-effective. I'm sure we make a lot from cancer.' Marcus: 'Yes. The patent holder is a client.'

Angel, to Illyria: 'Has it ever occurred to you that now might not be the best time for "when we were muck" stories?'

Illyria: 'When the world met me, it shuddered. Groaned. It knelt at my feet.' Spike: 'Dear *Penthouse*, I don't normally write letters like this, but . . .'

Marcus: 'It's profits that let you keep this plucky boatload-of-good above water. It's a business, boys, not a Batcave.' Lorne: 'I *still* like him better than Eve.'

Notes: 'Everything is a bit odd', notes Wesley at the beginning of this strangely structured and rather empty story. This, despite the inclusion of some interesting non-linear techniques as an aberration in the timelines, causes all sorts of malarkey for the regulars. 'Adaptation is a compromise' which, as Illyria states at one point, is the key phrase to understanding the episode's focus. This concerns questions of moral ambiguity, shifting memories and time paradoxes. Illyria is unstable in Fred's body and is, as Wesley discovers, about to self-destruct. Thus, the episode turns into a series of potted statements on how doing the right thing isn't, always, the right thing at all. A lot of this is well handled and some of the imagery on display is brilliant, particularly a quite startling and incendiary end-of-act-two massacre scenario that will, I guarantee, leave fans gaping at their television sets in a mixture of admiration and outright horror. But this and several other fine moments apart, 'Time Bomb' is, ultimately, a somewhat hollow tale with little substance to go with its bravura conceits and iconic characterisation.

While waiting to see Angel, Harmony offers The Fell Brethren a drink of organic cola which, after a moment's thought, they happily accept.

Critique: In a post-cancellation article on the series by Maureen Ryan, the writer highlighted Wesley's contribution to the series' on-going development: 'No character on the show (aside from Gunn) changed more; [Wesley] went from prissy, bookish über-Brit to a tough-yet-melancholy butt-kicker.'

Did You Know?: 'He's always tried to do North London,' Tony Head notes with reference to the accent that James Marsters created for Spike. 'It actually comes over as north-of-Watford!'

Cast and Crew Comments: From various press interviews given in the immediate aftermath of the cancellation of *Angel*, David Boreanaz appeared more relieved than upset to see the end of the show. 'As heavy or as light as it may be, it's not a negative,' he told *MSN*. 'It's a good thing!' While some fans were, perhaps understandably, surprised by this reaction, David sought to clarify his position in subsequent interviews, notably one with *TV Guide*. 'I don't wanna sound like I was cheering, but when Joss broke the news, it was like the burden of pressure came off me after five years,' he noted. 'It's a lot of responsibility. You don't realise how much until they say it's done and you can breathe.'

108
The Girl in Question

US Transmission Date: 5 May 2004
UK Transmission Date: 25 May 2004

Writers: Drew Goddard, Steven S DeKnight
Director: David Greenwalt
Cast: David S Lee (Alfonso), Carole Raphaelle Davis (Ilona),
Vikki Gurdas (Bartendress), Dominic Pace (Demon Bouncer),
Andrew Ableson (Italian Man), Irina Maleeva (Old Demon Woman),
Rob Steiner (Pirate)

Angel and Spike's Italian job is to travel to Rome and bring back the head of a dead demon. And, as a side issue, the self-preservation duo also attempt to save their former lover Buffy from the perceived sinister romantic clutches of their arch-nemesis, the charismatic and (allegedly) evil Immortal.

Dudes and Babes: Handsome, suave and, seemingly, a stallion between the sheets, the Immortal is, according to

Spike, the foulest evil that Hell ever vomited forth. In 1894, he had Angelus and Spike detained in Rome so he could have his wicked way with Darla and Drusilla (much to their delight). A century later, he is Buffy's new boyfriend.

A Little Learning is a Dangerous Thing: Angel had a Wolfram & Hart operative keeping tabs on Buffy in Rome until she put him in hospital.

The Conspiracy Starts at Home Time: Alfonso, the butler to the Goran demon clan, steals the head of the aged Capo di Famiglia which Angel and Spike were supposed to return to the Capo's family in LA for a resurrection ceremony. The Capo was tolerant of humans and more interested in profit than mayhem but, if he isn't revived in time, a rival clan will initiate a demon war. A huge admirer of the Immortal (whose book, he claims, changed his life), Alfonso sends a ransom demand to the Rome branch of Wolfram & Hart. The ransom is paid by Angel and Spike but, instead of getting the head, they are given a bomb.

Denial, Thy Name is Illyria: Fred's parents, Roger and Trish Burkle, arrive at Wolfram & Hart on their way to Hawaii. Illyria, much to Wesley's obvious distress, impersonates Fred to avoid seeing the Burkles' grief.

Denial, Thy Names Are Angel and Spike: Having argued about Angel's relationship with Nina (see **102**, 'Smile Time'), Angel and Spike decide to put their differences aside in an effort to save Buffy. However, when they see Buffy dancing with the Immortal, Spike seems ready to play the hero so that Buffy will take him back. Angel suggests this is *never* going to happen. Spike claims he knows as much, but that he still cares about Buffy and doesn't want to see her with a jerk like the Immortal. Or Angel, for that matter. Angel says, angrily, that his and Buffy's love is forever (see **8**, 'I Will Remember You'). Spike reminds Angel that *he* had a relationship with Buffy too. Sleeping together is not a relationship, says Angel. It is, argues Spike, if you do it enough times.

Subsequently, while waiting to pay the ransom, Angel notes that he saved the world. Spike says he did too. Angel claims he's done it more – he closed the Hellmouth. 'Done that,' responds Spike (see *Buffy*: 'Chosen'). Only, Angel adds, because Spike wore his necklace (**88**, 'Home'). And he helped to kill Mayor Wilkins (*Buffy*: 'Graduation Day' Part 2) and Jasmine (**87**, 'Peace Out'). Spike wonders if those *really* count as saving the world. Angel also stopped Acathla (see *Buffy*: 'Becoming' Part 2). Spike says that, actually, Buffy ran Angel through with a sword. Angel claims he made her do it, signalling her with his eyes. Spike remembers events differently, saying Buffy killed Angel and that he helped her, so that one counts as Spike's.

At Buffy's apartment, Andrew notes that Buffy hasn't been duped by some evil love-spell as Angel and Spike believe but, rather, fell for the Immortal on her own. She's happy. Angel, on the verge of tears, notes that she hasn't finished baking yet (see *Buffy*: 'Chosen'). Andrew then suggests that, while the Immortal is a cool guy, he *isn't* perfect, and that Buffy is moving on and Angel and Spike need to do the same. If they do, then one of them might catch her eventually. Buffy loves both of them but she has to live her life.

Work is a Four-Letter Word: Gunn telling Angel they don't want to lose another baby with the bath water refers to the climax of the previous episode. (Gunn still seems angry about the way Angel handled these events.)

It's a Designer Label!: Spike's leather coat – the one he took from Nikki Wood in New York (see *Buffy*: 'Fool for Love') – is destroyed when the bomb explodes. Ilona gets him a new one and arranges for ten identical items to be waiting for him in LA along with a fine assortment of shoes. For Angel, she obtains a garish red and white leather biker's jacket which, she insists, is the latest style and makes him look gorgeous. Even Andrew makes sarcastic comments about it.

References: Allusions to *Swamp Thing* ('the song of the green'), Eddie Izzard's *Dress to Kill* ('*Ciao!*'), the Titans of

Greek mythology, the Sistine Chapel (see **51**, 'Offspring'), *Highlander*, *The Godfather*, *The Simpsons*, Shemp Howard (see **28**, 'Guise Will Be Guise') and the PG Wodehouse character Jeeves (see **31**, 'The Trial'). Conceptually, the episode owes much to *Bring Me The Head of Alfredo Garcia*. There's a painting by Raphael in Ilona's office.

Bitch!: Gunn says recovery of the head is a delicate matter which has to be handled with finesse. He then asks why they are talking about sending Spike.

'West Hollywood?': Angel and Spike visit Buffy's apartment in Rome. Andrew has been living there since his own apartment was incinerated after what Andrew describes as a cultural misunderstanding. At the end of the episode an immaculately dressed Andrew has a date with two beautiful women, Caprice and Isabella. Maybe he's not gay after all. *Nah* . . .

Awesome!: Spike believes that their mission isn't complicated, unless the Immortal kills Angel. Which, Spike notes unconvincingly, would be sad. The brilliant trio of 1894 sequences: Angelus and William the Bloody menacing the Immortal's men (Angelus threatens to stick arrows up their arses); the discovery that their women have been (willingly) violated by the Immortal (Spike's incandescent cry of 'son of a *bitch*' is a series' highlight); their inability to get past the Immortal's bouncer to extract blood-vengeance. The moment, in the midst of a bar fight when Spike hits Angel – because he got confused. The monochrome clip of stylish 50s Spike and Dru. Andrew's moment of inspirational wisdom and, subsequently, the bitter final scene as Spike and Angel have trouble taking his advice.

'You May Remember Me From Such Films and TV Series As . . .': A former ice-skater, once ranked twelfth in the US, Julie Benz auditioned for the role of Buffy Summers in 1997. Although unsuccessful, her consolation prize was becoming Angel's sire, Darla. She also played Kate Topolsky in *Roswell* and appeared in *Taken*, *As Good As It Gets*, *Jawbreaker*, *A Fate Totally Worse Than Death*,

Darkdrive, *The Midget Stays in the Picture*, *Shriek if You Know What I Did Last Friday the 13th*, *Peacemakers* and *Satan's School for Girls*. David S Lee was in *Final Solution*, *Las Vegas* and *Alias*. Carole Raphaelle Davis's CV includes *Jack the Dog*, *The Rapture*, *Sex and the City*, *Clover*, *Mannequin* and *The A-Team*.

Vikki Gurdas appeared in *Totally Blonde* and *Cold Squad*. In addition to being the stand-in for Frankenstein's Monster in *Van Helsing*, Dominic Pace was also in *Forever Fever* and *NYPD Blue*. Andrew Ableson is the son of singer Frankie Vaughan. He has featured in *Numb*, *Gypsy Boys*, *Joan of Archadia* and *Charmed*. Irina Maleeva's CV includes *Hard Drive*, *Union City*, *The Yum-Yum Girls*, *Poly* and *Just Shoot Me*. Rob Steiner's movies include *Anger Management* and *Man on the Moon*.

Behind the Camera: One of the first industry jobs for *Angel* co-creator David Greenwalt was as Jeff Bridges' body-double, before becoming a director on *The Wonder Years*. This preceded a period as writer/producer on *The X-Files*, *Doogie Howser M.D.*, *The Commish*, *Profit* and, in 1997, *Buffy*. Since leaving *Angel* he's worked on *Miracles* and *Jake 2.0*. His film scripts include *Class*, *American Dreamer* and *Secret Admirer* (which he also directed). His sole acting role was as a cop in the 1981 horror-spoof *Wacko*.

A Haven For the Demons: Wolfram & Hart's Rome office appears virtually identical to the LA branch. The CEO is the gregarious Ilona Costa Bianchi. Her secretary is called Pietro. When Angel asks if there is an Italian version of Wesley, Ilona confirms there is, but he's currently having a nap.

Cigarettes & Alcohol: Angel's negative reaction to the miniature bottles on the Wolfram & Hart plane mirrors similar comments made by Spike in **104**, 'Shells'. Spike suggests that a vampire's constitution doesn't allow them to get drunk easily. When Illyria complains about how badly she feels, Lorne suggests she try a Seabreeze (see **93**, 'Life of the Party').

Sex and Drugs and Rock'n'Roll: In 1894, Angelus and
Spike return to their hotel to find that Darla has been,
apparently, raped by the Immortal. Angelus asks if the
Immortal hurt her. Not until she asked him to, Darla
replies, and she assures Angelus that it was just fornication. Really *great* fornication. Spike seems torn between
amusement and outrage, noting that Angelus should be
fitted for a pair of antlers as he's been made a cuckold.
Then, Drusilla asks if it's time for another pony ride.
Spike, in *obvious* denial, is horrified that the Immortal
violated their women in succession. Darla corrects him – it
was *concurrently*. A distraught Angelus notes that Darla
and Dru *never* let him and Spike do that! Darla suggests
Dru and she take a bath so the boys can weep in private.

In the Italian club, the bartendress describes Buffy as the
Immortal's new *ragazza*.

Logic, Let Me Introduce You to This Window: Several weeks
have passed since **103**, 'A Hole in the World'. Yet,
apparently nobody has bothered to notify Roger and Trish
that their daughter is dead. The last time Andrew encoun-
tered Angel and Spike (see **99**, 'Damage'), he threatened to
let loose a dozen Slayers on them because the new Council
of Watchers assumed they couldn't be trusted. Yet when the
vampires turn up on Buffy's doorstep, Andrew casually
invites them into the home of the Slayer and her sister. The
car chase takes place through what must be the most
deserted part of central Rome. When Angelus and Spike are
unconscious and chained up in 1894, both are hanging in
such a position that the balls of their feet are just touching
the ground. In the next shot, Boreanaz and Marsters can be
seen shifting their weight back onto their heels. Spike's first
line in this sequence, 'that right bastard' sounds like James
Marsters doing a bad impression of Boreanaz's bad Irish
accent. Spike says he's been wearing his coat for over thirty
years. He hasn't, he acquired it 27 years ago. One tiny
mention of how Dawn's doing would have been appreci-
ated. During the bar fight, when Angel first punches Spike,
the blow very obviously misses its target.

I Just *Love* Your Accent: Spike asks how one says 'w**k off' in Italian.

Motors: Escaping from the club, Alfonso steals Angel and Spike's (presumably hired) Ferrari. The vampires duly follow him on a Vespa scooter.

Quote/Unquote: Spike, to Angel: 'I just wanna see you happy. Well, not *too* happy, cos then I'd have to stake you. On second thoughts, have at it.'
Ilona: 'The Gypsies are filthy people . . . we shall speak of them no more.'
Angelus: 'Those were *my* nuns!'
Alfonso: 'Look, the Americans are relying on violence to solve the problem. What a surprise.'
Andrew: 'Is Angel crying?' Spike: 'No. Not yet.'

Notes: 'One more step and the head gets it!' 'The Girl in Question' is an *Angel* episode which has everything you could possibly want from this series: hilarious, continuity-driven bitching sessions between the leads and continuity-driven flashback sequences (seeing the return of two much-loved semi-regular characters from the past). It's also got clever sight-gags, subtle Fellini and Sam Peckin-pah allusions, a car/scooter chase and the return of Boreanaz's awful Irish accent. Best of all, the episode includes line after line of wonderful dialogue dripping with pithy, self-aware humour. An *Angel* buddy-cop adventure with liberal doses of characterisation alongside a more serious Wesley/Illyria subplot. The latter is there, one imagines, to remind everyone that *Angel* is still, at heart, and despite its comedy set-pieces and notions of absurdism, a series with a dramatic core. But, it's worth noting that laughing at oneself is far from being the worst crime in the world. Indeed, if the inevitable consequence of such self-deprecation is an episode as good as this, then it's a great pity other series don't try it more often. Best! Episode! *Ever!*
This is the second occasion Angel has been seen riding pillion on a motorbike (see **25**, 'First Impressions'). Angel's

almost pathetic babbling concerning cookies is a reference to his conversation with Buffy in *Buffy*: 'Chosen'. Spike and Drusilla were in Rome during the 1950s. The Immortal lived in Rome in the sixteenth century, once spent 150 years in a monastery, has climbed Everest several times and written a self-help book. On one occasion, in Frankfurt, his path crossed Angelus and Spike – he hatched some Rathruhn eggs and offered a group of nuns safe passage. He also once had Spike imprisoned for tax evasion while another time they met, Spike was beaten by an angry mob. Spike suggests he and Angel should lock Buffy up like they did with Pavayne (see **92**, 'Hellbound'). When Angel gets off the phone with his snitch in Rome, Spike asks what is it this time, mentioning übervamps (see *Buffy*: 'Never Leave Me'), demon gods and devil robots (see **94**, 'The Cautionary Tale of Numero Cinco'). Despite protestations to the contrary, Spike speaks at least two words of Italian. Trish mentions the events of **49**, 'Fredless'. Illyria notes that she was able to appear as Fred due to a simple modulation of her form. She can appear as, essentially, whatever she (or Wesley, for that matter) desires (see **110**, 'Not Fade Away').

The Italian exterior sequences were filmed at Universal Studios. The episode also features stock footage of Rome at night – specifically, the Colosseum and the Sant' Angelo bridge.

Soundtrack: 'Take Me in Your Arms' by Dean Martin accompanies the slow-motion parts of the bar-fight. There's a lovely contrast between this and the pounding techno music also heard during this sequence. The episode features a superb score with smooth night-club jazz and Carmine Coppola-style *tarantella* elements.

Critique: 'With three hours to go until the series' finale, *Angel*'s creative team gives us a comedy,' wrote *Dream-Watch*'s K Stoddard Hayes. 'Fortunately, it's an Angel/Spike showcase . . . The boys bicker, mope over Buffy and feel inferior to the Immortal, while the supporting characters chew the scenery with broad Italian accents.'

Did You Know?: One item of *Buffy*-related merchandise released during 2003 allowed Juliet Landau to follow in an established family tradition. 'I have an action figure [based on Drusilla]. My parents have that too,' she gleefully told *Xposé*. 'My sister was saying, "I'm the only one in the family without a doll; it isn't fair!" ' Juliet's mum and dad were, of course, TV icons of a previous generation, Barbara Bain and Martin Landau, the stars of *Mission: Impossible* and *Space: 1999*. As a consequence of the latter series being filmed at Pinewood, Juliet spent two years living in London during her childhood.

Cast and Crew Comments: 'We felt it was the last time to give Angel and Spike a chance to be out together and have some fun,' noted Steven DeKnight.

During an online interview, Alexis Denisof was asked if he enjoyed the direction that his character had taken over his five years of working on *Buffy* and *Angel*: 'It's a pleasure for an actor to have the chance to spend this amount of time with a character,' he noted. 'We didn't know where we were going when Wesley joined the show, but we knew that he needed to change. In a way, each time we reach a plateau, a new level, I feel like this is the starting point.'

109
Power Play

US Transmission Date: 12 May 2004
UK Transmission Date: 1 June 2004

Writer: David Fury
Director: James A Contner
Cast: Elimu Nelson (Ernesto), Joss Whedon (Mike Conley)[44]

Angel appears to have been sucked into the corrupting corporate lifestyle – playing racquetball with the devil and

---

[44] Uncredited.

being more interested in the acquisition of power than in helping the helpless. Has he reverted to his Angelus persona? Can he *possibly* have been responsible for Fred's untimely demise? Wesley, Spike, Gunn and Lorne wonder why Angel suddenly finds himself tying up loose ends and face the awful possibility that their champion has joined the growing ranks of darkness.

A Little Learning is a Dangerous Thing: Drogyn (see **103**, 'A Hole in the World') was attacked by a Sathari demon, who informed him, while being interrogated under torture, that Angel was responsible for Illyria's resurrection and Fred's death. The Truthsayer subsequently travelled to Los Angeles seeking out Spike to tell him of his friend's possible betrayal. Drogyn is captured by Marcus Hamilton and taken to a dungeon in what appears to be Wolfram & Hart's holding dimension (see **105**, 'Underneath'). There, Angel viciously kills him to prove his loyalty to The Circle of the Black Thorn.

The Conspiracy Starts at Home Time: Senator Helen Bruckner has been a client of Wolfram & Hart since the Holland Manners era. She requests their help in discrediting her election opponent, Mike Conley. Bruckner plans to run for president in 2008 and tells Angel that she didn't claw her way up from Hell and get installed in a human body only to lose her senate seat. She suggests that Dr Sparrow's brainwashing techniques could convince the public that Conley is a paedophile. Bruckner is also a member of The Circle of the Black Thorn, an elite group of evildoers who further The Senior Partners' agenda, including being the driving force behind the apocalypse. The Circle's other members include Archduke Sebassis (see **93**, 'Life of the Party'), Cyvus Vail (**106**, 'Origin') and Izzy, Angel's devilish racquetball partner (**100**, 'You're Welcome'). Wesley believes that Lindsey's true motive in returning to LA was to get himself noticed by The Circle.

Megalomania, Thy Name is Angel: It always begins the same, notes Illyria. A ruler turns a blind eye to battles which he cannot win and a deaf ear to the counsel of those closest to him. As his strength increases, so does the separation between him and his followers, because a corrupted ruler sees treachery and betrayal all around. This appears to be what is happening to Angel. He tells Wesley, Lorne, Gunn and Spike that if they spend their lives obsessed with good and evil they will, ultimately, become swallowed and lost in the minutiae. An ant with the best intentions or the most diabolical schemes is still just an ant. There is only one thing that matters: power. Until Angel has real global power, he is, and will accomplish, nothing.

Denial, Thy Name is Wesley: Wesley tells his friends that Angel has dedicated his life to helping others. Not because he had to but because it was a path he chose. If he has been swayed from that course, maybe there's still time for them to bring him back from the brink. Angel, Wes notes, would do the same for any of them, regardless of their actions.

Lies: Using a glamour to hide his conversation with Wesley, Gunn, Lorne and Spike from Marcus Hamilton (and anyone else who may be listening in), Angel reveals that his involvement with The Circle is part of a complex plan for revenge against The Senior Partners that he has set in motion. Everything they believe they know is a lie. It was Angel who sent Wesley the clue concerning The Circle through one of his sourcetexts. Angel did, indeed, send the assassin to kill Drogyn because he knew the warrior could handle himself. He confesses that he needed The Circle to believe Angel's own people didn't trust him; that a person as pure as Drogyn considered Angel an enemy; that he – indirectly – killed Fred. It was the only way to gain their confidence. Spike asks when all this started. Angel tells him it was two months ago when Cordelia kissed him (see **100**, 'You're Welcome'). It didn't hit Angel until later that evening but Cordy passed him a single vision of The Circle and their nefarious activities, just as Doyle once passed the visions to *her* through a kiss (**9**, 'Hero'). Cordelia showed Angel where the real power lies. Then Fred died and Angel decided to make her death matter. The scheme has, seemingly, worked. Angel has seen the faces of evil. He and his friends, he suggests, are part of a machine that's going to be there long after their bodies are dust. The Senior Partners will always exist in one form or another because mankind is weak. The powerful control everything, *except* man's will to choose. Lindsey may be a pathetic half-wit, Angel adds, but he's right about one thing – heroes don't blandly accept the way the world is. The Senior Partners may be eternal but their existence can be made painful. Angel wants to bring the machine's gears to a grinding halt, even if it's just for a brief moment, to show The Senior Partners that they don't *own* them.

Angel, however, wants his friends to be clear about what he's suggesting – killing every member of The Circle. He knows that they will not be allowed to walk away from such a course of action. The Senior Partners will rain their full wrath down upon them as an example to others. Power will endure. The others have to decide if laying down their lives is a price worth paying. Spike, Wesley and Gunn instantly agree. Lorne is more sceptical but eventually says he's in too.

Work is a Four-Letter Word: Nina attends the Southern California Academy of Arts and Design. Angel buys three plane tickets so that Nina and her family can leave the country before the coming apocalypse. Nina reluctantly agrees.

References: The episode shares a title with Martyn Burke's 1978 political thriller. Allusions to *The Lord of the Rings* (Gunn calling Drogyn Aragorn), the Keebler Elves (the cookie-baking mascots of Nabisco), *Ghost Story*, *The Wizard of Oz*, *Willie Wonka and the Chocolate Factory*, *Alice Doesn't Live Here Anymore*, *Yellow Submarine* (Spike describes Illyria as a Blue Meanie), Talking Heads' 'Burning Down the House', Jerome Kern and Oscar Hammerstein's 'Ol' Man River' (from *Showboat*), 'Man Was Made to Mourn' by Robbie Burns and Leona Helmsley (see **56**, 'Provider'). Angel recently fired six of Lorne's clients, some of whom were scheduled to appear in *Young Guns III*. Illyria and Drogyn play the video game *Crash Bandicoot* in Spike's apartment. Lorne alludes to a quotation by Baron Acton (1834–1902): 'Power corrupts, absolute power corrupts absolutely.'

Bitch!: Spike notes there are plenty of secret societies and cabals about. Most spend their time in basements paddling one another's bums to prove their manhood.

'West Hollywood?': Spike tells Illyria that he and Angel have never been intimate. Except once.

Awesome!: Angel and Izzy's game of racquetball. Lorne's description of The Circle as a sewing club for pirates. Illyria and Drogyn playing video games. Lorne's growing sense of disillusionment with the entire situation. Angel's two confrontations with Wes, Gunn, Lorne and Spike.

'You May Remember Me From Such Films and TV Series As . . .': Elimu Nelson appeared in *Love & Sex*, *The Shield*, *Pacific Blue* and *Love Don't Cost a Thing*. Stacey Travis's CV includes *Ghost World*, *Mystery Men*, *Caroline at Midnight*, *Intolerable Cruelty*, *Paranormal Girl*, *Traffic*, *Frasier*, *Nash Bridges* and *Earth Girls Are Easy*.

Not Exactly a Haven For the Sisters: Illyria suggests she has grown wary of this world since her powers were depleted (see **107**, 'Time Bomb') and that, although she's been made more human, this place remains strangely disconcerting.

Cigarettes and Alcohol: Angel shares a glass of wine with Izzy after his initiation ceremony.

Sex and Drugs and Rock'n'Roll: Angel and Nina enjoy what is, very obviously, a post-coital conversation in the episode's opening scene. Nina thinks they should take a vacation in Cabo, drink margaritas and make love on the beach.

Illyria notes that, subsequent to her assumption of Fred's persona (see **108**, 'The Girl in Question'), Wesley has ceased having intercourse with her. (Of course, she's talking about communication rather than sex.)

Logic, Let Me Introduce You to This Window: Who initiated first contact between Angel and The Circle? Doesn't anyone at the racquetball court find Izzy's horns and tail unusual? Drogyn pronounces the name Sathari differently twice within the same scene.

Cruelty to Animals: When meeting Bruckner, the senator asks for some blood for her vampire aide, Ernesto. A virgin, if possible. Harmony offers a crass apology, noting that they have a no-human-blood policy. She can, however, offer something in rodent including some fruity, unassuming vole.

Quote/Unquote: Spike, to Illyria: 'You may not think you're as powerful as you were, Highness, but looking like Fred, for some of us, it's the most devastating power you have.' And: 'You're wrong about Angel. Not that I don't think the sod could end up being a megalomaniacal bastard. It's just that if he did, I'd know it.'

Angel: 'We're in the business of business. Oil, software, worldwide wickets. The product doesn't matter. It's the game that matters.'

Lindsey, on The Circle: 'It's a secret society.' Gunn: 'Never heard of them.' Lindsey: 'That's cos they're *secret*.'

Notes: 'I spent years fighting to get somewhere. Now I'm close to it, I don't like what I see.' David Fury, from a standing start, produces the first plank in the scaffold that will form *Angel*'s climax. Given the job he had to do, it's a stunning achievement. With keynote themes of the nature of heroism, betrayal, power, corruption and lies, 'Power Play' flirts with a world of cynical demon politics and includes a fittingly magnificent series of performances from the regulars. It's also a *really* violent episode – particularly a truly grisly pre-title sequence. There's much internal continuity, a stunning plot twist involving Cordelia and a dark and claustrophobic sense of oncoming death and destruction. Beautifully directed by the always-reliable

James Contner, and with intricate set-pieces peppering a witty and involving script, 'Power Play' stands, proudly, as the last three-course meal before the execution.

Nina asks Angel about his Roman girlfriend suggesting that he revealed details of his and Spike's recent trip (see **108**, 'The Girl in Question'). He's also told Nina enough about his past that she knows if he achieves perfect happiness, she has to stake him. Wesley reports on a series of recent attacks by Boretz demons at an abandoned downtown amusement park called Funville. The latest victim was a teenage girl named Stacey Bluth. The Boretz tend to dress as transients to prey on the homeless. The leader of The Fell Brethren (see **107**, 'Time Bomb') is named Ed. Marcus Hamilton and Drogyn have previously met a long time ago. Wesley tells the others that Drogyn the Battlebrand was given eternal youth a thousand years ago. (Wes may have once done a paper on Drogyn for the Watchers' Council.)

Critique: 'I love the show, and think it's having a strong season. (I do miss Carpenter, but her exit was apparently unavoidable),' wrote Robert Biancho. The writer also noted that he would be willing to mourn *Angel*'s passing quietly and without comment if The WB had shown any ability to come up with a replacement that would be even half as good as the cancelled show. However, what really worried Biancho was the creativity drain which, he believed, had struck network television. 'Great writers have left over the last three years: Marshall Herskovitz and Ed Zwick, David Milch, Aaron Sorkin, and now, apparently, Joss Whedon.' The networks should be begging these people to stay, Biancho added. Instead they seem to be actively pushing them out.

Did You Know?: Since *Angel*'s cancellation, David Boreanaz's career has, literally, gone to the dogs. At least, that's the headline *TV Guide* used when reporting in July 2004 that David had been recruited by the pressure group People for the Ethical Treatment of Animals to appear in a public-service campaign urging dog owners not to chain their pets in the yard.

Cast and Crew Comments: 'The writing has been really good this year,' James Marsters told David Richardson. 'If you forget about your home turf and abandon your lead then your show is going to fail no matter how good the supporting cast is.'

110
Not Fade Away

US Transmission Date: 22 May 2004
UK Transmission Date: 8 June 2004

Writers: Jeffrey Bell, Joss Whedon
Director: Jeffrey Bell
Cast: David Figlioli (Bartender)

Angel and friends take on The Circle of the Black Thorn knowing that, even if they succeed in their endeavours, Wolfram & Hart's Senior Partners will not allow them to profit from the death of so many powerful demons. Facing almost certain death, they spend their final day in preparing for the coming apocalypse.

Dreaming (As *Buffy* Often Proves) is Free: Connor confesses to Angel that he is aware Angel is his father. He got his memories back when Wesley smashed the Orlon Window (see **106**, 'Origin'). The real memories, notes Connor, are mixed in with the replacement ones. They're like a strange, violent and, at times inappropriately erotic, dream (see also **73**, 'Apocalypse Nowish').

Apocalypse Now (Redux): Once Wesley, Gunn, Spike and Lorne agree to follow Angel's plan (see **109**, 'Power Play') Gunn wonders if they intend to take on The Circle as a single entity. Angel believes this is a bad idea. The Circle together could simply vapourise Angel and his friends. Separately, they're *just* demons. Angel recruits Lindsey to the plan, noting that he wants Lindsey to replace him at Wolfram & Hart – if Angel doesn't survive the battle – in a better-the-devil-you-know-type deal. Lindsey and Lorne are detailed to attack the Sahrvin (see **97**, 'Harm's Way'). Lorne agrees to this, but notes that, after completing the job, the others will never see him again. After Lindsey and Lorne defeat the Sahrvin, the full reason for Lorne's forthcoming disappearance becomes clear as he coldly shoots Lindsey noting that Lindsey can never be part of the solution.

Wesley is sent to Cyvus Vail under the cover of wanting to take Angel's place in The Circle. Illyria is told that Izzy (whom Angel refers to as Izzerial The Devil) and three other members of The Circle dine together. She says that she will make trophies of their spines. Gunn is sent to Senator Bruckner's campaign office in West LA to tackle the senator and her retinue of vampire aides. Spike's task is to retrieve the baby given to The Fell Brethren (see **107**, 'Time Bomb'), dismember the foster family and return the baby to its mother. Angel says he will kill Archduke Sebassis (whom, he notes, has over 40,000 demons under his command). This is also the story that he tells Harmony, knowing that she will betray him to her lover, Marcus (she is, after all, evil). Angel fires Harmony when her duplicity is revealed although, thoughtfully, he had already typed out a recommendation for her so at least she won't be left unemployed. In actual fact, Angel has already taken care of Sebassis by cunningly spiking the blood of his demon slave which poisons Sebassis when he drinks it. Angel's *real* fight is with the powerful Marcus whom he eventually defeats, with Connor's help, by drinking Marcus's blood to obtain some of the power that Marcus gained from The Senior Partners. Once the fight is over, the Wolfram & Hart building begins to collapse. Connor wants to go with Angel and help him in the even bigger battle to come but Angel sends his son home. Connor believes that they will destroy Angel. As long as Connor is OK, they can't, Angel assures him.

Denial, Thy Name is Gunn: Before the night of the long knives, Angel tells the others to spend the rest of the day doing whatever they want. Live the day like it's your last, he tells them. Because it probably is.

Gunn visits his friend Anne Steele (see *Buffy*: 'Lie To Me', 'Anne'; **34**, 'Blood Money'; **36**, 'The Thin Dead Line') who still runs the East Hills Teen Shelter – it's in the process of moving to a new site. Gunn asks if she has much trouble with vampires these days. Anne notes that the problem never goes away completely but the boys help out and that gives her time to concentrate on issues like crack, runaways, abuse victims and psychotics. They've had some good donations recently which allowed them to hire part-time psychiatric staff. Gunn asks what if he were to tell Anne that none of it matters. That everything is controlled by forces more powerful and uncaring than anyone could conceive. What would Anne do then? She replies that she would get this truck packed before the new stuff arrives.

Denial, Thy Name is Spike: Spike spends his final day in a demon bar. At first it appears he's merely getting drunk as a prelude to a massive fight with the other customers (he tells the barman that he needs another couple of shots of courage before making his presence felt). In fact the bar, McTarnan's, is having a poetry slam and Spike ends up on-stage, delivering a *devastating* version of 'Ode to Cecily' (see *Buffy*: 'Fool for Love' – it just goes to prove one *can* rhyme 'effulgent' with 'bulge in it' and get away with it if the delivery is good enough). This goes down an absolute *storm* with the punters. Spike intends to follow this triumph with the public debut of a previously unheard work, 'The Wanton Folly of Me Mum' (see *Buffy*: 'Lies My Parents Told Me'). Ah, bless – William was *always* a poet at heart, even when he was ripping people's lungs out.

Denial, Thy Name is Wesley: Wes tells Illyria that, unlike the others, he doesn't intend to smell the flowers, sky dive, or go to see Mistress Spanksalot. There *is* no perfect day for him. No sunset, painting or finely aged Scotch is going to sum up his life. Illyria realises that he wants to be with Fred. Wesley agrees. Illyria offers to assume Fred's persona for him but Wesley notes that the first thing a Watcher learns is to separate truth from illusion. The truth is that Fred is gone. To pretend anything else would be a lie.

Subsequently, Wesley receives a mortal wound when he attempts to assassinate Cyvus Vail. Illyria, having killed her own targets, rushes to be with him and, as he dies, she does assume Fred's persona and tells him that she loves him and that they will be together forever in the next world. Then, she finishes the job for Wesley by viciously killing Vail.

The Conspiracy Starts at Home Time: The Circle force Angel to sign away, in blood, any claim that he has to the Shanshu prophecy (see **22**, 'To Shanshu in LA').

Lies: Harmony claims that she was very popular in high school. Not with the Scooby Gang, she wasn't (see, for example, *Buffy*: 'Bewitched, Bothered and Bewildered', 'The Harsh Light of Day', 'Real Me').

References: The title is a rock'n'roll standard, a 1958 hit for Buddy Holly and the Crickets and subsequently covered by numerous acts including, most famously, the Rolling Stones.[45] There's also a possible allusion to a lyric by Joss Whedon's beloved Neil Young in 'My My Hey Hey' ('it's better to burn out, than to fade away'). Conceptually, some of the episode's inspiration appears to have come from two DC comic series, *The Sandman* (the conceit of a – literal – hope in Hell) and *Hellblazer*. Angel claims to have been at the taping of the first episode of *The Carol Burnett Show* in 1967. Also, references to 'MacArthur Park' (see **30**, 'The Shroud of Rahmon'; **81**, 'Orpheus'), *Reservoir Dogs*, Charles Manson and his 'Family' cult, Stephen King's *Golden Years*, *Pinocchio*, Lou Reed's 'Perfect Day', *Animal Farm*, *The Godfather* (Izzy stabbing Angel's hand), *The Devil's Advocate*, the nursery rhyme 'If Wishes Were Horses', TV psychic the Amazing Kreskin, and *Die Hard*. Among numerous biblical allusions are that

---

[45] 'Not Fade Away' was also, as several media commentators noted at the time of the episode's broadcast, often performed live by one of Boreanaz's favourite bands, the Grateful Dead.

old stand-by I Timothy 6:12 (see 1, 'City Of'), Isaiah 48:22 ('no rest for the wicked'), Mark 5:9 ('we are legion'), Exodus 20:17 (Lindsey mentions that Angel covets his neighbour's ass), Genesis 2 (Angel telling Eve that it appears they're getting kicked out of the garden) and Matthew 26 (when Angel informs his friends that one must betray him, Spike asks if he can deny Angel three times).

'West Hollywood?': Angel tries to persuade Lindsey to join his team for the big fight. 'I want you,' he notes, then adds that he's thinking of rephrasing that statement. Lindsey says he'd be more comfortable if Angel did.

Awesome!: Harmony's musings on missing hearing her heartbeat. Spike's eagerness to be the one that betrays Angel. Illyria's reaction to Wesley talking about Mistress Spanksalot. The return of William (the bloody *great*) poet. Lindsey's shock when it turns out to be Lorne, rather than Angel, who kills him, and dying, as he lived, with *great hair*. Gunn and Wesley's parting handshake and the sorrow that Angel, Spike and Gunn show when Illyria tells them that their friend is dead. Angel firing Harmony (but giving her a recommendation anyway). Angel's amazing fight with Marcus and Connor's unexpected intervention. Gunn killing Bruckner with an axe. Wesley dying in Illyria's arms. The end, in a rain-drenched alley. 'Good night, folks'.

'You May Remember Me From Such Films and TV Series As . . .': Julia Lee played the title role in *Ophelia Learns to Swim*. She was also in *Grind*, *Hellborn* and *Charmed*. David Figlioli appeared in *The American Shame*, *Dating Rosie* and *The X-Files*.

Logic, Let Me Introduce You to This Window: Illyria's bandage comes loose in one shot but, a moment later, it's back in place. In the scene when Illyria becomes Fred, her face is Fred yet the shot of her arm is still Illyria. When Angel talks about attending the first episode of *The Carol Burnett Show*, he mentions that Tim Conway was on fire that night. Although comedian Conway *was* a regular guest on the show, he was not featured in the first episode (when Carol's guest was singer Jim Nabors). Conway's first appearance was actually in episode four. Angel reminds Lindsey that he – Angelus at least – was the biggest mass-murderer Lindsey ever met. Surely Darla, who had a 150-year head-start on Angelus, killed more people than he. And Lindsey knew her. Very well. If the timescale established in **109**, 'Power Play' is correct (it being two months since the events of **100**, 'You're Welcome') then Amanda's baby can only be, literally, a few days old (she still hadn't had the child in **107**, 'Time Bomb' and the events of the subsequent three episodes seem to cover little more than a week). Yet the child whom Spike rescues from The Fell Brethren is clearly much older than that.

Quote/Unquote: Lindsey: 'What are you thinking about?' Eve: 'Angel.' Lindsey: 'You simply couldn't have said a worse thing.'

Harmony: 'Are you firing me?' Angel: 'Among other things, yes.'

Illyria, to a dying Wesley: 'Would you like me to lie to you now?'

Marcus: 'My blood is filled with their ancient power.' Angel: 'Can you pick out the one word there you probably shouldn't have said?'

This is Where it All Ends: In the alley behind the Hyperion, Angel, Spike, Illyria and an injured Gunn face the vast armies of Hell, including a dragon. Gunn suggests that the others should take the 30,000 on the left. Illyria tells him that he will last ten minutes at best, but Gunn believes that he can make those minutes really count. Spike asks what the plan is. We fight, replies Angel. Then he adds, 'Personally, I wanna slay the dragon. Let's go to work!'

Notes: 'You're not part of the solution. You never will be.' The deliberate ambiguity of the episode title is the key to understanding and, perhaps, to appreciating, the full drama of the *Angel* finale. There was, quite simply, no other way to end this series – unlike *Buffy*, these characters, in this particular city, could not fade from the screens and into the comforting arms of our dreams and continuing fan-fiction. This *had* to be the last word on a series that always tried to show that fighting the good fight seldom ends in a happy ever after. If I had one disappointment, it's that Wesley died in the penultimate scene and, therefore, wasn't with his friends as they faced the final curtain. But, given the 'hero's journey' nature of his story, perhaps *that* was inevitable too. A couple of decent cameos and a lot of tied-up loose ends (like the Shanshu prophecy) battle for prominence with a great performance by Adam Baldwin and what is, unquestionably, Alexis Denisof's finest 43 minutes. 'Not Fade Away' is also, quite remarkably, given much of the subject matter, very funny – one of *Angel*'s less well-documented strengths being its uncanny ability to laugh in the face of horror. But, ultimately, what the episode is about is one noble death and another disturbingly unexpected one, a – wholly expected – betrayal from within and an ending that, with hindsight, was signposted five years ago in **9**, 'Hero'. 'Try not to die', Illyria tells Gunn, but you know that such an option isn't really viable to a show that always dealt with the black and white areas of heroism and honour. Not with a whimper, then, but with a bang. Did we make it? Goodnight . . .

Angel doesn't remember what it was like when he was human – it was too long ago. According to Angel, Nina makes great pottery. He has never written a résumé before, though he claims to have nice handwriting. Connor considers this a girlish trait. Lindsey asks Eve if she remains worried by Lorne's dire prediction of her future (see **103**, 'A Hole in the World'). Lorne reminds Lindsey that he's heard him sing (see **40**, 'Dead End'). Lindsey suggests that Angel is about to pick the nastiest fight since mankind drop-kicked the last demon out of this dimension (see *Buffy*: 'The Harvest'). When Gunn meets Anne, he mentions Rondell (see **36**, 'The Thin Dead Line'; **41**, 'Belonging'; **47**, 'That Old Gang of Mine'). Harmony recalls that she became a vampire at her high school graduation (see *Buffy*: 'Graduation Day' Part 2). Hamilton taunts Angel about the friends he's lost: Doyle (see **9**, 'Hero'), Cordelia (**100**, 'You're Welcome') and Fred.

The original US broadcast was followed by a short montage of clips from various episodes and a voice-over which explained that Angel had lived for 277 years and thanking viewers for spending the last five with them. This concluded with a caption thanking everyone involved in *Angel* 'from your friends at The WB'.

Soundtrack: Andy Hallett belts out a stunning rendition of Leslie Bricusse and Cyril Ornadel's 'If I Ruled the World' (based, the actor noted, on James Brown's arrangement of the song). 'They sent me the piano tracks,' Andy told *DreamWatch*. 'I laid down the vocals at my house.'

Critique: '*Angel* ends its WB run tonight,' wrote David Bianculli in the *New York Daily News*. 'It's a premature, somewhat-rushed goodbye, because co-creator Joss Whedon and company would prefer to have continued the show a few more seasons. But give *Angel* this: The show, like its characters, goes out swinging.'

'For those who loved *Angel*, parting will be hard,' noted *USA Today* on the eve of the final episode. 'Not just because the show has been so good, or because its end is untimely. The real sorrow is that Joss Whedon, one of TV's best and most dedicated writers, is now out of television – and there's no guarantee he'll ever return.'

In a rather spiteful if, sadly, somewhat typical review on the *Television Without Pity* website, the reviewer, Strega (almost certainly not his or her real name), whose dislike for Wesley had never been remotely concealed, noted that the character died as he had lived, 'delusionally'.

Did You Know?: *Angel* fandom was horrified by the news in May, shortly after the final episode was shown, that Andy Hallett had been hospitalised due to a viral infection complicated by exhaustion. Andy was subsequently transferred to the ICU at Cedars-Sinai Medical. Thankfully, a few days later he was released.

Cast and Crew Comments: 'I'm so pleased for everyone that we've made this journey,' Alexis Denisof noted shortly after the final episode had been filmed. 'I'm really happy with the work that we've done. It's a great accomplishment to have made 100 [plus] episodes and most of them are pretty damn good.' In another interview, with *Dream-Watch*, Alexis added that, 'There's no way to sum up the six years of playing Wesley and working on this show. It's been my life. I don't know how else I can convey the depth and breadth of what the journey has been.'

The final episode itself, noted Denisof, had been written some time previously while the prospect of a sixth season was still a possibility. 'There was no need to make many adjustments to it once the announcement came from The WB that we weren't coming back. In fact, Joss has left it open-ended.'

The Frog Chronicles: In July 2004, WB Chairman Garth Ancier hinted at a WB event that *Angel* may still have been with us today, had 20th-Century Fox given the network until May to make a final decision. 'We [were forced] to make the decision early based on their request.' However, in an attempt to mollify fans, Ancier noted that he would like to see the show back as a series of TV movies. 'Certainly, Joss would like to,' he noted. 'David [Boreanaz] will take a bit more coaxing, but I think he will do it.' Ancier, and The WB's new entertainment president David Janollari, were heavily criticised in the press after the event for their admission that they had never watched several of their own Network's shows. Janollari (a former producer of *Six Feet Under*), noted that 'it would be great to have a show that galvanizes an audience in [as] big a way as *Buffy the Vampire Slayer*'. As was subsequently pointed out by many fans, they actually used to have one. Whatever happened to it . . .?

Joss Whedon's Comments: 'The whole point of *Angel* is the idea of the fight and how it never stops,' Joss had told the press at the time of the cancellation announcement.

The Legacy: 'In ten or twenty years, I think people will look at *Angel* in a different light to *Buffy*,' David Boreanaz noted. 'It's a broader show. It takes place in a major city. The characters are different. I think people will say "Wow, they did some fantastic things." It will live on.'

'The last episode of *Angel* didn't garner the gallons of ink and fawning farewells of other shows,' wrote Marijke Rowland. She continued that: 'What was brilliant about Whedon's work is that you were able to look past the vampires and demons, to see the human stories underneath. The universal themes we all struggle with – love, loss, loneliness, lust – came across more real than anything on "reality" television.' 'As much as I liked *Buffy*, I have come to like *Angel* even more,' noted John Ginn. 'Some of its plotlines have touched on far darker and morally ambiguous themes than *Buffy* ever went near. On *Angel*, the heroes won many battles, but rarely achieved an overwhelming victory in the ongoing war against evil.' The *Chicago Tribune*'s Maureen Ryan wrote that, 'The evil weasels at The WB cancelled *Angel*. If there was a hell dimension handy, we'd toss [them] into it.' The series was not exactly *CSI: Los Angeles*, Ryan continued, but noted that this was one of the things that made *Angel* great – that it couldn't be accused of being a copycat show.

This was a theme also commented upon by *USA Today*, which observed: 'What *Angel* had in abundance, is heart. There wasn't a line in *The West Wing* – a show that used to crank out lump-in-your-throat dialogue weekly – that could touch Illyria's when she was holding the dying Wesley. If you weren't a fan, it won't make sense. If you *were*, it was heartbreaking.' Describing the show as 'a phenomenal series', the *Globe and Mail*'s Nikki Stafford noted that *Angel* explored the deepest emotions of people 'and how they can be crushed. [It] taught us that just because something's a demon doesn't make it a monster, and showed how important familial love and friendship can be.'

'The show had a deceptively simple premise: Evil bad. Fighting evil good,' wrote *Toronto Star*'s Malene Arpe.

'But, as Angel learned many times over the past five years, understanding what that means is far from simple.' Unlike *Buffy*, which ended on a sunny note, Arpe added, *Angel* was allowed to stay true to its darker roots. 'There was to be no redemption for Angel, just a rainy alley . . . [and] one final stand.'

What Might Have Been . . .: Shortly before the final episode aired, Joss Whedon said in an online interview, 'This year was about, if you're inside of a structure, be it corporate or societal, that is by its nature corrupt, do you affect it or does it affect you?' If the series had continued, Whedon noted, the sixth season would have had, as a main focus, the consequences of this. 'When you buck the system and you do your best to make it collapse and it does, the next season would have been some serious chaos.'

Angel and the Internet

To a series like *Angel*, the Internet is the only fan forum that actually *matters*. Let's put this another way: *Buffy* has been described as 'television's first true child of the Internet age'. If this is an accurate description (and it pretty much is), then *Angel* should be considered the medium's first grandchild – a series not only born *on*, but also (due to the instantaneous nature of fan reaction) *by*, the net. Within weeks of *Angel*'s debut in 1999, a flourishing net-community had spawned numerous newsgroups, mailing lists, posting boards and websites, often as annexes to already existing *Buffy* domains. With the demise of the series many of these groups have branched out into discussion of the work of *Buffy*verse *alumni* and of the short-lived, but much-loved, Joss Whedon show *Firefly* and its eagerly awaited big-screen resurrection, *Serenity*. As with most fandoms much of what has emerged is great – passionate, enthusiastic and intelligent – but there's also some downright scary stuff out there that the uninitiated should be aware of. This is a rough guide to some of what you can find.

Newsgroups: The usenet newsgroup alt.tv.buffy-v-slayer allows posters to discuss all aspects of the *Buffy*verse. In the past, it's been a stimulating forum with debate openly encouraged. However, it has also, occasionally, attracted an aggressive contingent and, that curse of usenet, trolls (people who send offensive messages simply to stir up some trouble). Hell hath no fury, it seems, like overgrown schoolchildren with access to a computer. A relevant case in point: when a previous edition of *Slayer* was published in 2002, it was criticised by some newsgroup regulars because they regarded the above one-line description of trolling as a personal insult to them. This generated a heated thread with over 150 messages. All of which, kind of, proves my point. As with many fandoms the users of a.t.b-v-s like to talk about *Buffy*, but some of them, actually, prefer talking about *themselves*. A lot. uk.media. tv.buffy-v-slayer is, as the name suggests, a British equivalent and features broadly similar topics.

The *Angel* newsgroup, alt.tv.angel, began even before the series did, as a consequence of David Boreanaz's undoubted popularity on *Buffy*, though it had somewhat humble origins (many initial posts were from fans of the series *Touched By An Angel* wondering why everyone was talking about vampires). It's grown nicely along with the show and appears to have acquired little of the pale cynicism and annoying self-aggrandisement of the *Buffy* group. alt.fan.buffy-v-slayer.creative is a fan-fiction forum carrying a wide range of missing adventures, character vignettes, 'shipper-fic (relationship-based erotica) and slash-fic (same-sex erotica), some of it of a very high standard indeed. There are also lively newsgroups in Europe (alt.buffy.europe) and Australia (aus.tv.buffy) where *Buffy* has big followings.

Mailing Lists: Much more relaxed than usenet, at http:// groups.yahoo.com/ you'll find access to numerous *Buffy* and *Angel*-related lists. Simply type the name of your favourite character or actor into the 'search groups' box and you'll enter a world you only dreamed about! Be warned, however – mailing lists can be extremely addictive, so resist the temptation to join too many. It's also worth noting how many members a group has before you join. Some of the larger groups are *very* high volume; for example, *The Bloody Awful Poets Society* (motto: 'Spike *HAS* been redeemed, dammit!') has over 3,000 members and generates hundreds of messages every day. Especially recommended is the *JossBTVS* list which features daily newsflashes on the activities of the *Buffy* and *Angel* cast and crew. *Buffy-Christian* are a group who pride themselves on being 'Christians who love *Buffy*' and reject small-minded bigotry in all its forms. If you're up for a lively debate, join the fun at *conversebuffyverse*. Fans of gossip can catch the latest media articles and news from other forums at *spoiler-crypt*. Other lists include *angelseries*, which has over 600 members and *BuffyWatchers*, which is basically a group of friends, including this author, who are happy for visitors to join us for after-dinner chats. A *Buffy* version of *The Algonquin*, if you will. (We're currently in the process of a complete week-by-week rewatch of *Buffy* and *Angel*.) In short there's a list for just about everything: each character, actor and writer will have a yahoo group somewhere. You will get the option of having posts sent to you or of checking the list via a weblink.

Live Journal Communities: Increasingly, groups of *Buffy* and *Angel* fans are gathering on the LJ network (www.livejournal.com). Here you can sign up for a free Live Journal and, if you provide a list of your interests, you will be offered a range of individuals and communities whose tastes match your own. The primary purpose of Live Journals is as a kind of online diary, but it also abounds in discussion, fanfic and artwork, some of it of a very high standard.

Posting Boards: The original official *Buffy* Posting Board, *The Bronze*, is sadly no more, and is much lamented. But its spirit lives on at www.bronzebeta.com. This board includes occasional contributions from Joss Whedon himself and from other members of the production team (Jane Espenson, David Fury and Steven DeKnight have all posted there, for example). It's a fast, cliquey forum and, to a newcomer, it can seem somewhat bewildering at first, with its shout-out lists and obscure in-jokes. But it's worth sticking around as you'll find yourself participating in some fascinating discussions. *All Things Philosophical On BtVS* (www.voy.com/14567/) is also well worth a visit. For daily news, chat, caption competitions and the ever popular 'More Naked Angel' photo-feature, try the *An Angel's Soul* board (www.voy.com/14810/), though you should be advised that they have regular 'newbie flogging' sessions.

Many fansites have their own posting boards like http://forums.morethanspike.com/, a haven for all-things-

Marsters, the amusing www.bloodyspike.proboards16. com/index.cgi or the fascinating http://pub165.ezboard. com/ftheducksversefrm1, the home to The Ducks, a loyal fan community devoted to 'classic *Buffy*' (for which, read 'Buffy and Angel, tru-luv-4ever'). A somewhat amusing diversion is to visit a number of 'shipper-sites and note the wildly differing reactions to the same episodes or events that you'll find there. What is absolute nirvana to a Bangel (a Buffy/Angel 'shipper) will, likely, utterly infuriate a Spuffy (Buffy/Spike 'shipper) while The Redemptionistas (see www.tabularasa.com) battle it out with The Ducks and The Evilistas in a seemingly never-ending game of 'my vampire's better than your vampire.' Fans argue, endlessly, about the amount of screen time devoted to their favour- ites. Even those who've fallen out of love with the series have their own forums, known as 'ranting rooms'. If all of this sounds a bit silly then, yes, it probably is. But it's mostly good fun, especially if you remember to take much of what you read with a healthy pinch of salt. You will, however, be amazed that television shows can inspire such passion and devotion. And, within a few weeks, you'll probably be taking sides, joining in the discussions and wondering how you ever lived without knowing this world existed.

A good rule of thumb for newbies on *all* forums is to arrive, introduce yourself, read the rules, then lurk about for a few days watching what goes on. It's very easy to make new friends but certain issues can bring out an element of insane-troll-logic in everyone. So, don't be 'a Bezoar'. Or you'll get flamed. And, if you're feeling really brave, go and play hardball at www.televisionwithoutpity.com where cynicism among both the episode reviewers and the posters seems to have developed into something of an art form. They take no prisoners; their proud motto is 'spare the snark, spoil the networks'. You can, however, practice on somewhat gentler forums like www.scoopme.com first.

Websites: There are, literally, thousands of sites relating to both *Buffy* and *Angel*. What follows is a (by no means definitive) list of some of the author's favourites. Many of these are also part of webrings that link to other related sites. Remember, an hour's surfing can get you to some very interesting places. Joss Whedon confirmed in a recent online interview that he often surfs the net specifically looking for comments to see which subjects fans are discussing among themselves. 'What they're liking, not liking, all of that stuff. I'm fascinated by it,' he noted.

A necessary disclaimer: websites are transitory at the best of times and this information, though accurate when written, may be woefully out of date by the time of publication.

UK Sites: The BBC's *Buffy Online* (www.bbc.co.uk/cult/buffy/index.shtml) has become a breathtaking resource with one of the most up-to-date *Buffy* and *Angel* news services on the net. It also features numerous exclusive interviews and a plethora of other goodies. Check it daily.

US Sites: *Little Willow's Slayground* (http://slayground.net) is a delightful treasure-trove of photos, articles and reviews, plus all the latest news. It also includes 'Who Says?' the VIP archive of the *BtVS Posting Board*, fun sections like 'The Xander Dance Club', filmographies and official webpages for *Buffy* regulars Danny Strong (Jonathan) and Amber Benson (Tara). There's also a useful link to the *Keeper Sites* (www.stakeaclaim.net/), a webring with numerous pages. It's possible to find something new on each visit.

If you want to discover *anything* related to what's happening in the world of *Buffy* and *Angel* and all of those associated with it, *Whedonesque* (www.whedonesque.com) should be your first port of call. The site also boasts a large, and impressive, fan forum. Dan Erenberg's *Slayage* (www.slayage.com) should be your second, boasting a massive archive of interviews, articles, reviews and media resources.

The Angel Annex Presented by The Sunnydale Slayers (http://rhiannon.dreamhost.com/angel/) is part of the SUNS group and was, according to the authors, set up by 'a gang of people . . . who wanted to talk about, lust after and discuss in depth *Buffy*'. It includes fiction, well-written reviews and biographies. Chrystal's *Angel's Secrets* (http://www.geocities.com/angelsecrets) is a long-running site devoted to all-things-Boreanaz and is always worth a visit. It includes a news section with numerous links to obscure interviews. *The Sanctuary Devoted to David Boreanaz and Angel* (http://sanctuary.digitalspace.net/) prides itself on being 'the most comprehensive site on *Angel* on the Net'. It's certainly very impressive, with extensive fan-fiction and a section containing detailed episode summaries and reviews.

Two Demons, A Girl & A Bat Cave (http://angel.fcpages.com/) is an intelligent domain that shares many qualities with the equally impressive *Complete Buffy Episode Guide* (www.buffyguide.com) featuring full episode synopses, reviews and character studies. It does take a while to load, however, so be patient. http://www.ayelle.net/thecityofangel/ (*The City of Angel*) is another highly entertaining and enthusiastic site with a big section on 'creative fandom' (fiction and artwork). *An Angel's Soul* (www.angelicslayer.com/angelsoul/main.html) is a spin-off from the legendary *Buffy Cross and Stake* (www.angelicslayer.com/tbcs/main.html) and has an impressive media section containing interviews and lots of good links. http://cityofangel.com/ (*City of Angel*) is beautifully designed and has lots of unique content, with production staff and comics-related interviews, a 'behind the scenes' section and excellent news coverage.

www.slayerfanfic.com (*The Slayer Fanfic Archive*) is, as the name suggests, dedicated to *Buffy* and *Angel* fan-fiction of all kinds with links to many related pages. www.buffysmut.com (*Bad Girls*) is a *must* for those adult readers who are yet to discover the joys of 'shipper-fic and slash-fic. More fan-fiction can be found at the likes of *Slashing the Angel* (ficbitch.com/slashingtheangel/), *The Darker Side of Sunnydale* (www.tdos.com), *Weetabix & Alcohol* (http://weetabixandalcohol.freewebtools.com) and *The Sandlot* (www.the-sandlot.com/). 'I love fan-fic', Jane

Espenson told the *Posting Board*. 'There's some great stuff out there. Also some crappy stuff, but people should feel free to read/write that as well.' On the same forum, Joss once commented: 'On the subject of fanfic, I am aware that a good deal of it is naughty. My reaction to that is mixed; on the one hand, these are characters played by friends of mine, and the idea that someone is describing them in full naughtitude is a little creepy. On the other, eroticising the lives of fictional characters you care about is something we all do, if only in our heads, and it certainly shows that people care. So I'm not really against erotic-fic and I certainly don't mind the other kind. I wish I'd had this kind of forum when I was a kid.'

Marti Noxon, meanwhile, is full of praise for the genre. 'We're in a weird position,' she told the *Washington Post*. 'It's flattering because a universe you're part of has inspired people to continue imagining.' The *Buffy* and *Angel* writers, however, have to be careful as a TV story with similarities to a previously published piece of fanfiction could result in accusations of plagiarism. 'Because of legalities, we have to be judicious how much we read.'

Both Charisma Carpenter and David Boreanaz have numerous unofficial websites: www.charisma-carpenter.com (*Charisma-Carpenter.com*) and www.david-boreanaz.com (*David-Boreanaz.com*) are among the best. There are also several impressive Alexis Denisof pages like *Go Wes Go* (http://naturalblues.org/gowesgo/) and *AD Unofficial* (http://ad.elusio.net/). Among the vast plethora of James Marsters fansites are www.JamesMarsters.com (*The Official James Marsters site*) which has an excellent archive from the, now-defunct, *Spike Spotting*, as well as regular updates and shout-outs to fans from the man himself. For up-to-date Marsters news, check out www.morethan-spike.com.

Christian Kane has a terrific unofficial website *Christian-Kane.net* (http://christiankane.cjb.net/) which includes details on his musical activities. Fans of everyone's favourite empath demon will enjoy www.andyhallett.com. Curiously, one of the best general *Angel* sites around is dedicated to a former cast member. Tara O'Shea's *Doyle – Glenn Quinn* (http://ljconstantine.com/doyle/) is a beautiful celebration of both the series and the much-missed actor.

Miscellaneous: Space prevents a thoroughly detailed study of the vast array of *Buffy* and *Angel* websites from around the world, but a few deserve to be highlighted.

For European readers the following sites offer impressive local coverage:

- France's *Black Angel* (www.ifrance.com/blackangelfan/)
- Germany's *Angel Investigations* (www.angelinvestigations. de/)
- *The Italian Angel Page* (www.buffysweetslayer.com/ italianangelpage/)
- *Buffy in Ireland* (www.//bite.to/Buffy)
- *Dutch Buffy* (http://members.tripod.lycos.nl.dutchbtvs)
- Iceland's *Blódsugubaninn Buffy* (http://oto.is/buffy/ inngangur.htm)
- Portugal's *Buffy, a Caça Vampiros Page* (www.geocities/ edilal/novaseries.htm)
- Sweden's *Totally Buffy* (http://medlem.spray.se/Totally_ Buffy)
- *Buffy in Israel* (www.geocities.com/TelevisionCity/ Station/9409)

Readers down under are advised to check out:

- *Angel's Southern Cross* (www.angelfire.com/wa2/angel-thorn/).
- Danny Sag's excellent *Buffy and Angel Episode Title Explanations* (www.geocities.com/glpoj/buffy/)
- www.buffy.com.au/

If intellectual debate is your thing then head for *Tea at the Ford* (www.teaattheford.net), where *Buffy*, *Angel* and mythology meet and mingle. Also recommended for *Angel*'s intelligentsia is *Slayage The Online Academic Journal* (www.slayage.tv). The site sponsors several academic conferences and is guaranteed to boggle even the brightest brain by analysing the shows in quite mind-melting detail. For excellent episode summaries and guides try *Angel's Acolyte* (www.angelsacolytecom). *Countdown to Redemption* (http://angelsredemption.mainpage.net/) also has several unique features. *Mutant Boosters, Obsessed, Vocal, Organised* (www.mutantboosters.com) is an attractive and informative site with a host of forums dedicated to the cast, crew and writers. It's packed with news and information and has an impressive links section. *Cold Dead Seed* (www.forum/colddeadseed.com) is a very funny, irreverent and good-natured Spike/Angel forum.

At www.google.com, just a few clicks will take you from the useful and informative to the downright bizarre (ever wanted to know what would happen if Spike and Cap'n Jack Sparrow met? If so, you'll find it). Finally, there's www.buffysearch.com ('your portal to the *Buffy* and *Angel* community'), a truly invaluable search engine that includes links to most of the above sites and, literally, thousands more. Happy surfing.

Select Bibliography

The following books, articles, interviews and reviews were consulted in the preparation of this text:

Abery, James, 'Where Angel Fears to Tread', *Shivers*, issue 71, November 1999.

Abery, James, 'Fallen Angel?', *Shivers*, issue 102, January 2003.

'A Charismatic Exit?', *TV Zone*, issue 173, February 2004.

Acker, Amy, and Denisof, Alexis, 'Angel's Angels', interview by Jenny Cooney Carrillo, *DreamWatch*, issue 103, April 2003.

Acker, Amy, 'The Rose of Texas', interview by Grant Kempster and Judy Sloane, *Starburst*, Special #60, October 2003.

Acker, Amy, 'Science Vixen', interview by Steven Eramo, *TV Zone*, issue 175, April 2004.

Adalin, Josef, and Schneider, Michael, 'Plots are hot-spots for Net', *Daily Variety*, 23 September 2001.

Adalin, Josef, 'A trail of modest moves', *Daily Variety*, 6 January 2004.

Adams, Michael, *Slayer Slang: A Buffy the Vampire Slayer Lexicon*, Oxford University Press, 2003.

Amatangelo, Amy, '*Angel* raises the stakes with familiar faces in new setting', *Boston Herald*, 1 October 2003.

'Angel Restores Faith', *DreamWatch*, issue 68, April 2000.

'Angel's Darkest Day', *DreamWatch*, issue 103, April 2003.

'*Angel*: Magic, Mystery & the Unknown', *Xposé*, issue 85, May 2004.

Anthony, Ted, '12 Weeks After Columbine, Delayed "Buffy" airs', *Associated Press*, 12 July 1999.

Appelo, Tim and Williams, Stephanie, 'Get Buffed Up – A Definitive Episode Guide', *TV Guide*, July 1999.

Arpe, Malene, '*Angel* fights to the bleak, bitter end: Joss Whedon's last show bows', *Toronto Star*, 20 May 2004.

Arpe, Malene, 'Television's afterlife: In the world of fan fiction, great characters never die. They just get new scripts', *Toronto Star*, 22 May 2004.

Atherton, Tony, 'Fantasy TV: The New Reality', *Ottawa Citizen*, 27 January 2000.

Atkins, Ian, 'Fallen Angel', *Cult Times*, issue 47, August 1999.

Atkins, Ian, 'I Will Remember You' review, *Shivers*, issue 77, May 2000.

Ausiello, Michael, '*Angel* Mystery: Will Cordy Wake Up?', *TV Guide*, 26 May 2003.

Baldwin, Adam, 'Partners in Crime', interview by K Stoddard Hayes, *DreamWatch*, issue 119, August 2004.

Baldwin, Kristen, Fretts, Bruce, Schilling, Mary Kaye and Tucker, Ken, 'Slay Ride', *Entertainment Weekly*, issue 505, 1 October 1999.

Barratt, Brian, 'Rm W/a Vu', 'Sense and Sensitivity', 'The Bachelor Party' and 'I Will Remember You' reviews, *Xposé*, issue 42, January 2000.

Barratt, Brian, 'First Impressions', 'Untouched', 'Dear Boy' and 'Guise Will Be Guise' reviews, *Xposé*, issue 52, January 2001.

Barratt, Brian, 'Darla', 'The Shroud of Rahmon', 'Trial', 'Reunion' reviews, *Xposé*, issue 53, February 2001.

Barrett, Brian, 'Waiting in the Wings' to 'Sleep Tight', *Xposé*, issue 67, May 2002.

Barrett, David V, 'Far more than a teenage fang club', *Independent*, 3 January 2002.

Bell, Jeffrey, 'Ringing the Changes', interview by Bryan Cairns, *Cult Times*, Special #28, November 2003.

Benz, Julie, 'Little Miss Understood', interview by Ed Gross, *SFX Unofficial Buffy Collection*, 2000.

Benz, Julie, 'Princess of the Night', interview by Ian Spelling, *Starlog*, issue 14, June 2001.

Bernstein, Abbie, 'A date with destiny', *DreamWatch*, issue 113, February 2004.

Bianco, Robert, 'The good, the bad and the ugly of 2002 TV', *USA Today*, 22 December 2002.

Bianco, Robert, 'TV shows worth making time for', *USA Today*, 21 November 2003.

Bianculli, David, 'Fallen *Angel*: A Grand Finale', *New York Daily News*, 19 May 2004.

Billings, Laura, ' "Like, Duh," says Gen Y', *St Paul Pioneer Press*, 10 October 2000.

Binns, John, 'Times Past', *Cult Times*, issue 93, June 2003.

'Blood-thirsty scholars gulp *Buffy*-related concoctions', *Chicago Tribune*, 7 November 2002.

Bone, James, 'Declaration of Ignorance as American teenagers flunk July 4 Quiz', *The Times*, 4 July 2001.

Boreanaz, David, Landau, Juliet and Marsters, James, 'Interview with the Vampires', interview by Tim Appelo, *TV Guide*, September 1998.

Boreanaz, David, 'Leaders of the Pack', interview (with Kerri Russell) by Janet Weeks, *TV Guide*, November 1998.

Boreanaz, David, 'City of Angel', interview by David Richardson, *Xposé*, issue 35, June 1999.

Boreanaz, David, 'Aurora Boreanaz', interview by Sue Schneider, *DreamWatch*, issue 69, May 2000.

Boreanaz, David, 'Good or Bad Angel?', interview by David Richardson, *Shivers*, issue 77, May 2000.

Boreanaz, David, 'Moving On Up', interview by Christina Radish, *DreamWatch*, issue 80, May 2001.

Boreanaz, David, 'Dead Man Talking', interview by Jenny Cooney Carrillo, *DreamWatch*, issue 96, September 2002.

Boreanaz, David, 'Voice of an Angel', interview by Jean Cummings, *Cult Times*, issue 86, November 2002.

Boreanaz, 'Reflections of the Undead', interview by Joe Nazzaro, *Starburst*, Special #57, March 2003.

Boreanaz, David, 'Avenging Angel', interview by Steven Eramo, *TV Zone*, issue 166, July 2003.

Bradney, Anthony, 'Choosing Law, Choosing Family: Images of Law, Love and Authority in *Buffy the Vampire Slayer*', in *Web Journal of Current Legal Issues*, 2002.

Breznican, Anthony, 'Sci-fi convention life or death for Hollywood's superheroes', *South Florida Sun-Sentinel*, 28 July 2004.

Britt, Donna, 'The Truth About Teen TV', *TV Guide*, 28 October 2000.

Brown, Anthony, Eramo, Steven and May, Dominic, '*Angel* Cancelled', *TV Zone*, issue 174, March 2004.

'Buffy roots out the adolescent demon in all of us', *This is Leicestershire*, 24 January 2003.

Bunson, Matthew, *Vampire: The Encyclopaedia*, Thames and Hudson, 1993.

Campagna, Suze, 'Website of the Month', *Intergalactic Enquirer*, March 2000.

Campagna, Suze, 'Bite Me: The History of Vampires on Television', *Intergalactic Enquirer*, October 2000.

Campagna, Suze: 'The World of Joss Whedon', *Intergalactic Enquirer*, February 2001.

Campagna, Suze, 'TV Tid Bits', *Intergalactic Enquirer*, March 2001.

Carpenter, Charisma, 'Charismatic', interview by Jim Boulter, *SFX*, issue 40, July 1998.

Carpenter, Charisma, 'Femme Fatale', interview by Mike Peake, *FHM*, issue 117, October 1999.

Carpenter, Charisma, 'Charisma Personified', interview by Jennifer Graham, *TV Guide*, 1 January 2000.

Carpenter, Charisma, 'In Step With . . .' interview by James Brady, *Parade*, 5 March 2000.

Carpenter, Charisma, 'Charisma!', interview by Ed Gross, *SFX*, issue 75, March 2001.

Carpenter, Charisma, 'Heaven Sent', interview by Jenny Cooney Carrillo, *DreamWatch*, issue 103, April 2003.

Carter, Bill, '*Dawson's Clones*: Tapping into the youth market for all it is, or isn't, worth', *New York Times*, 19 September 1999.

'Celebrity Shame', *Dolly*, October 2000.

Chan, Paul, '*Angel* faces do it all for laughs', *Huddersfield Daily Examiner*, 17 July 2002.

'Chase is On, The', *Cult Times*, issue 82, July 2002.

'Cheers and Jeers', *TV Guide*, 2 December 2000.

Chin, Richard, 'Single-minded viewers: Some folks tune in to television for one – and only one – show. How do they do that?', *St Paul's Pioneer Press*, 22 April 2003.

Collins, Scott, '*Buffy* star goes to the woodshed over remark about sticking with The WB', *Los Angeles Times*, 30 January 2001.

Cornell, Paul, Day, Martin and Topping, Keith, *The Guinness Book of Classic British TV*, second edition, Guinness Publishing, 1996.

Cornell, Paul, Day, Martin and Topping, Keith, *X-Treme Possibilities: A Comprehensively Expanded Rummage Through the X-Files*, Virgin Publishing, 1998.

Cornell, Paul, '20th Century Fox-Hunting', *SFX*, issue 63, April 2000.

Danford, Natalie, 'Pop Goes Philosophy', *Publishers Weekly*, 3 February 2003.

Darlington, David, 'Heartthrob' to 'Fredless' reviews, *Shivers*, issue 94, December 2001.

Darlington, David, 'Billy' to 'Dad' reviews, *Shivers*, issue 95, February 2002.

Darlington, David, 'Waiting in the Wings' to 'Sleep Tight' reviews, *Shivers*, issue 97, May 2002.

Darlington, David, 'Deep Down' to 'Slouching Towards Bethlehem' reviews, *Shivers*, issue 101, November 2002.

Darlington, David, 'Supersymmetry', to 'Spin the Bottle' reviews, *Shivers*, issue 102, January 2003.

Darlington, David, 'Soulless' to 'Salvage' reviews, *Shivers*, issue 104, May 2003.

Darlington, David, 'Life of the Party' to 'Destiny' reviews, *Shivers*, issue 110, February 2004.

Darlington, David, 'Harm's Way' to 'Damage' reviews, *Shivers*, issue 111, March 2004.

DeKnight, Steven, 'DeKnight in Shining Armour', interview by Joe Nazzaro, *DreamWatch*, issue 103, April 2003.

DeKnight, Steven, 'Creatures of DeKnight', interview by Joe Nazzaro, *TV Zone*, issue 167, August 2003.

DeKnight, Steven, 'DeKnight's Tale', interview by Steven Eramo, *Xposé*, Special #26, July 2004.

Denisof, Alexis, 'A Revival of Spirit', interview by Simon Bacal, *Xposé*, issue 43, February 2000.

Denisof, Alexis, 'Vogue Demon Hunter', interview by Matt Springer, *Buffy the Vampire Slayer*, issue 7, Spring 2000.

Denisof, Alexis, 'Half Price', interview by Paul Spragg, *Xposé*, issue 65, March 2002.

Denisof, Alexis, 'The Right Pryce', interview by Steven Eramo, *TV Zone*, issue 150, April 2002.

Denisof, Alexis, 'Denisof On One', interview by Jean Cummings, *Cult Times*, issue 86, November 2002.

Denisof, Alexis, 'Paying the Pryce', interview by Abbie Bernstein, *DreamWatch*, issue 119, August 2004.

Dougherty, Diana, 'Angel – Season One', *Intergalactic Enquirer*, July 2000.

Duffy, Mike, 'All seems to be rotating perfectly on Planet Buffy', *TV Weekly*, October 1999.

Dushku, Eliza, 'Keeping Faith', interview by Ed Gross, *SFX Unofficial Buffy Collection*, 2000.

Ellis, Martin, 'Bad Girl Does Good', *Shivers*, issue 104, May 2003.

Eramo, Steven, 'Exterminating Angel', *TV Zone*, issue 175, April 2004.

Espenson, Jane, 'Superstar Scribe', interview by Joe Nazzaro, *DreamWatch*, issue 74, November 2000.

Espenson, Jane, 'The Write Stuff', interview by Joe Nazzaro, *DreamWatch*, issue 103, April 2003.

Ferguson, Everett, *Backgrounds of Early Christianity* [second edition], William B Eerdmans Publishing, 1993.

Francis, Rob, '*Buffy the Vampire Slayer* Season 4', *DreamWatch*, issue 71, August 2000.

Francis, Rob, 'TV Heroes', *TV Zone*, Special #45, April 2002.

Francis, Rob, 'Pop Idols' in *Buffy the Vampire Slayer: the Official 2002 Yearbook*, Pocket Books, 2002.

Fretts, Bruce, 'City of Angel', *Entertainment Weekly*, April 1999.

Frutkin, AJ, 'Generation Next', *Media Week*, 3 February 2003.

Fury, David, 'Interview with the Vampire Producer', interview by Cherise Huang, *Northwestern Chronicle*, 30 October 2003.

Gabriel, Jan, *Meet the Stars of Buffy the Vampire Slayer: An Unauthorized Biography*, Scholastic Inc., 1998.

Gammage, Jeff, 'Guardian Angel', *Inquirer*, September 2000.

Gellar, Sarah Michelle, 'Staking the Future', interview by John Mosby, *DreamWatch*, issue 61, September 1999.

Giglione, Joan, 'Some Shows Aren't Big on TV', *Los Angeles Times*, 25 November 2000.

Ginn, John, 'Take a bite out of bad media', *Corvallis Gazette-Times*, 20 May 2004.

Gottlieb, Allie, '*Buffy*'s Angels', *Silicon Valley Metro*, 2 October 2002.

Gray, Ellen, 'There's nowhere that *Angel* star fears to tread', *Knight Ridder Newspapers*, 24 February 2002.

Green, Michelle Erica, 'Darla and Topolsky Are More Than Bad Girls', *Fandom Inc*, September 2000.

Greenwalt, David, '*Angel* delivers a devil of a time', interview by Charlie Mason, *TV Guide*, 14 August 2001.

Greenwalt, David, 'Angel's Guardian', interview by James Abery, *Shivers*, issue 98, July 2002.

Greenwalt, David, 'Miracles Do Happen', interview by David Richardson, *Xposé*, issue 76, January 2003.

Gross, Ed, 'The Trial', 'Reunion' reviews, *SFX*, issue 75, March 2001.

Hallett, Andy, 'Angelic Host,' interview by Pat Jankiewicz, *Starburst*, issue 272, April 2001.

Hallett, Andy, 'Smells Like Green Spirit', interview by Tom Mayo, *SFX*, issue 81, August 2001.

Hallett, Andy and Lutz, Mark, 'The two gentlemen of Pylea', interview by Nick Joy, *Starburst*, issue 289, July 2002.

Hallett, Andy, 'Jolly Green Demon', interview by Steven Eramo, *TV Zone*, issue 173, February 2004.

Hallett, Andy, 'The Final Curtain', interview by Abbie Bernstein and Chloe Richards, *DreamWatch*, issue 119, August 2004.

Hanks, Robert, 'Deconstructing Buffy', *Independent*, 1 July 2002.

Hannigan, Alyson, 'Willow Pattern', interview by Kate O'Hare, *Sydney Herald News*, 1 February 2003.

Hayes, K Stoddard, 'Destiny' reviews, *DreamWatch*, issue 113, February 2004.

Head, Anthony Stewart, 'Heads or Tails', interview by Paul Simpson and Ruth Thomas, *DreamWatch*, issue 69, May 2000.

Heldenfels, RD, 'Doomed *Angel* still good TV', *Beacon Journal*, 17 February 2004.

'Hell is for Heroes', *Entertainment Weekly*, issue 505, 1 October 1999.

Hibbs, Thomas S, 'Forget about the world . . . *Buffy* saved TV', *The National Review*, 22 May 2003.

Hiestand, Jesse, 'Push to Speed Up Scripts Working, DGA Says', the *Hollywood Reporter*, 12 July 2004.

Holder, Nancy, *Angel: city of – a novelisation of the series premiere*, Pocket Pulse, December 1999.

Huddleston, Kathie, '*Angel* Season Five Premiere: Running the LA branch of an evil law firm adds a whole new level of complication to helping the helpless', *Science Fiction Weekly*, 15 October 2003.

Huff, Richard. 'WB Net Returns to Gender-Build on Initial Appeal Among Young Women', *New York Daily News* 14 September 1999.

Jervis, Lisa, 'Decoding Hot Girl-on-Girl Action', *LiP*, July 2004.

Johnson, Allan, 'Willow's Soulful Visit Illuminates *Angel*', *Chicago Tribune*, 19 March 2003.

Katner, Ben with Michael Ausiello, 'Is *Angel* Livin' On A Prayer?', *TV Guide*, 5 May 2003.

Katz, Paul S, 'Fans rally for their favorite vampire', *TV Guide*, 12 April 2003.

Kaveney, Roz [ed], *Reading the Vampire Slayer: An Unofficial Critical Companion to Buffy and Angel*, 2001.

Kempster, Grant, 'Preview *Angel*', *Cult Times*, Special #28, November 2003.

Kiesewetter, John, '*Angel*, *Buffy*, *Dawson* may end', *Cincinnati Enquirer*, 13 January 2003.

Landau, Juliet, 'Dear Girl', interview by David Richardson, *Xposé*, Special #26, July 2004.

Lenk, Tom, 'The Geek Makes Good', interview by Joe Nazzaro, *Starburst*, Special 60, November 2003.

Levin, Gary, 'WB plans fresher approach to programming', *USA Today*, 14 July 2004.

Littlefield, Kinney, 'Avenging Angel', *The Orange County Register*, October 1999.

Love, Lorie, 'Los Alamos to Hollywood: Goddard finds success as television writer for popular series', *Los Alamos Monitor*, 2 February 2004.

Lowry, Brian, 'WB Covers A Trend Too Well', *Los Angeles Times*, 29 June 2000.

MacDonald, Ian, *Revolution in the Head* – second edition, Fourth Estate Ltd, 1997.

MacFarlane, Melanie, 'It's not easy being green: WB could croak on its new lineup', *Seattle Post-Intelligencer*, 16 January 2004.

MacIntyre, Ben, 'Anti-globalist child of Seattle?', *Statesman*, November 2003.

Madden, Michelle, 'Total Faith', *Mean*, July 2001.

Malcolm, Shawna, 'Angel Bites', *TV Guide*, 4 May 2002.

Malcolm, Shawna, 'The Big Fang Theory', *TV Guide*, 6 September 2003.

Malcolm, Shawna, 'Interview with the Vampire', *TV Guide*, 31 January 2004.

Malcolm, Shawna, 'Goodbye, *Angel*', *TV Guide*, 16 May 2004.

Marsters, James and Caulfield, Emma, 'Vamping It Up', *Alloy*, Summer 2000.

Marsters, James, 'I, Spike', interview by Ed Gross, *SFX Unofficial Buffy Collection*, 2000.

Marsters, James, 'Life at the Sharp End', interview by John Reading, *TV Zone*, issue 164, June 2003.

Marsters, James, 'Dead Man Talking', interview by Steve Dexter, *DreamWatch*, issue 107, August 2003.

Marsters, James, 'Marsters' Mind', interview by Steven Eramo, *TV Zone*, issue 177, May 2004.

Marsters, James, 'Marsters and Commander', interview by Steven Eramo, *TV Zone*, issue 178, June 2004.

Martino, John, 'Dead, Sexy', *Shivers*, issue 96, March 2002.

Mason, Dave, 'When Bad Things Happen To Good Vampires', Scripps Howard News Service, 22 October 2002.

Mauger, Anne-Marie, 'Staking their Claims', *Sky Customer Magazine*, January 2001.

May, Dominic, '*Angel* co-creator says show's future is secure', *TV Zone*, issue 150, May 2002.

May, Dominic, and Spilsbury, Tom, 'Return to Sunnydale High for Buffy Season 7', *TV Zone*, issue 153, July 2002.

May, Dominic, *Angel* 'I Quit', *TV Zone*, issue 154, August 2002.

McCamish, Tom, 'TV or not TV? That is the question', *The Age*, November 2003.

McCollum, Charlie, 'Joss Whedon gets so many ideas, he feels overwhelmed', *Mercury News*, 19 August 2002.

McIntee, David, *Delta Quadrant: The Unofficial Guide to Voyager*, Virgin Publishing, 2000.

McLean, Gareth, 'Channel Surfing: Why *Buffy* is the best show ever', *Guardian*, 13 November 2002.

McNab, Mercedes, 'Vamping it Up!' interview by Steven Eramo, *Xposé*, issue 81, November 2003.

Middendorf, Tracy, 'Insider: The Next Guest Thing', interview by Shawn Malcom, *TV Guide*, 15 January 2000.

Minear, Tim, '*Angel*: Year One', interview by Ed Gross, *SFX Unofficial Buffy Collection*, 2000.

Mollen, Jenny, 'Never Work with Boyfriends, Werewolves or Puppets', interview by Bryan Cairns, *Xposé*, Special 26, July 2004.

Moore, Jennifer, 'Copyright Protection or Fan Loyalty – Must Entertainment Companies Choose? Addressing Internet Fan Sites', *North Carolina Journal of Law and Technology*, 2002.

Mosby, John, 'UK-TV', *DreamWatch*, issue 71, September 2000.

Mosby, John, 'Last Writes', *Impact*, issue 127, July 2002.

Nelson, Resa, 'Angel makes us ask: why do bad boys make us feel so good?', *Realms of Fantasy*, February 2000.

Nelson, Resa, 'To Live and Die in LA', *Science Fiction World*, issue 1, June 2000.

Norton, Phillip, 'Fang-tastic fans of *Buffy* question star', *Grimsby Telegraph*, 30 April 2003.

Noxon, Marti, 'Soul Survivor', *DreamWatch*, issue 63, November 1999.

Nussbaum, Emily, 'Confessions of a Spoiler Whore', *Slate*, 4 April 2002.

O'Hare, Kate, 'WB's Core Series *Buffy* and *Angel* Cross Time and Space', *TV Weekly*, 12 November 2000.

O'Hare, Kate, 'While *Buffy* Rages, *Angel* Still Flies', *St Paul Pioneer Press*, 15 April 2001.

O'Hare, Kate, 'The sun sets on *Buffy the Vampire Slayer*', *St Paul Pioneer Press*, 18 May 2003.

Pearce, Gareth, 'Alyson Hannigan: She Shoots, She Scores', *The Times*, 13 July 2003.

Pierce, Scott D, 'Spike is in, Cordelia is out', *Deseret News*, 26 May 2003.

Queenan, Joe, 'Cross-Checked By An Angel', *TV Guide*, 15 April 2000.

Richards, J August, 'Gunn Fighting', interview by Mark Wyman, *Cult Times*, Special #16, 2000.

Richards, J August, 'Smoking Gunn', interview by Steven Eramo, *TV Zone*, issue 136, February 2001.

Richards, J August, 'Real Gunn Kid', interview by Paul Simpson and Ruth Thomas, *SFX*, issue 81, August 2001.

Richards, J August, 'Gunn Fighter', interview by Jennifer Dudley, *Sydney Herald Sun*, 29 January 2003.

Richards, J August, 'Charles in Charge', interview by Steven Eramo, *TV Zone*, issue 160, February 2003.

Richards, J August, and Kartheiser, Vincent, 'Younger Guns', interview by Jenny Cooney Carrillo, *DreamWatch*, issue 102, March 2003.

Richardson, David, 'The House Always Wins' to 'Spin the Bottle' reviews, *Xposé*, issue 76, January 2003.

Richardson, David, '*Angel* Hits 100', *TV Zone*, issue 173, February 2004.

Richardson, David, '*Angel*'s Happy 100th?', *Shivers*, issue 111, March 2004.

Richardson, David, 'Why We Fight', to 'Shells' reviews, *Xposé*, issue 85, May 2004.

'Right Said Fred, Angelic Amy Acker has a lot at stake in *Angel*', *Femme Fatales*, February 2004.

Robins, Max J, 'To Be Or WB? It's No Longer A Question', *TV Guide*, 1 January 2003.

Robson, Ian, 'Action Reply: Buffy's Show'll Slay You' ('City Of' review), *Sunday Sun*, 9 January 2000.

Romanov, Stephanie, 'The Rise of the Romanov Empire', interview by Nick Joy, *DreamWatch*, issue 96, September 2002.

Romanov, Stephanie, 'Naughty, But Nice', interview by Steven Eramo, *TV Zone*, issue 162, April 2003.

Roush, Matt, 'The Roush Review', *TV Guide*, 11 December 1999.

Roush, Matt, 'The Roush Review: Alluring *Angel* Stingless Scorpion', *TV Guide*, 17 February 2001.

Roush, Matt, 'The Roush Review: Great Performances – Andy Hallett', *TV Guide*, 21 April 2001.

Roush, Matt, 'Daddy Darkest', *TV Guide*, 13 April 2002.

Roush, Matt, 'Roush Rave', *TV Guide*, 8 March 2003.

Roush, Matt, 'Touched by *Angel* fans', *TV Guide*, 11 April 2004.

Rowland, Marijke, 'Sadly floating away from last of the Buffyverse', *Modesto Bee*, 28 May 2004.

Ryan, Maureen, with Raoul Mowatt, 'Touched by *Angel*; A fond farewell to the small but superb show that proved vampires are people, too', *Chicago Tribune*, 19 May 2004.

Sangster, Jim and Bailey, David, *Friends Like Us: The Unofficial Guide to Friends* [revised edition], Virgin Books, 2000.

'Sarah gets a spanking: *Buffy* star forced to eat humble-pie after "Quit" gaff', *Daily News*, 31 January 2001.

Sepinwall, Alan, '*Buffy* Network Switch Could Slay TV Industry Practices', *St Paul Pioneer Press*, 29 April 2001.

Shaar Murray, Charles, 'A passionately perverse sexiness', *The Word*, issue 4, June 2003.

Simpson, Paul, *CSI: The Files – An Unofficial and Unauthorised Guide to the Hit Crime Scene Investigation Shows*, Virgin Books, 2003.

Simpson, Paul and Thomas, Ruth, 'Interview With The Vampire', *DreamWatch*, issue 62, October 1999.

Simpson, Paul and Thomas, Ruth, 'The Lizard King', *SFX*, issue 80, July 2001.

Smith, Jim, 'This Hollywood Life', *Starburst*, issue 283, February 2002.

Speck, Rebecca, 'Farcical end to worst kept secret of century', *Daily News*, 28 May 2003.

Spelling, Ian, 'Biting Talent – An Interview With Charisma Carpenter', *Starlog*, May 2000.

Stafford, Nikki, 'Farewell, it's been fun', *Globe and Mail*, 1 May 2004.

Stanley, TL, 'Is It the End of the Road for *Buffy-Angel* Connection?', *Los Angeles Times*, 21 May 2001.

Streisand, Betsy, 'Young, hip and no-longer-watching-Fox', *US News & World Report*, 15 November 1999.

Thompson, Sarah, 'All About Eve', interview by Steven Eramo, *Xposé*, Special #26, July 2004.

Topping, Keith, *Slayer: The Revised and Updated Unofficial Guide to Buffy the Vampire Slayer*, Virgin Books, 2000.

Topping, Keith, *High Times: The Unofficial & Unauthorised Guide to Roswell*, Virgin Books, 2001.

Topping, Keith, *Inside Bartlet's White House: An Unofficial and Unauthorised Guide to The West Wing*, Virgin Books, 2002.

Topping, Keith, *Beyond the Gate: The Unofficial and Unauthorised Guide to Stargate SG-1*, Telos Publishing, 2002.

Topping Keith, *Slayer: The Next Generation: An Unofficial and Unauthorised Guide to Season Six of Buffy the Vampire Slayer*, Virgin Books, 2003.

Topping, Keith, *A Day in the Life: The Unofficial and Unauthorised Guide to 24*, Telos Publishing, 2003.

Topping, Keith, *Slayer: The Last Days of Sunnydale: An Unofficial and Unauthorised Guide to Season Seven of Buffy the Vampire Slayer*, Virgin Books, 2004.

Topping, Keith, 'Angel Delight', *DreamWatch*, issue 65, January 2000.

Topping, Keith, '*Sed Quis Custodiet Ipsos Custodes*?', *Intergalactic Enquirer*, May 2001.

Topping, Keith, 'Has *Buffy* Jumped the Shark?', *Shivers*, issue 97, May 2002.

Topping, Keith, '*Les Cirques des Vampires*', *Shivers*, issue 100, September 2002.

Topping, Keith, 'Reviews 2002: *Angel*', *TV Zone*, Special #45, October 2002.

Topping, Keith, *Angel* Season Four reviews, *TV Zone*, issues 157–164, November 2002–June 2003.

Topping, Keith, 'So Let Me Rest in Peace', *TV Zone*, issue 158, December 2002.

Topping, Keith, 'Do You Know This Man?', *TV Zone*, issue 160, February 2003.

Topping, Keith, 'This town ain't big enough . . .' *Shivers*, issue 107, September 2003.

Topping, Keith, '*Angel*'s Return', *Shivers*, issue 108, October 2003.

Topping, Keith, *Angel* Season Five reviews, *TV Zone*, issues 169–178, October 2003–June 2004.

Topping, Keith, 'A Long Dark Journey into Right', *Xposé*, Special #26, July 2004.

Topping, Keith, '*Angel* Top 25 Episodes', *Xposé*, Special #26, July 2004.

Torres, Gina, 'Heaven Scent?', interview by Paul Spragg, *Cult Times*, issue 93, June 2003.

Tsai, Michael, 'Slaying stereotypes, one fan risks ridicule to defend *Buffy*', *Honolulu Advertiser*, 26 May 2003.

Tucker, Ken, 'Angel Baby', *Entertainment Weekly*, 3 December 1999.

Udovitch, Mim, 'What Makes Buffy Slay?', *Rolling Stone*, issue 840, 11 May 2000.

Udovitch, Mim, 'We Like Spike', *New York Magazine*, 9 December 2002.

van Beek, Anton, 'Bite Me!', *Total DVD*, issue 21, January 2001.

'Veteran shows chase lost glory with fresh faces, new angles', *USA Today*, 16 December 2003.

Walton, Rob, 'Earth Angel: Naked Charisma', *Playboy*, June 2004.

'WB shows class with *Jack & Bobby*', *Alameda Times-Star*, 17 July 2004.

Weir, William, 'Wesleyan Mafia Racks Up Credits: New Center For Film Studies Is Evidence Of A College Program Building On Success', *The Hartford Courant*, 30 December 2002.

'*West Wing* dips, *Angel* soars', *USA Today*, 20 May 2004.

Whedon, Joss, 'How I Got To Do What I Do', interview by Wolf Schneider, *teen movieline*, issue 1, March 2000.

Whedon, Joss, 'Whedon, Writing and Arithmetic', interview by Joe Mauceri, *Shivers*, issue 77, May 2000.

Whedon, Joss, 'Blood Lust', interview by Rob Francis, *DreamWatch*, issues 71–72, August/September, 2000.

Whedon, Joss, 'Prophecy Boy', interview by Matt Springer with Mike Stokes, *Buffy the Vampire Slayer*, issue 20, May 2001.

Whedon, Joss, 'Buffy, R.I.P.?', interview by John Mosby, *DreamWatch*, issue 84, September 2001.

Whedon, Joss, 'The Wonderful World of Whedon', interview by Ian Spelling, *Cult Times*, issue 79, April 2002.

Whedon, Joss, 'Tales from the Crypt', interview by Ian Spelling, *Starburst*, Special #60, November 2003.

Whedon, Joss, 'Life after *Buffy*', interview by Camilla and Neil, *The Face*, issue 84, January 2004.

'Whedon Reflects Post-*Buffy*', *TV Zone*, issue 164, June 2003.

Wigmore, Gareth, 'Powers That Be Wanted Us Here', *TV Zone*, issue 154, August 2002.

Wilcox, Rhonda V and Lavery, David [eds], *Fighting the Forces: What's at Stake in Buffy the Vampire Slayer*, Rowan & Littlefield Publishers Inc., 2002.

Wilde, MJ, 'The TV Queen', *Albuquerque Tribune*, 1 October 2002.

Williams, Zoe, 'The lady and the vamp – a buff's guide to *Buffy*,' *Guardian*, 17 November 2001.

Williamson, Kevin, 'Cancellation Bites', *Calgary Sun*, 18 February 2004.

Woodward, Jonathan, 'Conversations with a Frequently Dead Person', interview by Bryan Cairns, *Xposé*, Special #26, July 2004.

Wright, Matthew, 'Endings and New Beginnings', *Science Fiction World*, issue 2, July 2000.

Wyman, Mark, 'Buffy Joins The Banned – A Fable for the Internet Age', *Shivers*, issue 68, August 1999.

Wyman, Mark, 'The Thin Dead Line', 'Reprise', 'Epiphany' reviews, *TV Zone*, issue 140, July 2001.

Wyman, Mark, 'Who's The Daddy?', *TV Zone*, issue 150, April 2002.

Wyman, Mark, 'The Price' to 'Tomorrow' reviews, *TV Zone*, issue 152, June 2002.

Wyman, Mark, '*Buffy* and *Angel* in 2003', *Xposé*, Special #24, December 2003.

Wyman, Mark, '*Angel* Season Four', *TV Zone*, Special #54, December 2003.

Zinn, Howard, *A People's History of the United States*, Harper & Row, 1980.

Grr! Arrrgh!

'There's no better way to end the five-year run of a series than for people to protest [about] its cancellation,' James Marsters noted, pithily, in May 2004. 'I want to thank all those who took the time to make their voices heard. It proves to The WB that there's still an interest in *Angel*. Who knows what might come of that?'

'I've enjoyed working with these actors that have become like family and this great crew that holds the whole thing up and makes it run,' Alexis Denisof told Abbie Bernstein. 'In every area, it's been people working to their outermost limits and giving it their all. It's felt like we've made little movies that air on TV once a week.'

For David Boreanaz, the end of the show brought mixed emotions. Using a somewhat challenging metaphor of drinking cranberry juice (beneficial but, sometimes, bitter), David told *SFX* that he was looking forward to being able to play other characters. However, he expressed his love for the fans of *Angel*, and his disappointment that the production had been unable to give them a season-long example of closure rather than to see the series end in a rush. 'The decision to cancel was purely a business one,' David noted. 'However, I felt sure that we could have done another season with what they did in terms of retooling the show for this year.' Interestingly, Charisma Carpenter, interviewed by *TV Guide* around this time, said that, while she understood the disappointment of the fans, she believed the series *had* reached a natural conclusion and she certainly wasn't interested in reprising the role of Cordelia in any proposed spin-off: 'Not because of David or anyone I worked with. I just think we're all done.'

In May, *E!Online*'s *Watch with Kristin* column obtained an interview with The WB's president Jordan Levin. Their first question, inevitably, concerned the cancellation of *Angel* and why, in Kristin's own words, one of the best-written shows on television had been replaced with what the critic described as 'unoriginal offerings from Jeff Foxworthy and Drew Carey'. 'The big problem with *Angel* is it didn't repeat well,' Levin commented. 'It wasn't growing its audience, but it was a show we adored. Joss Whedon came to me in February and said, "If you don't think the show is going to come back, I'd rather know it now, so I can end it appropriately." When we looked at our schedule, with *Charmed*, *7th Heaven*, *Gilmore Girls*, *Angel* and *Smallville*, we realised we had a lot of veteran series. One of the challenges of any schedule is to let your veterans retire so you can make room for the rookies.'

TV Guide's Matt Roush believed that there was a 'genuine regret at The WB network that *Angel* was axed prematurely, for whatever reason, especially after development of some new fantasy franchises failed to deliver.'[46] But with Joss Whedon busy making *Serenity*, his movie spin-off of *Firefly*, Roush believed that it would be 'a while' before any *Angel* movies (TV or otherwise) could move into production. 'I hope we'll see more *Angel* stories down the road,' noted Roush, 'but we're going to have to be patient.'

In July 2004 James Marsters revealed on the Australian chat show *Rove Live* that Joss Whedon had approached him with a proposal to star in a Spike-based TV movie. According to Marsters, Whedon hoped to make four hour-long TV movies, each focusing on a different character within the *Buffy*-universe, but with all four being linked by one common plot thread. Even more exciting, for fans of *Buffy* and *Angel*, is the possibility that one or more of these TV movies could function as a back-door pilot for a new spin-off series. James did add, however, that the Spike movie would only be made if the other three were as well and that, while he had provisionally agreed to become involved, he could not speak for the participation of any other actors.

Nevertheless, we have, perhaps, yet to see the final curtain for a legacy that has produced over 250 episodes

---

[46] A reference to *Dark Shadows*, seemingly.

and a vast, loyal and vocal fanbase. These are fans who have passionately devoured and kept alive the spirit of the series made by Joss Whedon and his talented team of writers, craftsmen and actors. If there are any *Buffy* or *Angel*-related stories left to tell, then you can rest assured the fans will be there to watch them.